Globalization and Development in East Asia

Routledge Studies in Emerging Societies

Series editor: Jan Nederveen Pieterse,
University of California, Santa Barbara

The baton of driving the world economy is passing to emerging economies. This is not just an economic change, but a social change, with migration flows changing direction towards surplus economies; a political change, as in the shift from the G7 to G20; and over time, cultural changes. This also means that the problems of emerging societies will increasingly become world problems. This series addresses the growing importance of BRIC (Brazil Russia India China) and rising societies such as South Korea, Taiwan, Singapore, Indonesia, South Africa, Turkey, the UAE and Mexico. It focuses on problems generated by emergence, such as social inequality, cultural change, media, ethnic and religious strife, ecological constraints, relations with advanced and developing societies, and new regionalism, with a particular interest in addressing debates and social reflexivity in emerging societies.

1 **Global Modernity, Development, and Contemporary Civilization**
Towards a Renewal of Critical Theory
José Maurício Domingues

2 **Globalization and Development in East Asia**
Edited by Jan Nederveen Pieterse and Jongtae Kim

Globalization and Development in East Asia

Edited by
Jan Nederveen Pieterse and
Jongtae Kim

Routledge
Taylor & Francis Group
NEW YORK LONDON

First published 2012
by Routledge
711 Third Avenue, New York, NY 10017

Simultaneously published in the UK
by Routledge
2 Park Square, Milton Park, Abingdon, Oxon OX14 4RN

Routledge is an imprint of the Taylor & Francis Group, an informa business

Library of Congress Cataloging-in-Publication Data

Globalization and development in East Asia / edited by Jan Nederveen Pieterse and Jongtae Kim. — 1st ed.
p. cm. — (Routledge studies in emerging societies ; 2)
Includes bibliographical references and index.
1. East Asia—Economic policy. 2. Economic development—East Asia. 3. Globalization—Economic aspects—East Asia. 4. Globalization—Social aspects—East Asia. I. Nederveen Pieterse, Jan. II. Kim, Jongtae.
HC460.5.G667 2012
338.95—dc23
2011053385

ISBN13: 978-0-415-80703-6 (hbk)
ISBN13: 978-0-415-53739-1 (pbk)
ISBN13: 978-0-203-11057-7 (ebk)

Typeset in Sabon
by IBT Global.

Cover photo by Seok-Jin Kim.

Contents

Figures

Tables

Acknowledgments

Most of the chapters in this book were presented as papers at the third annual Global studies conference that was held in June 2010 in cooperation with Pusan National University in Busan, South Korea. The conference theme was Global Rebalancing: East Asia and Globalization. We would like to express our gratitude to Professor Seung Kuk Kim, our host at Pusan National University, for his kind and generous cooperation, and to Common Ground Publishing for co-organizing the annual Global Studies conferences.

An earlier version of the chapter by Nederveen Pieterse was published in *Development and Change* (2011, Vol. 42, No. 1). An early version of Jongtae Kim's chapter was published in *Sahoe Gwahak Yeongu* [Social Science Studies] (2011, Vol. 19, No. 2). An earlier version of Min Gong's chapter was published in the *e-Journal of Global studies* (2011). An early version of Peilin Li's chapter was published in *China: An International Journal* (2011, Vol. 9, No. 1).

Introduction

Jan Nederveen Pieterse and Jongtae Kim

East Asia holds a special place in historical globalization as well as in contemporary globalization. In historical globalization East Asia's global role long preceded that of the West; oriental globalization predates occidental globalization and stretches over a much longer time. East Asia led world trade long before the West entered the picture. East and South Asia have been driving forces of the world economy from 1000 CE to 1800 (or from 1100 to 1850 by other assessments), as discussed in a wide range of literature (Frank 1998; Pomeranz 2000; Hobson 2004). China held world treasure before with the world's largest holds of silver, as it does now with the world's largest external account holdings. Against this backdrop the 20th-century rise of Asia is a comeback, a "Resurgent Asia" (Arrighi et al. 2003). Given the deep history of East Asia in globalization, its contemporary resurgence holds profound significance and should not be underestimated.

It was underestimated when Japan was dismissed as another copycat industrializer—until the "Japanese challenge" took over from the American challenge (which changed again for post-bubble Japan for a long period of stagnation and slow growth). It was underestimated when the tiger economies were dismissed as overseas sweatshops of American multinational corporations that enjoyed a temporary demographic "sweet spot" of abundant labor, without enhancing productivity or innovating (Krugman 1994). It was underestimated when the 1997 to 1998 Asian crisis was interpreted through the lens of Asian crony capitalism, which was deemed inferior to Anglo-American capitalism and its free market virtues—until the Enron series of corporate scandals unveiled American crony capitalism and the subprime mortgage crisis showed the flipside of "free market" policies. It may be underestimated again in current assessments of China as an export-dependent, overheated economy that fights inflation, experiences a property bubble, overinvests in infrastructure, and lags in innovation.

East Asia's comeback began with Japan's rise starting in the late-nineteenth century, its victory in war with Russia, and its rise as an economic powerhouse after its defeat in World War Two, an "economic miracle" on a par with postwar Germany. Phase two was the rise of the tiger economies, South Korea, Taiwan, Hong Kong, and Singapore, which the World Bank dubbed the "East Asian miracle." The tiger cubs of Southeast Asia followed. The next phase has been the momentous rise of China.

For developing countries, "Looking East" toward Japan and East Asia has been the norm for almost two decades. The East Asian experiences have also been a major inspiration for the human development approach of the United Nations Development Program. East Asian societies have been able to achieve rapid development, industrialization, and urbanization while building relatively equal societies, thus mitigating some of the wrenching consequences of modernization. The role of developmental states in East Asia, initiated by Japan, parallels industrial policy in Europe and the catch-up policies of Central and East Europe. The notion of the developmental state has now evolved beyond East Asian authoritarianism to the idea of active states that are democratic and flexible.

The Asian momentum was interrupted by the "Asian crisis" of 1997 to 1998 (which did not affect China, Taiwan, and Japan); East Asia has since reinvented itself and recovered. Along with Germany, the East Asian economies represent the leading exporters of manufactured goods, the world's leading factory economies. Energy exporters are the other main category of surplus economies (such as Saudi Arabia, the Gulf emirates, Russia, and Norway). East Asia is on the upside of global economic imbalances, in trade balance and current accounts, while societies that have deindustrialized, have invested outward rather than inward and have become import-dependent, particularly the postindustrial economies of the U.S. and U.K., are the main deficit economies. The "great recession" of 2008 to 2011 reveals these differences. As Warren Buffett remarked, when the tide is down you can see who has been swimming naked. East Asia is widely regarded as the main "winner" in contemporary globalization. The East Asian economies are the leading new industrializing nations and emerging economies. Emerging relatively unscathed from the economic crisis of 2008, emerging societies have become the drivers of the world economy.

While 20th century globalization was led by the West, the 21st century ushers in different dynamics. That "the next phase of globalization will most likely have an Asian face" is a cliché (Stephens 2006). Yet, there is no "Asian model," and of course, East Asian societies are arenas of struggle, so besides a general sense of direction what there would be to emulate is not clear. Various social, cultural, and political economic ideas and experiments are being tried out in East Asia. Japan and Korea have achieved prosperity comparable to the West while maintaining relatively harmonious and equitable societies. Despite rapid economic growth, traditional cultural and social values that emphasize social cohesion are widely implicit in their societies. Japan has been pursuing its identity of "uniqueness," seeking to build a socially harmonious postmodern society while maintaining global economic power. The Chinese pursue an "alternative modernity" with a mixed economy of "socialism with Chinese characteristics." With the "harmonious society" framework adopted in 2003 and its recent five-year plans China seeks to achieve a more balanced development. In South Korea, International Monetary Fund intervention in the late 1990s was followed by a neoliberal turn in government policies, ushering in another phase of the "post-developmental state." While Korea has recovered from these setbacks, market-oriented policies continue. While Korea ranks high in global brands, global market reach, and innovation policies it is also highly export-dependent. A view on Wall Street is, "Korea is the quintessential leveraged bet on global trade . . . The moment there's any form of doubt in worldwide growth or exports or trade, the Korean market is susceptible to a selloff" (quoted in Ramstad 2011). Analysts view South Korea as "a proxy for global growth in trade" (Sender 2011).

Challenges of the "next Asia," according to Stephen Roach (2009, xvii), are "Asia's critical role in the globalization debate, the rebalancing imperatives of the Chinese economy, a new pan-regional framework of integration and competition, and a frank discussion of the risks of trade frictions and protectionism." What is required is "a consumer-led, lighter, greener Asia" (ibid.). Part of global rebalancing is that "Asian savers become spenders and American consumers become savers" (Roach 2009, 395; Nederveen Pieterse this volume; Ciochetto this volume; Peilin, this volume).

East Asia has been affected by the global-scale trends of the rise of China and the decline of American hegemony. China has become the biggest trade partner of many countries, from Brazil to South Korea and Japan, and China's significance in the region has grown across a broad spectrum. The development of the Association of Southeast Asian Nations with Japan, South Korea, and China (ASEAN+3), ASEAN's free trade agreement with China, and the possible emergence of ASEAN+6 (with the addition of India, Australia, and New Zealand) lends further momentum to pan-regional economic integration. Thus, the theme of an East Asian community, which has a considerable lineage in the region (Sakamoto 2000; Seung Kuk Kim, this volume) has received a major economic boost.

"Asia's China-centric supply chain has become a new and important source of pan-regional growth for most of its major economies, especially Japan, Korea, and Taiwan" (Roach 2009, 399). But this new regional identity carries two risks: China dependence, or as long as China is on the upside, Asia is fine; and second, as the region has become more integrated it has also become more export dependent, "with export shares of Developing Asian GDP having soared from 36 percent in the late 1990s to 47 percent in 2007" (Roach 2009, 399), so it remains tethered to a post-bubble world economy that is contracting. According to Thomas Palley, "the possibility of global development via export-led growth is now exhausted." The key problems are waning consumer markets in developed economies, emerging markets' exports hindering the recovery of industrialized economies, crowding out of the exports of other emerging markets, increasing South-South competition, declining prices of manufactured goods, and the ability of multinational corporations to shift production to lower cost countries (Palley 2011, 4–5). Thus, even as East Asia emerges as a major beneficiary of contemporary globalization, sustainable prosperity poses new challenges. A consumer-led "next Asia" also involves addressing the problems of "environmental degradation and widening income disparities" (Roach 2009, 401; cf. Nair 2011). This volume seeks to address these various dilemmas.

If the world is talking about East Asia, what is East Asia talking about? In this volume we turn to local reflexivities in China, South Korea, and Japan and across the region. We know how East Asia is looked at from the outside; what does it look like from within? What are the key debates in sociology and political economy in East Asia, and what are the perspectives on globalization? The thrust of the treatments is, of course, far from triumphalist and reflects enduring concerns in various countries.

Most chapters in this volume were presented as papers at the third annual Global Studies conference, held in cooperation with Pusan National University in Busan, South Korea's second city. Given Asia's importance in globalization, past and present, reemerging Asia's visions of development and perspectives on globalization carries special weight. So while East Asian perspectives on globalization are a central question, in most contributions the dominant motifs are regional and national, rather than global perspectives. Rather than reflecting outright on East Asian agendas for 21st-century globalization, most attention focuses on national and regional issues. This may be due, first, to sociology as the disciplinary background of most contributors, rather than macroeconomics, global studies, or international relations, so social questions occupy the foreground. Second, it may reflect a point made by Mahbubani (2008, 5): what "the irresistible shift of global power to the East" means also depends "on how the West reacts to the rise of Asia." Third, an implication is that at this stage the relation to the global is mediated through regional dynamics, and East Asian interactions and cooperation shape its engagement with global futures.

THE CHAPTERS

The volume opens with general chapters as an entrée to East Asia. John Hobson discusses oriental globalization in a long-term framework and situates the rise of East Asia in a wider time frame. Jan Nederveen Pieterse takes up the "East-South turn" in 21st-century globalization and places East Asia alongside other emerging societies in the dynamics of global rebalancing. Lynne Ciochetto explores the BRIC thesis in terms of a "triple bottom line" of profit, people, and planet with a focus on the environmental implications of the new consumerism in emerging societies.

Chapter 1 discusses globalization in a long-term historical perspective. Rejecting both Orientalist and Occidentalist understandings of globalization, which put excessive weight on the role of the West and the East, respectively, John Hobson argues that the "promiscuous" interactions of the East and the West are themselves the processes of globalization. Orientalization and Occidentalization are "constituent parts of globalization." Hobson traces the beginning of globalization back to circa 500 CE and distinguishes four historical phases varying in the relative strengths of Orientalization and Occidentalization. The first phase is from 500 to 1450 when the extensity, intensity, velocity, and impact propensity of Afro-Eurasian interactions were sufficient to qualify as "proto-globalization." In this phase Orientalization was dominant in the sense that the "proto-global network was crucial for delivering Eastern resource portfolios into Europe." In the second phase, "early globalization" (1450/1492–1830), "the diffusion of 'resource portfolios' from East to West" led to the "fundamental re-organization of societies across the world including Europe." This period is characterized as "Orientalization dominant and Occidentalization emergent." The third phase, "modern globalization" (1830–2000), witnessed "Occidentalization in the ascendance, with the West being the dominant civilization," which was achieved by colonization and neocolonial globalization (i.e., Western capitalism). The current phase is "post-modern globalization" that witnesses "the return of China to the center of the global economy." In relation to global futures, Hobson is optimistic in the sense that the Chinese, unlike the West, "explicitly eschew the cultural conversion of societies according to a Chinese standard of civilization."

In Chapter 2, Jan Nederveen Pieterse zeroes in on current globalization, or Hobson's fourth phase, and discusses the rise of emerging markets. He argues that "North–South relations have been dominant for 200 years, and now an East–South turn is taking shape." This global turn and the economic and financial crisis of 2008–2011 are part of a process of "global rebalancing." An ideological element and a hegemonic perspective that is implicit in "global rebalancing" is that it is premised on a fiction of balance. Yet, in his view, "actual ongoing global rebalancing means dynamic imbalance or transitions from one type of imbalance to another." Nederveen Pieterse identifies two main scenarios arising from this global turn: one is "global plutocracy with Anglo-American capitalism and financial markets in the West back in the lead, and emerging markets joining the club" and the other is "emancipatory multipolarity" in which "countries representing the majority of the world population have joined the global head table." He argues that the first scenario is unlikely due to several weaknesses. "The Anglo-American financial sector is vast, politically embedded and out of control" and "because of decades of deregulation and structural deficits the Anglo-American institutions are crisis-prone and the appeal of western institutions has been receding." He raises the question whether the rise of emerging societies is mainly "a matter of their 'joining the club' or whether it implies genuine advances for the majority of the population." In his view, "the rise of emerging societies is likely to be *on balance* emancipatory in the sense of benefiting the majority of the domestic population and the world majority." It involves the rise of forms of capitalism that are, potentially, more viable and more equitable than Anglo-American capitalism.

In Chapter 3, Lynn Ciochetto examines the dynamics of Asian countries in the light of profit, people, and the planet. Noting that economic growth does not guarantee equity and sustainability to people and the planet, she challenges conventional notions of economic growth obsessed with profit for economic growth based upon profit-driven development models tends to damage social equity and the environment. The economic dynamics of Asian countries raise concerns about people and the planet, especially because they concern a large portion of the world population. "The environmental implications of future growth in the JKIC [Japan, Korea, India, and China] economies are potentially disastrous." Thus, she argues for actively taking the values of people and the planet into account in the assessment of development. With regard to people, she emphasizes that "the management of economic development needs to encompass equity and issues of social justice." With regard to the planet she suggests that "instead of treating the environment as an invisible and infinite resource, the real costs and benefits of development and growth need to be incorporated into analysis." For Ciochetto, changing the methods of assessing development is not a matter of choosing between the market and the planet but, rather, necessary for both: "the market needs to tell the ecological truth or there will not be a market."

Two chapters offer overall perspectives on East Asia. Jongtae Kim considers distinctive national identities that have recently emerged in South Korea, Japan, and China and compares the discourses of Korean *seonjinguk*, Japanese *nihonjinron*, and Chinese new nationalism. It shows how each has assimilated or negotiated western notions of development and constructed the images of the West in their modernization processes. Seung Kuk Kim discusses prospects for an East Asian community.

In Chapter 4, Jongtae Kim provides a comparative view of East Asian countries' national identity in relation to the West, the most significant "other" in their modernization processes. He focuses on distinctive discourses that have taken shape in Korea, Japan, and China, the discourses of *seonjinguk*, *nihonjinron*, and new nationalism. Through a comparative analysis of these nationally popular discourses he shows that, despite their geographical proximity, each country has distinctive national identities and perceptions of the West and modernity. With regard to representations of the West, the Korean discourse respects the West by designating it as *seonjinguk* (advanced country). In contrast, the Japanese discourse tends to regard the West as culturally deficient, and Chinese views treat the West as somewhat hostile. With regard to national identity vis-à-vis the West, he argues that the Korean discourse is disposed to "catching up" with Western modernity while Japanese and Chinese discourses focus on their "uniqueness" and "alternativeness," respectively. Koreans tend to interpret their own modernity as insufficient in relation to the Eurocentric framework of modernity, while the Japanese highlight non-modernity and post-modernity, and the Chinese promote a concept of "alternative modernity." He argues that these differences in national identity in relation to the West offer important cultural perspectives on their different interpretations of and responses to contemporary globalization.

In Chapter 5, Seung Kuk Kim considers prospects for an East Asian community and sets forth a vision of East Asian regionalism from a postmodern, post-universalist, and post-Eurocentric perspective. For Kim, envisioning East Asianism is a desirable project for building a more cooperative, harmonious, and peaceful region. Developing the idea of the "self-fulfilling prophecy," he considers that the imagination of alternative regional characteristics would give great momentum for the realization of the community. Rather than establishing a regional boundary, his project for East Asianism is a hybridizing process that should encompass the merits of both the East and the West. Noting that the contemporary world has long been dominated by the excessive universalism, rationalism, and materialism of the West, he argues that the rise of East Asianism has a great potential for counterbalancing and compensating for these negative aspects: "since the East has been excessively westernized or modernized under the prevalence of Eurocentrism, EAC [East Asian Community] has to correct the imbalance by the medium of East Asianism as hybridizing force." While distancing himself from any effort to essentialize society and culture, he argues that East Asian cultural values and heritages such as Confucianism, Buddhism, and Taoism are common grounds for establishing an East Asian community. Alternatively the East Asian Community may be imagined as based upon political autonomy, economic basic needs, social cooperation, cultural particularism, and religious transcendentalism. He proposes "five functional value orientations" for an East Asianism that can overcome Western modernity and shape a better, hybrid modernity: "post-statist pacifism for a peaceful life," "post-materialist idealism for a simple life," "post-competition mutual aid for a caring and sharing life," "post-universalist particularism for a hybrid life," and "post-secularist mysticism for an imaginative life." On these grounds he envisions an East Asian community as a "hybrid society in which cosmopolitanism has become more of a popular phenomenon than an elite mission."

The next chapters focus on specific countries, Japan, China, and South Korea. In Chapter 6, Hidetaka Yoshimatsu discusses Japan's external and internal responses to globalization. He identifies two important developments in East Asia in the current trends of globalization: East Asia's economic dynamism and the ascendancy of the Chinese economy. Japan employed outward-looking policies to integrate it into East Asian dynamism, notably the government's strategies for deploying integrated infrastructure systems and international standardization. Japan also adopted inward-looking policies to "transform domestic systems and regulations in order to take East Asian dynamism in the domestic economy." These policies include neoliberal reforms such as tax reforms and the promotion of free trade agreements (FTAs) and economic partnership agreements (EPAs), which mainly aim to attract foreign investments to Japan and to boost advantages from international trade. Despite fierce domestic opposition to these policies, especially to FTAs, he argues that "to open up the Japanese economy and integrate it into East Asian dynamism conditions are necessary to regain the vitality of Japanese industry in the long run." Japan has also adopted various polices to respond to the rise of China, which offers Japan both challenge and opportunity. Thus Japan employs a dyadic strategy of "competition and cooperation" in relations with China. While the Japanese government "implemented strategic policies to counter China's regional influence," for instance in the Mekong region, it also "launched cooperative initiatives to sustain the sound development of the East Asian and Chinese economies." As to prospects for an East Asian community, he emphasizes the importance of these two countries' cooperation, arguing that "Sino-Japanese partnership is required to develop regional cooperation into the phase of community-building."

Two chapters focus on China. Li Peilin discusses social inequality and China's new post-crisis development policies, and Min Gong reflects on the imbalances in the world economy and criticizes the idea that they could be remedied by China appreciating the value of its currency, the renminbi. In Chapter 7, Li discusses China's imbalance between economic growth and domestic consumption and China's next stage of development. China now promotes "changing the mode of development," which hinges on the importance of three socioeconomic elements: domestic consumption, technological innovation, and the environment. The Chinese inclination toward savings rather than spending has contributed to its "high-investment and high-growth" development mode. The Chinese rate of consumption as a share of gross domestic product declined from 52 percent in 1958 to 35.4 percent in 2008, and is far below that of the U.S. at 70 percent and Japan at 65 percent. Thus, "The 300 million American people consume more than $10 trillion's worth of commodities every year, while 1.3 billion Chinese people consume only over $1 trillion every year." In his view, China's over-saving type of economy is as undesirable as the U.S. over-consumption type of economy and would eventually undermine China's socioeconomic development. In his words, "long-term high investment is bound to cause excessive production capacity, reduced investment gains, redundant construction, and increase in non-performing bank loans." He argues for changing the structure of income distribution to boost domestic consumption and proposes three policies: "to establish a mechanism for the normal growth of labor wages"; to implement "such levers as finance, taxation, social security, and social benefits"; and "to provide public products and services more effectively and universally." China has reached the stage for a different development strategy. "If the high-speed growth of China's economy in the past 30 plus years relied mainly on investment and exports, then its growth in the next 30 years should rely more on the growth of domestic consumption." He proposes expansive socioeconomic reform: "to fully promote and deepen the social reform will become a hallmark of the new stage of growth and a major task for China to accomplish in that stage."

In Chapter 8, Min Gong examines global economic imbalance with a focus on the trade imbalance between China and the U.S. On the basis of theories of global division of labor and comparative advantage, Gong argues that "global specialization in the process of economic integration is a key factor contributing to global imbalances." China's joining the World Trade Organization in 2001 facilitated China's role as a "trade bridge" in the regional and world economies. "China has played a unique role as a trade bridge (an essential assembling center) for many exports from Asia (Japan and South Korea) to the U.S. and EU." In other words, China has become a world factory in which Asian industrialized countries" capital is invested for manufacturing goods that are exported to Western countries such as the U.S. Thus, the global imbalance represented by the trade imbalance between China and the U.S. mainly derives from structural factors that are inherent in the specialization of the global economy. She points out that "a change in the roles of China and East Asian economies in the U.S. trade deficit is the result of relocation of production from the East Asian economies to China in response to the Asian financial crisis, as well as a stagnant Japan." Thus, the increasing U.S. trade deficit and job loss cannot be attributed to a particular country's policy, such as China's currency policy. "The U.S. trade deficit with China resulting from inter-industry and completely specialized trade is irreversible because labor-intensive industries in the U.S. cannot be revived due to high labor costs there." The U.S. trade deficit associated with China's trade surplus is irreversible in today's global political economic structure. "If U.S. imports from China decrease because of renminbi appreciation, Americans will buy more from India, Vietnam, Mexico, Indonesia, Bangladesh, and other low labor-cost economies instead." Thus, global economic imbalances represented by China-U.S. trade imbalances are a global structural problem. To improve global economic imbalances she argues for the need for structural adjustment on a global scale.

In Chapter 9, Hyun-Chin Lim and Jin-Ho Jang examine democracy in South Korea, which has been an ongoing concern since Korea's emergence from military rule and the democracy movement of the 1980s. Reviewing the long processes of democratization in Korea for the past decades, Lim and Jang argue that the recent trend of neoliberal globalization has significantly encroached on "liberal democracy" in Korea by weakening labor forces and restricting civil rights. It has widely expanded the political economic power of big businesses such as *chaebol* across various fields in the country. The weakening of progressive social forces and the strengthening of capital has been promoted by various neoliberal reforms in Korea; thus their argument addresses the sociopolitical effects of neoliberal globalization. They note that "globalization has worked as a force to form a neoliberal alliance to drive democratic governments to pursue neoliberal economic reforms resulting in negative socio-economic outcomes." the negative effects of globalization on various socioeconomic aspects of Korea culminated in the election of the conservative party candidate Lee Myung-Bak as president in 2008. Restrictions on civil rights under the Lee administration go well with neoliberal transformations, which are promoted by a neoliberal alliance formed in the processes of neoliberal globalization. Thus, neoliberal globalization has been a significant deterring factor for democracy in South Korea. They conclude that "South Korea's experience shows the complicated possibilities and difficulties of democratic progress in the process of globalization."

Wiebe Nauta's concluding Chapter 10 provides a comparative view on the development of democracy and civil society in South Korea and South Africa. Nauta compares labor and social movements in South Korea and South Africa and notes the intensive use of the internet in South Korea and its significance in shaping civil society. Considering that both countries have had similar experiences of struggling for democracy from the 1970s to the 1990s, he asks what explains the stark divergence between the two from the 2000s in terms of the deepening of civil society. The two countries had similar demographic and socioeconomic conditions around 1980 and shared similar experiences of democratization until the 1990s, such as bloody uprisings (the 1976 Soweto Student Uprising and the Kwangju Uprising of 1980), the establishment of massive labor organizations (the National Coalition for Democracy Movement and the Mass Democratic Movement in the 1980s), and the presidential election of Nobel Peace prize-winning opposition political leaders (Kim Dae-Jung and Nelson Mandela in the 1990s). He identifies three periods in both countries' democratization processes: "the struggle for freedom" in the late 1970s and 1980s, the "period of democratic transition" in the 1990s, and the "era of the internet" since 2001. In the last period the two countries begin to diverge markedly. Focusing on the role of information technology in the deepening of civil society and the public sphere he argues that the development of strong civic organizations and participatory internet culture in Korea has played a vital role in promoting its qualitative development of civil society and democracy. Advances in information technology "contribute to the increasing capability of subordinate groups to shape South Korean politics and give voice to those who were rather voiceless before the age of the internet." But "there are huge differences between South Korea and South Africa concerning the advances in information technology." Contemporary trends of globalization and the "East-South turn" might in the future connect the two countries. "A Korean wave on the African continent . . . could assist processes of democratic deepening by strengthening civil society as public sphere."

REFERENCES

Arrighi, G., T. Hamashita, and M. Selden, eds. 2003. *The Resurgence of East Asia: 500, 150 and 50 Year Perspectives*. New York: Routledge.

Frank, A. G. 1998. *ReOrient: global economy in the Asian age*. Berkeley: University of California Press.

Hobson, John M. 2004. *The Eastern Origins of Western Civilisation*. Cambridge: Cambridge University Press
Krugman, Paul. 1994. "The Myth of Asia's Miracle." *Foreign Affairs* 73(6): 62–79.
Mahbubani, Kishore. 2008. *The New Asian Hemisphere*. New York: Public Affairs.
Nair, Chandran. 2011. *Consumptionomics: Asia's Role in Reshaping Capitalism and Saving the Planet*. New York: Wiley
Palley, Thomas. 2011. "The End of Export-Led Growth: Implications for Emerging Markets and the Global Economy." Friedrich Ebert Stiftung Shanghai Briefing Paper 6, Shanghai.
Pomeranz, Kenneth. 2000. *The Great Divergence: China, Europe and the Making of the Modern World Economy*. Princeton: Princeton University Press.
Ramstad, E. 2011. "Global Woes Land a Punch in Korea." *Wall Street Journal*, August 17: C5.
Roach, Stephen S. 2009. *The Next Asia: Opportunities and Challenges for a New Globalization*. Hoboken: John Wiley.
Sakamoto, Y. 2000. "An Alternative to Global Marketization: East Asian Regional Cooperation and the Civic State." In *Global Futures: Shaping Globalization*, edited by Jan Nederveen Pieterse, 98–117. London: Zed.
Sender, H. 2011. "Asian Domestic Demand Won't Make Up for Global Slack." *Financial Times*, August 19: 18.
Stephens, Ph. 2006. A perilous collision between nationalism and globalisation. *Financial Times*, March 3: 13.

1 Orientalization in Globalization

A Sociology of the Promiscuous Architecture of Globalization, c. 500–2010

John M. Hobson

INTRODUCTION

In this chapter I seek to provide a critique of the conventional conception of globalization which views it as a pure expression of Westernization or Americanization. My aim is to provide an alternative non-Eurocentric approach to globalization, which, while not dispensing with Western agency in the making and reproduction of globalization, nevertheless raises the ontological status of Eastern agency; something which has been entirely obscured by, or erased from, the conventional Eurocentric narrative. In recent years a non-Eurocentric school has emerged, which has tended to bend the polemical stick to the opposite Occidentalist pole, reifying Eastern agency and dismissing Western agency. At the same time, the paradox emerges that for the latest period of globalization (c. 1830–2000), the non-Eurocentric school has implicitly deferred to the Eurocentric position by assuming that contemporary globalization is in effect pure Westernization. And so in this chapter I seek to go beyond the polarities or antinomies of Eurocentrism and non-Eurocentrism (as well as to iron out the inconsistencies within the non-Eurocentric school) by providing an alternative non-Eurocentric third-way position. In this way, then, I seek to produce a fresh research agenda for globalization theory.

One of the key problems is that the Eurocentric analysis of "globalization proper" is highly presentist, insofar as its birth-date is usually located to the 1945/1973 period (and sometimes as late as the post-1989 era). One of the major themes of the non-Eurocentric school is that it reaches back in time, locating the birth of globalization either to the post-1500 era or even as far back as the post-500 era. In the process it reveals the Eastern role in the making of globalization through the longue global durée. My proposed resolution that I outline here involves rethinking globalization in its past, present, and future incarnations. In order to bring in a genuinely poly-civilizational approach that reifies neither Western nor Eastern agency, I propose that we begin by separating out the processes of Occidentalization, Orientalization, and globalization.

I treat globalization as a set of infrastructures upon which transnationalization or trans-spatialization is based. These include the usual list of suspects, including global modes of transportation, global communications networks, global institutional integration, and so on. While these infrastructures give rise to the physical base or *form* of globalization, Occidentalization and Orientalization provide its *content*. Importantly, the very content of globalization will vary at any one point in time depending on which of these two generic processes is dominant. And moreover, the content of both Occidentalization and Orientalization themselves vary through time. Thus, for example, Orientalization in the pre-1800 era was more offensive, insofar as it entailed the projecting outwards of Eastern technologies and institutions, whereas between 1800 and the present much of its rationale was defensive, aiming to resist the pressures of Occidentalization by seeking to preserve heterogeneity in the world. Nevertheless, Occidentalization has since 1492 been far more offensive, consistently seeking to promote the homogenization of the world according to a Western standard of civilization. And precisely because these civilizational processes have varied in absolute and relative intensities, so globalization itself will be configured differently over time.

It is no less significant to note that in one important sense there is no such thing as pure Orientalization or pure Occidentalization, given that these processes mutually or promiscuously entwine, thus complicating the picture even further. Thus, while the dominant reductive definition of globalization-as-Occidentalization produces a monolithic vision and linear account of globalization in the last 60 years and implicitly in the last 500, so my alternative narrative will revision globalization as a highly protean or promiscuous phenomenon that undergoes major discontinuities over time as it crystallizes in numerous forms. Accordingly, I propose to offer a more historically sensitive poly-civilizational account to the extant Eurocentric ahistorical and monological approach which dominates globalization theory and analysis. But given all this conceptual complexity the trick, then, is to sociologically chart these historical phases which exhibit continuities and discontinuities, while not getting lost in a mire of particularistic detail. To achieve this I propose to treat globalization as developing through a four-phase historical lineage, from c. 500–2010.

The article is set out in two main sections. In the first I lay out in summary form the Eurocentric literature and provide a brief discussion of the alternative non-Eurocentric approaches. The second section will lay out my alternative third-way non-Eurocentric framework for mapping the changing architecture of globalization as it reflects the changing intensities—relative and absolute—of Orientalization and Occidentalization.

NARRATIVES OF GLOBALIZATION

The Dominant Eurocentric Big Bang Theory of Globalization

The dominant narrative of globalization is sub-divided into pro-global liberal and anti-global Marxist approaches. But, when viewed through a non-Eurocentric lens, both appear as variations on a common Eurocentric theme. For both approaches view globalization as the expression of the *triumph of the West* over all non-Western societies, even if this is celebrated by many liberals (e.g., Fukuyama 1992; Friedman 1999; M. Wolf 2005) and lamented by Marxists (e.g., Wallerstein 1984; Cox 1996; Gill 1995; Bromley 1999). And both view globalization as a specifically post-1945 phenomenon, equating it with the Pax Americana and its aftermath. However, while most conventional theorists largely ignore the pre-1945 era, all implicitly subscribe to what might be euphemistically dubbed the "Eurocentric big bang theory of globalization." This approach invokes, in effect, a two-step (a)historical narrative of globalization, where the first step refers to the autonomous rise of the West before it exports its civilizational attributes through globalization to the East (the second step).

The first step of the big bang theory holds that by, or during, the 16th century Europe had risen to the top of the world material power hierarchy by its own accord. The key point here is that the vast majority of liberals and Marxists assume that the West is a *self-made civilization*, which developed through what I call the Eurocentric *logic of immanence* (Hobson 2004, ch. 1). That is, it is argued that Europe contained within itself the seeds of its own rise, such that it had all the necessary social energies and ingenuities to be able to *self-generate*. Indeed, Europe (and later the U.S.) is thought to have been entirely "exceptional." In the process the story of the rise of the West is related in terms of an endogenous, evolutionary unfolding intra-European process. Thus development into modernity was inscribed within the social structure of European civilization such that its rise to the top was but an (a)historical *fait accompli*.

Reflecting this Eurocentric endogenous approach, standard accounts tread a familiar path by painting a picture of European development as akin to a journey of the Western "developmental train"—sometimes euphemistically dubbed the "Oriental Express" (Blaut 1993; Frank 1998; Hobson 2004). Typically, the train sets off from Ancient Greece and then passes through a series of Western way-stations. Thus having passed through Ancient Rome the train steams on through European feudalism, through the Italian way-station that was marked by the commercial and financial revolution of the post-1000 era and on to the Renaissance, before it tracks north-westward, up to the Netherlands and Dutch hegemony, and then onto British industrialization and the Pax Britannica via the French Revolution, whence the global baton was transferred to the great Western ship which delivers the baton to the highest stage of civilization in the very far West—U.S. liberal-capitalism and the Pax Americana. Of course for Marxists, this represents the penultimate stop before the ship pulls into the terminus of communism.

No less critically for many, though not all, Eurocentrics, such a developmental journey is entirely absent in the East. This is because the East is

Eurocentrically constructed as the West's inferior opposite Other and is denied the progressive ability to self-generate. Thus the East is said to be governed by irrational regressive institutions—for example, Oriental despotic states rather than Western liberal states, mystical other-worldly religions rather than rational Protestantism, collectivist rather than individualist social structures, superstitious mentalities rather than scientific ones, and so on. All of which culminates in the point that for many social theorists, because the East is deemed to be incapable of self-development, it was incumbent upon the West to engage in an imperial or global civilizing mission in order to "jump-start" the East onto the developmental track that would eventually deliver it to the terminus of (Western-based) civilization.[1] And so it is precisely at this point that the second-step of the Eurocentric big bang theory cuts in.

Once the first step had been completed so it is assumed that the second step immediately cuts in, whereby the West expands outwards to remake the world in its own image. Or, to complete the metaphor: the big bang of capitalist development exploded in Europe in the 16th century and thereafter Western civilization diffused outwards to make the earthly universe in its own image. Of course, the obvious conundrum here lies in the seemingly awkward chronology of these two occurrences: that the West had moved to the top by the 16th century but that globalization only "properly" emerged after 1945 within the Eurocentric narrative. However, the chronological gap is explained, often implicitly, through the deployment of another Oriental Express, or Western relay-race, metaphor. Thus the intervening period is viewed in effect as a period of *Western proto-globalization.* To use the latter metaphor, it is assumed that the global baton of power was passed from one Western imperialist runner to the next. That is, the Iberians ran the first leg after 1492/1497, spreading Western institutions and normative practices outwards to the Americas in the far West (via Columbus in the first instance) and to Asia in the East (via Da Gama in the first instance). The baton of global power was then passed to the Dutch in the 17th century before it was handed over to the British in the 19th century, culminating with the American anchor man who ran the final leg in record time after 1945. The essential task performed by these Western runners in the period between 1492 and 1945 was to smash down the obstructive walls or "civilizational barriers" that allegedly divided East from West. This was a form of proto-globalization or, perhaps better still, *primitive globalization* (to adapt Marx's notion of the primitive accumulation of capital) insofar as it prepared the essential groundwork for the initiation of "globalization proper" under American hegemony, thereby giving the Americans a running jump into their project of globalizing the world.

All in all, whichever way we carve up the chronology, whether it be that globalization appeared miraculously after 1945 as some kind of "Western virgin birth" or whether it evolved more gradually under Western proto- or primitive-globalization, it is clear that the dominant Eurocentric narrative insists that globalization was *made in the West*. And it is assumed that by the end of the 20th century the world operates according to the singular rhythm of Western civilization.

The Non-Eurocentric Narrative of Globalization

In the last decade or so, the Eurocentric approach to globalization has been challenged by the rise of a non-Eurocentric school, which has developed largely within historical sociology and world history. The first wave was pioneered by the likes of Marshall Hodgson (1974), Eric Wolf (1982), Janet Abu-Lughod (1989), André Wink (1990), and James Blaut (1993). However, with the exception of Abu-Lughod, their task was not to produce an explicit account of globalization. Globalization emerged in their writings very much as the backdrop to other concerns, whether these be, for example, developments within the Islamic world (Hodgson 1974), or relations between the Islamic world and India (Wink 1990), or the rise of the West (Blaut 1993). Abu-Lughod provides the exception insofar as her primary concern is to argue that a global economy emerged *before* European globalization. Critically, her argument is that this was pioneered mainly by Islamic traders as they set up or revitalized three key trading routes, which integrated the world into one continuous loop of interactions. This brings to the fore two key insights that underpin the non-Eurocentric school of globalization: first, that globalization has deep historical roots that predate American or European hegemony (i.e., the "Orient first" thesis), and second, that globalization has been made or at least shaped by Eastern agents (the thesis of Eastern agency).

The second wave of non-Eurocentric globalization theory has been developed by a number of scholars.[2] And to this can be added various non-Eurocentric scholars who assume implicitly that globalization has had an Eastern input.[3] While I situate myself within this school, I want to refine my earlier (Hobson 2004) claims in this chapter, not least because there is a core essentialist problem that haunts this school as much as it does the Eurocentric one. Jan Nederveen Pieterse precisely articulates this problem when he states that "at times the oriental globalization literature reverses the current of Eurocentrism by centring the East and marginalizing the West, thus replaying East-West binaries in reverse" (2006, 64–65). Indeed, while the dominant mainstream account of globalization exhibits a one-sided Orientalist exaggeration of the West, much of the non-Eurocentric school turns out to oscillate between a one-sided Occidentalist exaggeration of the East in the early period and an implicit Orientalism for the post-1800 era. Clearly, then, countering the one-sided

Eurocentric approach with an equally one-sided Occidentalist account is merely to reproduce the problem that the non-Eurocentrics set out to solve in the first place. The question then becomes: how to produce an account that apportions agency to both East *and* West, while producing much greater coherence to the non-Eurocentric approach. This is, to put it mildly, an extremely challenging task, though it is one that I believe should form the basis of the next stage of globalization theory, especially that of non-Eurocentric theory. In what follows I want to sketch the outlines of my proposed solution.

Because this chapter is concerned primarily to set out a chronological-conceptual framework for analyzing globalization over the longue durée, it makes sense to briefly summarize the different chronologies that extant non-Eurocentric approaches to globalization produce. At the risk of over-simplification, there are three broad chronologies offered in the non-Eurocentric school. First, in my own work I located the birth-date of what I called "Oriental globalization" to the post-500 era in the "Afro-Eurasian Age of Discovery" (Hobson 2004, ch. 2–4).[4] I also argued that "Oriental globalization" lasted between 500 and c. 1800/1830. Thus it is implicitly assumed that after about 1830 Oriental globalization ended and was replaced by Occidental globalization which remains to the present day (though I never stated this and nor have I ever felt that the modern period could be uniformly reduced to Westernization, as I shall explain later).

A second chronology dates Eastern-led globalization to the 13th/14th centuries and was terminated after 1350 when the Black Death undermined a key trading route that linked China to Europe via India and the Middle East (Abu-Lughod 1989). Interestingly, Abu-Lughod is explicit that after 1500 the global economy was dominated by Europe, thereby converging with the Orientalist position thereafter. This conception is complemented by James Blaut (1993) who views East and West as on an equal footing up to 1492 but then diverges thereafter as the West becomes hegemonic in the world. Finally, Kenneth Pomeranz (2000) and Andre Gunder Frank (1998), implicitly in the former case and explicitly in the latter, envisage Eastern-led globalization as dominant prior to 1800 but that thereafter Western-led globalization takes over until Oriental globalization returns at the beginning of the 21st century.

All in all, while this "Oriental global" approach has the advantage of ascribing a major pioneering role to the East its major disadvantages are two-fold: first that it underplays the role of the West in the early phase of historical globalization, thereby lapsing into an Occidentalist narrative, and second, that it (implicitly) ascribes too much weighting to the West after either 1492 (Blaut 1993; Abu-Lughod 1989) or 1800 (Frank 1998; Pomeranz 2000), thereby lapsing into an Orientalist/Eurocentric narrative. Ironing out these problems is a key task of this chapter.

BEYOND THE ANTINOMIES OF ORIENTALISM AND OCCIDENTALISM: NON-EUROCENTRIC LINEAGES OF GLOBALIZATION, c. 500–2010

There are two ways of delineating the historical development of globalization. As already explained, the first is to talk about Oriental globalization in the 1450/1492–1830 period (or even c. 500–1830) and Occidental globalization from c. 1830–2000, and then the return of Oriental globalization after 2000. The second is to analytically break down globalization into its core civilizational constituents—Orientalization and Occidentalization. Of course, one could talk about Oriental globalization as well as Occidental globalization co-existing in differing degrees and intensities. Or one could look at Orientalization and Occidentalization as constituent parts of globalization. Here I shall run with the latter approach. And the reason for this is that to paint the period between 1492 and 1800 as defined by a pure Oriental globalization and the period between 1800–2000 as a pure Occidental globalization is reductive, leading to an Occidentalism in the former period and an Orientalism in the latter period.

Jan Nederveen Pieterse (2009) has produced an interesting chronology of globalization from 500. Here I would like to adapt it in order to produce my own non-Eurocentric chronology of the changing, promiscuous architecture of globalization from 500 CE through to 2010 and beyond (see Table 1.1). And in what follows I shall take each phase briefly in turn.

Table 1.1 The Changing Architecture of Globalization, c. 500–2010

Phase of Globalization	*Relative Strengths of Occidentalization and Orientalization*	*Central Nodes*
Proto-Globalization c. 500–1450	Orientalization dominant	Middle East/North Africa primary up to 1100, China primary after 1450, Middle East/N. Africa and India secondary
Early Globalization 1450/1492–1830	Orientalization dominant; Emergent Occidentalization	China dominant, but Middle East/ North Africa and India important; Europe emergent
Modern Globalization 1830–2000	Occidentalization dominant; Orientalization subordinate	U.S. and Europe dominant; the return of Japan and China
Postmodern Globalization 2000–?	Occidentalization receding; Orientalization resurgent	China and India in the ascendance; U.S. and Europe in decline

Figures 1.1 and 1.2 juxtapose my non-Eurocentric account with that of the conventional Eurocentric one. Given that I view the Eurocentric "hockey stick" representation of globalization as a "convenient myth" (Figure 1.1), I propose an alternative dual-vision of globalization as based on two very broadly based "S-curves" that chart the changing developments of Orientalization and Occidentalization in the making of globalization (Figure 1.2). And while, of course, Eurocentric critics will view this as a heretical betrayal of Western civilizational superiority, I view it simply as an "inconvenient truth." Consequently, my "heretical" narrative forms the basis of the subsequent discussion, which is broken down into four sub-sections, one for each phase of globalization.

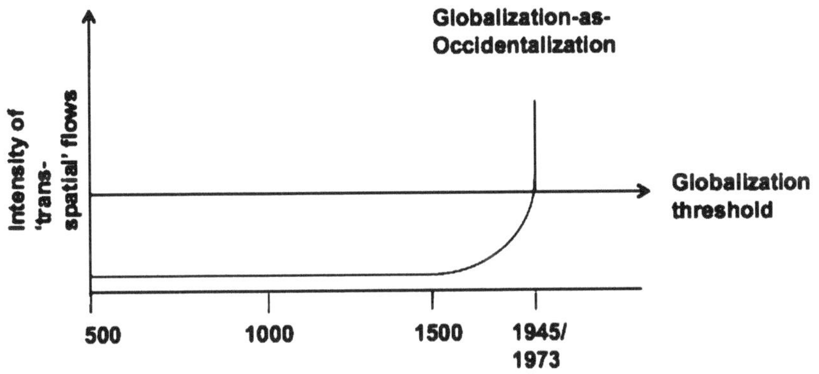

Figure 1.1 The Eurocentric "hockey stick" representation of the rise of globalization.

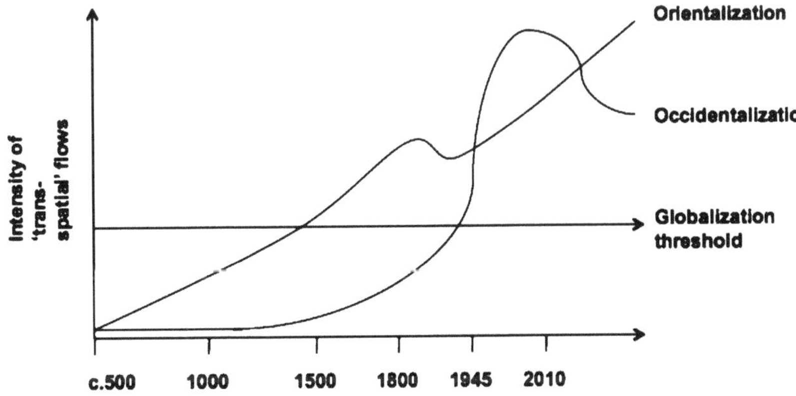

Figure 1.2 Non-Eurocentric S-curves representation of the rise of globalization.

Phase I Proto-Globalization: Orientalization Dominant

As I have already noted, in previous work I referred to the 500–1800 period as governed by "Oriental globalization" (Hobson 2004, ch. 2–4). Here I break this long phase into two: "proto-globalization" between 500–1450/1492 and "early globalization" between 1450/1492 and c. 1830. The immediate question then, is why has the earlier period up to 1450 been conceptually downgraded from globalization to proto-globalization? One of the key arguments made in *Global Transformations* (Held et al. 1999) is that globalization can only be said to exist if there is a sufficient degree of *extensity* in "transnational" or global exchanges; by which they mean that exchanges have to be conducted between countries, groups, and individuals right across the world. They make two specific arguments here as to why extensity was at insufficient levels before 1850 so as to render moribund the idea that globalization existed at *any time* before 1850, let alone before 1450/1492. First, they argue that before 1492 the Americas were not part of the global trading system (see also Flynn and Giráldez 2006); and second, that the trade that did exist was in luxury goods which were consumed by the elites, or the top 10 percent of societies. Thus if the Americas were not in, and 90 percent of the rest of the world's population were also excluded, then *ipso facto* globalization could not have existed between 1450–1830 let alone between 500–1450.

My response here is that Held et al. (1999), as well as Flynn and Giráldez (2006), are correct with respect to the exclusion of the Americas but wrong with respect to the "luxury goods" thesis. That is, globalization could not have existed prior to 1492 since the Americas were not in; hence why I describe the period between 500–1450/1492 as *proto*-globalization. But one of the themes of Afro-Eurasian trade prior to (and after) 1492 was that everyday goods were traded at least as much as luxury goods, which meant that probably the majority of the world's population consumed goods that were traded in the Afro-Eurasian trading system.

It is also important to note that standard Eurocentric historiography discounts the existence of globalization proper at any point before 1945 on the grounds that it had insufficient degrees not just of extensity but also of intensity, velocity, and impact propensity (Held et al. 1999). With respect to extensity, I have already conceded that the omission of the Americas before 1492 warrants the discounting of globalization in that period, though I believe that proto-globalization very much existed. Thus in the 500–1450/1492 phase I would argue that Afro-Eurasian extensity was sufficient to qualify for the label of proto-globalization. Trade, especially in everyday consumer goods, as already noted, was exchanged between the majority of the Afro-Eurasian population. Movements of peoples, especially from the East, across the whole of the Afro-Eurasian economy were profound. Indeed the relative numbers in the period between 500–1000 would easily have surpassed those experienced in the last 50 years. Diseases too migrated across regions, having impacts that were sometimes far more devastating than the current AIDS epidemic. One can think of the impact of the Black Death, for example, which devastated populations right across the Afro-Eurasian economy after about 1320 (with about a third of Europe's total population wiped out); or equally, the impact of European diseases after 1492, which decimated 90 percent of the South American population following the Spanish encounter.

It is obviously the case that the intensity of interactions (i.e., the regularity of exchanges) and velocity (i.e., the speed of exchanges) were nowhere near as high back then as they are today. But the key point is that Afro-Eurasian transactions were of sufficient scale as to lead to changes in societies throughout this area—that is, that they qualify in terms of high *impact propensity*—thereby ticking *the* major box that Held et al. (1999) delineate as a defining property of globalization. Moreover, such exchanges were not simply confined to goods, diseases, and demographic migrations, but extended to all manner of "resource portfolios" (including technologies, institutions, and ideas). Indeed as I have argued in book-length form (Hobson 2004), the rise of the West was only made possible by the earlier rise of the Rest, given that at each major turning point Eastern resource portfolios, having diffused from East to West were then assimilated to enable the rise of the latter, as I explain shortly. But before considering this dimension it is necessary to outline the Eastern origins of proto-globalization between c. 500 and 1450/1492.

A key development in the rise of Afro-Eurasian led proto-globalization was the formation of a series of inter-linked regions or empires. These comprised T'ang China (618–907), the Islamic Ummayad/Abbasid Empire in West Asia (661–1258), the Ummayad polity in Spain (756–1031), and the Fatimids in North Africa (909–1171). Moreover the kingdom of Śrīvijaya in Sumatra was important in that it constituted the vital entrepôt that connected China to the Indian Ocean between the 7th and 13th centuries. These inter-linked regions were vital in promoting an extensively pacified space that fostered considerable trade and enabled the transmission of Eastern resource portfolios. While a number of capitalist agents were important here—including Africans, Jews, Indians, Chinese, and Javanese—the prime role was performed by the West Asian Muslims. The Afro-Eurasian economy comprised three prime trade routes, though the two most important ones were the Middle and Southern ones (Abu-Lughod 1989). The Middle route had a land component, which linked the Eastern Mediterranean with China and India, and a sea route that passed through the Persian Gulf. The Southern route linked the Alexandria-Cairo-Red Sea complex with the Arabian Sea and then, as with the Middle sea route, the Indian Ocean and beyond to Southeast Asia, China, and Japan. These routes ensured that Europe was fundamentally connected to the Afro-Eurasian economy after about the eighth century. And *contra* Eurocentric world history, this situation continued throughout the period between 1000–1800 when the various leading European powers were at their height.

With the "Fall of Acre" in 1291 the Venetians, who were the key intermediary that fed Eastern trade across to Europe, came to rely on the dominant Southern route which was presided over by the Egyptians. As Abu-Lughod claims, "Whoever controlled the sea-route to Asia could set the terms of trade for a Europe now in retreat. From the thirteenth century and upto the sixteenth that power was Egypt" (Abu-Lughod 1989, 149). Moreover, Venetian trade did not dry up after 1291 but continued on, especially given that the Venetians managed to circumvent the Papal ban and secured new treaties with the Sultan in 1355 and 1361. And right down to 1517, Venice survived because Egypt played such an important role within the global economy. Moreover, after 1517 Venice continued its trading connection through the Ottomans.

This proto-global network was crucial for delivering Eastern resource portfolios into Europe. These included the iron horseshoe, iron stirrup, and crop rotation systems, which were vital technologies that enabled the European feudal revolution; the square hull and stern-post rudder, lateen sail, astrolabe, and manifold navigational systems, all of which promoted the Voyages of Rediscovery (a term that I shall explain shortly), in the absence of which the Europeans would most likely have remained confined to the Islamic Mediterranean Sea. All in all, I call this period "proto-globalization" simply because the Americas (as well as Australasia) were not included. Another term, then, might be that of Afro-Eurasian regionalization.

Early Globalization 1450/1492–1830: Orientalization Dominant, Occidentalization Emergent

My dating the birth of globalization to c. 1450/1492 will at first sight appear to dovetail with the Eurocentric narrative, which views the origins of (primitive) globalization as coinciding with the rise of the West to the world's leading civilization. But as I shall argue, the West only emerged at the top during the 19th century and that between 1500–1800 it lagged behind India, China, and North Africa/West Asia (see Hobson 2004, ch. 2–8; also Frank 1998; Pomeranz 2000). Indeed, Eurocentric theory assumes that 1492 provided a radical break with the past, insofar as it saw the Europeans "discover the world" and initiate the primitive accumulation of globalization through the breaking down of the Eastern civilizational walls. And although the post-1450/1492 era witnessed new processes underpinning globalization, nevertheless these built upon the developments that had already been made during the era of Oriental-led proto-globalization or Afro-Eurasian regionalization. Thus the appearance of globalization after 1450/1492 should not obscure the continuities with the previous era. To advance my argument here it makes sense to treat the Eurocentric narrative of the post-1492 era as my foil.

The Eurocentric assumption is that prior to 1492 the world was segmentalized into separate and more-or-less self-constituting civilizations that were isolated from each other. But, in the light of what has just been argued, it would seem much fairer to say that the Europeans discovered nothing in that all the major Eastern civilizations had been in continuous contact with each other since the Afro-Asia Age of Discovery in the sixth century. Accordingly, the so-called Voyages of Discovery might better be labeled the European Voyages of *Rediscovery*.

Here we encounter perhaps the most profound dual-paradox of Eurocentric world history. For it is an axiom that after 1434 the Chinese withdrew from international trade owing to the proclamation of the official Ming ban on all foreign trade. This is thought to have created a vacuum into which the newly charged Iberians poured through the so-called Voyages of Discovery so as to initiate the phase of Western primitive- or proto-globalization (Landes 1998; Roberts 1985). The first paradox is that the Chinese did *not* withdraw from international trade after 1434 but in fact moved toward the center of an emergent global trading system shortly thereafter (Hobson 2004, ch. 3). And, no less profoundly, the second paradox emerges in the point that European trading connections intensified after 1492 in significant part thanks to the role played by the Muslims and Indians but, above all, the Chinese. Nevertheless, it would be problematic to conclude from this that the Europeans played only a passive role in the emergent global economy. For my aim here is to counter the antinomies of Orientalism and Occidentalism. The immediate question, though, must be: how did China move to the center of an emergent global economy?

The conversion of the Chinese economy onto a silver standard in the mid-15th century was the seminal moment (which is why I delineate *1450*/1492 as the birth-date of early globalization). For this in turn created a huge demand for silver that would later flood in after the Europeans had arrived in the Americas. This huge demand was in turn a function of the strength of the Chinese economy, which had undergone a kind of industrial miracle in the 10th and 11th centuries (Hobson 2004, ch. 3). This created a strong base for Chinese exports as well as a strong gravitational pull for the world's silver, especially given that China enjoyed a trade surplus with all other regions. A pure Eurocentric narrative would interpret all this through awarding the Europeans a monopoly of pioneering agential power, recounting the story in terms of how the Europeans discovered the Americas and the Far East and then wove them together through their trading activities. What, then, might an alternative to this look like?

Prior to 1492 the Europeans were largely peripheral players in the Afro-Eurasian economy, receiving Eastern goods that entered Europe via Alexandria as well as through the West Asian trading corridor. After 1492, for the first time the Europeans directly joined the extant Afro-Eurasian trading system. Having discovered silver (and gold) in the Americas in the 16th century, it was later left to the British to construct the famous "triangular trading system." This, of course, linked up West Africa with the Americas and with Britain. There is no doubt that this was an important development in the establishment of a global economy. It was also the Europeans (specifically the Spanish) who extended a trade route from the Americas to China via the Philippines.[5] However, though significant, it would be wrong to exaggerate this European global-agential role. Certainly the Chinese demand for silver coupled with the European trade deficit provided a major causal factor both in the mining of silver in the Americas (much of which was exported to China and India) and the extension of the trade route to China. Most importantly, in recent years a number of non-Eurocentric works have emphasized the rise of the "Black Atlantic system" (i.e., the triangular trading system) within which Europe was socialized by all manner of non-European influences (e.g., Gilroy 1993). But the key point is that the Pacific and Indian Ocean economies that were dominated by Asian merchants provided a strong input into the reproduction of the Atlantic economy. This is not to eradicate the European role in the Atlantic system. But it is to say that the Pacific/Indian Ocean trading systems helped suck the Europeans into both these systems as well as to sustain Europe's role in the Atlantic system. Moreover, while the Europeans clearly played an agential role in the Americas, it is also the case that in the Asian trading systems they played a subordinate role, at all times before 1800 being dependent upon local Asian knowledge, Asian capital (much of which was provided by rich Indian Banians), and the goodwill of Asian rulers. Indeed they even had no choice but to cooperate with the Asians in such matters as the sharing of trading ships (Hobson 2004, ch. 7).

But it was not just the fact of a European trade deficit with China that provided the impetus to the linking up of the Atlantic, Pacific, and Indian Ocean trading systems into one coherent global system. There were in addition two other factors of importance here. First, the fact that the Chinese economy was the strongest in the world and that it was based on a silver standard meant that the price of silver relative to gold in China was about twice that of the equivalent figure in Europe (1:6 in China, 1:12 in Europe). As Flynn and Giráldez (1994) argued, this gave rise to a global arbitrage system, where American silver was shipped by the Europeans into China where it was exchanged for gold. This was then shipped back to Europe where it was exchanged for twice the amount of gold, before this was then shipped back to China where the process began anew. And profits were realized at each stage of the process, thereby fanning the development of the Chinese and European economies. Moreover, despite all the talk of Europeans monopolizing the spice trade, the fact is that the majority of European profits—around 75%—were derived from their place in this global arbitrage system (or what I call the *global silver recycling process*). Second, the Europeans relied for much of the rest of their profits not by monopolizing Asian trade but by acting as intermediaries within the intra-Asian trading networks (or the "inter-country trade"). Either way, although the Europeans played an important role in linking up the global economy, much of the impetus to this was provided by the Asians.

Of course, standard Eurocentric narratives would deny that the period between 1450/1492 and 1830 qualified for the label of "global" (along the lines described earlier). It is certainly true that the quantity of trade in this era was well below that of the post-1945 era. But trade was only one factor of relevance here. Most important of all was the diffusion of "resource portfolios" from East to West. As I mentioned earlier, all the key developments that we associate with the rise of the West were significantly enabled by the borrowing or assimilation of Eastern resource portfolios. For this post-1450/1492 era these include Chinese, Indian, and above all West Asian ideas that underpinned the Renaissance and scientific revolution;[6] the full development of the gun, cannon, and gunpowder all of which diffused across from China; and, last but not least, Chinese technologies that gave rise to the European agricultural and industrial revolutions (Hobson 2004, ch. 8–10).

The significance of this discussion is two-fold. First, it dispenses with the first-step of the Eurocentric big bang theory of globalization, which presumes that the West was *self-made* as a result of its own exceptional qualities. Rather, the West was to an important, though by no means complete, extent "Other-made," thereby yielding the idiom that *without the Rest there might be no West*—certainly not the one that we witness today. And second, it reveals that the rise of the West occurred in significant part during the early global age in which Orientalization was the dominant process and Occidentalization the subordinate one. That is, the assimilation of diffused Eastern resource portfolios provides a significant litmus test for the presence of globalization in this period, since clearly it evoked a strong impact propensity insofar as it led to the fundamental re-organization of societies across the world including Europe.

Modern Globalization, 1830–2000: Occidentalization Dominant, Orientalization Subordinate

Although the period of early globalization that saw Orientalization dominate Occidentalization went into a reversal after about 1830, nevertheless Orientalization remained important. The seminal moment in this transition that usually goes un-noticed was the reversal of the British trade deficit with China in 1828. This was a key moment also because it signals the centrality of Western imperialism along with a host of Western double standards that accompanied it. In essence, the British drugged the Chinese into relinquishing their trade surplus, given that it was the exporting of Indian opium that the British had planted there, coupled with the export of tea that was also grown in India by the British imperial hand, which led to this reversal. The double standards that go with this are manifold. But the most obvious one is that while today the West wages a war on drugs, back then it was through the pushing of drugs into China that they waged their war on the Chinese trade surplus. Moreover, when the Chinese quite reasonably tried to ban opium consumption and its importation from India (led by Commissioner Lin), the British used this as a pretext for war. And in the aftermath of the Arrow Wars, the British imposed a series of *unequal treaties*, which gave them all manner of trading advantages. Even so, it would be wrong to exaggerate the British impact on China—aside of the drug-pushing!—given that they gained only limited penetration of the vast Chinese economy, much of which carried on behind the backs of the British. And moreover, it would be wrong to conclude that Chinese Orientalization ended with the arrival of the British given that the Chinese business diaspora continued through the 19th and 20th centuries to weave together much of South and East Asia through its trading and investment activities.

Nevertheless, the period between 1830 and the late 20th century has witnessed Occidentalization in the ascendance, with the West being the dominant civilization. This was achieved first in the era of colonization (c. 1800–1960) and thereafter through the logic of neo-colonial globalization—that is, Western-dominated neoliberal capitalism. Given that this is a well-rehearsed argument that forms the center-piece of the mainstream Eurocentric account of globalization, I shall not repeat all the details here. One key difference between Orientalization prior to 1830 and post–1830s Occidentalization was that the former saw the expansion of Eastern processes across much of the world though there was no central attempt to impose an Eastern standard of civilization. In strong contrast, Occidentalization has attempted to impose a monolithic homogenizing logic on the world, as the West sought to universalize its civilization. In this respect, modern Occidentalization represents something new both in world politics and globalization.

Given the undeniable fact that the West has played the dominant role since 1830, this necessarily poses a challenge to the non-Eurocentric school of globalization, which has for the most part failed to even consider this phase of globalization. It is as if the school has conceded implicitly that the East bowed out after about 1830, not to be seen again until the late 20th century, when it came crashing back onto the global scene with the "rise" or *return* of Japan and China. As I have already explained, such a characterization would be problematic as it defers far too much to Eurocentrism as far as this phase of globalization is concerned. My task here is not so much to downgrade Occidentalization, but rather to upgrade, or make visible, the role of Orientalization in the "modern" period. For what is equally the case is that in standard Eurocentric narratives of modern globalization (and implicitly within non-Eurocentric narratives), the East plays no agential role in the making of modern globalization whatsoever. It is, instead, viewed either as a passive victim of Western neo-imperial globalization (Marxist and critical theories) or as a passive beneficiary of Western largesse (liberalism).

Although there are a number of arguments I could make by way of illustration here, I shall reveal two key moments of Eastern agency that have had profound implications for the global economy: decolonization and the Organization of Petroleum Exporting Countries (OPEC) oil shocks. I could provide many more examples, but these two illustrate the essential point that I am seeking to make. Turning first to decolonization it is noteworthy that dominant Eurocentric narratives tell the story very much in terms of pure Western agency. Overall, they have in common the idea that decolonization represents the "triumph of the West." Liberal-inspired accounts emphasize how the East passively emulated or endogenized the "superior" Western ideas of sovereignty and self-determination, many of which were "learned" by Eastern elites who had the good fortune to be schooled in Britain or the U.S. (e.g., Bull and Watson 1984); or that the West merely handed over sovereignty to the colonies as it "had always planned to" (consistent with the imperialist trusteeship rhetoric of Article 22 of the League of Nations Covenant concerning the Mandate System). By contrast, Marxist-inspired accounts relate decolonization as a moment in which the baton of global power was finally passed from Britain to the U.S. That is, decolonization enabled the replacement of formal colonial exploitation by the far more "effective" informal vehicle of neo-imperial exploitation. As Immanuel Wallerstein put it, in typical "critical" Euro-functionalist language, the East

> had to be decolonized in order to mobilize productive potential in a way that had never been achieved in the colonial era. Colonial rule after all had been an *inferior* mode of relationship of core and periphery, one [that was] no longer desirable from the point of view of the new [American] hegemonic power. (Wallerstein 1974, 412)

Although neo-imperialism did indeed come to replace formal colonialism, nevertheless it seems an extraordinary leap of 20–20 hindsight to claim that this was the clear intention behind decolonization as it actually played out at the time. Either way, though, in one sense this claim is merely the flip-side of the liberal apologists' Eurocentric argument that the end of empire was brought about by the autonomous policy of the imperial powers. For in both cases, Western agency and Eastern passivity remain the lowest common denominator. In such ways, then, even such a significant moment of Eastern agency is converted into yet another chapter in the ongoing Eurocentric saga of the "triumph of the West."

Undoubtedly many of the factors that enabled decolonization after 1945 can be traced back to the pre-World War I period. Crucial here was the Japanese defeat of Russia in 1905, an event that had an epistemic-transforming impact both within the West and in the East. In the West many peoples now became gripped by a sense of anxiety about the "rising tide of colour" (Stoddard 1920), while the image of the West as infallible and superior began to crack in the eyes of the Eastern peoples. This was crucial in stimulating the nationalist revolt against the West, which developed rapidly in the inter-war period such that by 1960 the colonial powers realized that the great colonial game was up. While there were many localized uprisings concentrated in the periods of 1919–1922, 1929–1932, and 1936–1938, yet more important was the *rhetorical* challenge to empire. Though not wishing to discount physical resistance, nevertheless this occurred in no more than a dozen countries. What mattered far more was the strategy of Eastern mimesis or *mimetic challenge*, wherein the nationalist movements appropriated Western civilizational rhetoric as a means to delegitimize empire. They used, for example, the key third point of the Atlantic Charter which asserted that the signatories (Roosevelt and Churchill) "respect the right of all peoples to choose the form of government under which they will live; and they wish to see sovereign rights and self-government restored to those who have been forcibly deprived of them." Although Churchill believed that this should apply to countries *outside* of Britain's empire, nevertheless the opinion leaders in the colonies used this to push for emancipation. The attack on racism was pivotal.

The allies had fought Nazism under the anti-racist banner. The paradox, however, was that "people of color in their overseas possessions were asked to support a struggle against the very doctrine which, in more benevolently paternalist form, underlay the European colonial enterprise" (Abernethy 2002, 145). Moreover, the experience of being on the receiving end of racism was a humiliating experience for the colonial over-lords. This rendered them morally weakened in the face of the colonial tactic of challenging white racism and paternalism. In the end, the Eastern nationalist movements successfully prosecuted the West in what in effect amounted to a Western "social court of justice" and won the case for decolonization.

The ultimate significance of revolutionary Eastern mimetic challenge is two-fold: first, that it undermines the point that the colonial peoples had merely endogenized Western ideals for freedom, and second, that it reveals the agency of Eastern peoples in breaking down the walls of empire. Indeed, as noted previously, it is commonly believed that the rise of nationalism and sovereignty in the East was the product of a *passive* mimicking of Western ideals. But Eastern nationalism was fundamentally different to that of the European variety given that it was mobilized against the colonial powers. And sovereignty was fought for precisely so as to furnish the East with a *bulwark* against future aspiring Western colonizers rather than as something that would enable them simply to join the Western club. Moreover, sovereignty was to an extent reconceptualized within the Asian setting, thereby suggesting that the ex-colonies did not passively endogenize the Western concept. Thus while within the European context "positive sovereignty" prevailed (which allowed for intervention only in order to maintain the balance of power within the West), by contrast the ex-colonies embraced the norm of "negative sovereignty" which was based on strict demands for self-determination to prevent future Western intrusion. And, the specific local context through which sovereignty was filtered meant that multilateral defense pacts in Asia were resisted (Acharya 2005), something that was institutionalized at the 1955 Bandung Conference.

The significance of all this as far as globalization is concerned is straightforward. For one of the key developments after 1945 that enabled the intensification of globalization was precisely the end of empire. For under formal imperialism most of the world had been divided up into semi-autonomous imperial islands or segments that were largely self-contained. The end of formal empire meant that the whole world became much more open to further integration—that is, the East, albeit unwittingly, secured the achievement of yet deeper levels of global extensity. It is indeed surprising that standard globalization accounts give little, if any, consideration to the end of empire even if it hovers implicitly within their approaches (given their emphasis on the Pax Americana). Nevertheless, Eurocentrics might well respond by arguing that even if decolonization was important (though they would most probably deny the role of the East in all of this), it was, nevertheless, the West that actively sought the integration of the world in the aftermath of formal imperialism, and that if the East had done anything here it was merely to prepare the way that would be filled by Occidentalization after 1960.

I could provide all manner of examples here to counter this portrayal of the post-1960 period, but the one that I choose to develop here, by way of my second example of Eastern agency or *defensive* Orientalization in modern globalization, concerns the OPEC oil shocks. It is well-known that the 1973/1974 and 1979/1980 oil shocks were initiated primarily by the West Asian Muslims in order to punish the West. The former crisis was a response to American military support of Israel in the 1973 Yom Kippur war, while the latter was connected to the Khomeini Revolution in Iran that stood against the American-imposed Shah. Crucial here was the creation of a contemporary triangular trading system, centered on the Middle East, extending to the West at the second pole and the Third World at the third pole. This contemporary triangular trading system reorganized the global economy in fundamental ways.

These two crises sent out shock waves throughout the world. There are two key outcomes that are of prime concern here. First, these waves washed up on the shores of the West in the form of a tsunami of petro-dollars, which were then deposited in Western banks and the Eurocurrency markets. This glut of capital was then lent out, particularly to the Third World. As is well-known, this proved to be a time-bomb that eventually went off in late 1982 in Mexico. Interestingly, the debt crisis was a function of Eastern and Western policies. Thus about a third of Third World debt was ratcheted up in order to pay for the massive increase in the price of oil that was imposed by the OPEC countries. In turn, the profligate lending of Arabic and Persian money to the Third World by the West, coupled with the massive increase in American interest rates in 1980/1981 (in order to attract Japanese investment to support the wary American taxpayer in the face of a rapid escalation of U.S. military expenditures), also played an important part. In other words, both Orientalization and Occidentalization entwined to produce the crisis. Ultimately, though, once the Third World debt crisis had fully exploded, so the global economy had to be reorganized to deal with the problem (e.g., the International Monetary Fund was revived as the major institution that would deal with this and subsequent crises). Of course, this choice was made by the West, principally the U.S., but it occurred as a response to the shocks that were imposed by the East.

Second, the oil shocks had a profound impact on the West. Above all, the two shocks were an important causal factor in the development of recession in the West. The recession of the 1970s was a seminal moment not just for the West but also for the global economy. With the creation of stagflation, Western political economy shifted rightward as a response, seeing an end to Keynesianism and the rise of monetarism and neoliberalism. And, of course, this new epistemic modality of political economy became enshrined in the Washington Consensus. This enabled the hitherto defensive West to go back onto the counter-offensive as it sought to *culturally convert* the Third World along neoliberal Western lines to cure the "ailment" of Eastern cultural "deviancy." By no means is this to say that the oil shocks created Reaganism, Thatcherism, and the Washington Consensus. Rather, the point is that the recession that the oil shocks helped substantially create were responded to in the West by the shift to neoliberalism. The conclusion then is two-fold: first, that the resistance strategies deployed largely by the West Asian Eastern oil states against the West had the effect of further intensifying the integration of the world economy, albeit largely in unanticipated ways. And second, the actions of West Asia served to retrack the West, both in terms of its inner and outer trajectories.

This latter point raises a key conceptual issue when developing my non-Eurocentric theory of modern globalization. For while the modern period witnessed a largely one-way dialogical flow of resource portfolios from West to East (thereby reversing the one way flow that went from East to West between 500–1830), this "dialogue of civilizations" was increasingly complemented by a new logic of inter-civilizational relations—what one scholar calls the "dialectic of civilizations" (Nederveen Pieterse 1989; see also Hobson 2007). In order to clarify this let me outline these two concepts that underpin my non-Eurocentric inter-civilizational analysis of globalization.

The *dialogue of civilizations* refers to the manifold ways in which each civilization develops through the borrowing and assimilation of "resource portfolios" (ideas, technologies, and institutions) that emanate from other civilizations. This process has been going on since at least 500 CE and embodies a largely non-conflictual relationship (as I discussed earlier). Here I suggest that in the dialogue, the meeting point of civilizations is a two-way "dialogical zone" that generates poly-civilizational hybridity through what Mary-Louise Pratt (1992) calls "transculturation," and which amounts to a form of "dialogical negotiation" (as opposed to a monologic one-way passive receptivity).

But the "edges" of civilizations can simultaneously be conceptualized as *imperial dialectical frontiers*. This emerges in the *dialectics of civilizations* where Western imperialism/neo-imperialism and Eastern resistance dialectically engage and entwine. At first sight this might seem reminiscent of Huntington's "clash of civilizations" thesis. Huntington's civilizational edges are likened to volatile "fault lines" where self-constituting, monolithic civilizations meet and clash (Huntington 1996). But in Huntington's conception there is no possibility for a two-way trans-cultural socialization process since civilizations retain their autonomous, self-constituting "natural cultural essences" after social interaction. In my alternative formulation, which I adapt from the pioneering analysis in Nederveen Pieterse's (1989) book, *Empire and Emancipation*, these "edges" can better be imagined as *permeable two-way dialectical frontiers* where civilizations once again shape and retrack each other, thereby coming to constitute and guide each other's internal and external developmental trajectories. In contrast to Eurocentric monologism, this process of "dialectical negotiation" reveals, as Nederveen Pieterse emphasizes, a bottom-up logic of emancipation/resistance entwined with a top-down logic of imperial/neo-imperial domination. Indeed, the Eastern peoples never simply lay passively underneath the empire "thinking of England" as the British and Americans went about their imperial exploitation, but always played an active constitutive role in the globalization and imperial processes.

Returning now to the theme being discussed previously, my key point here is that once Western imperialism had begun mainly in the post-1800 period, the dialogues of civilizations (which became largely Western-led) were complemented by the dialectics of civilizations, where Eastern resistance agency retracked the West, which in turn responded through new imperial strategies, which were then resisted by the East, such that these "negotiations" went back and forth, in the process remaking both East and West as well as globalization more generally. This is applicable to decolonization as much as it is to the story of the OPEC oil shocks.

Postmodern Globalization: Occidentalization Receding, Orientalization Resurgent

Finally, in the last few decades of the 20th century, Occidentalization had reached its nadir as Orientalization proved to be not only resurgent but in the ascendance, first through the Japanese miracle and later at the turn of the 21st century with the second Chinese industrial miracle. The "return of Japan" (given that Japan had attained great power status by the end of the 19th century) was evident not just in terms of Japan's colossal trading power and the rise of Japanese investment across the world, but also through the Western emulation of Japanese management practices, Just-in-Time production system (or what is termed "Toyotism"). But the key development, of course, is the return of China. I call this the "return" rather than the "rise" of China because as I discussed earlier, China was the leading economy between 1100–c. 1830. Indeed the first Chinese industrial miracle, which occurred after 960 during the Sung dynasty (Hobson 2004, ch. 3), is now coming "full circle" almost exactly 1,000 years later with the contemporary (second) Chinese industrial miracle that can be dated to the post-1978 era CE (see also Jones et al. 1993). Thus while the 150 year interlude between 1830 and 1980 saw an eclipse of China, first by Britain and later Europe and the U.S., nevertheless China and the West seem to be trading places once again as we enter the 21st century.

Much of the debate within the discipline of International Relations concerns the issue as to whether China will become the next hegemon and that its power in the world is read or filtered by Western scholars through this "hegemonic" lens. There are, however, two key problems with this approach. First, the jury is still out on this issue not least because for many Chinese, as was the parallel case with Japan in the 1980s, there is no clear desire to "rule the world." Thus to quote the title of one important recent book, *When China Rules the World* (Jacques 2009), it would appear to be more "whether" rather than "when." And second, viewing China through the lens of a potential Pax Sinica is to look in the wrong place for signs of Chinese power in the world today. More important is the role of Chinese global *structural power*, which entails the ability of China to shape the global economy even if it is not (yet) the leading power in the world and even if it does not seek to form a world hegemony either at present or in the future. Owing to a lack of space, I shall reserve my discussion for a consideration of one of the key signs of Chinese structural power.

One of the key questions concerning the return of Orientalization to the center of the global economy is whether this is "just another episode in the rise and decline of nations, another reshuffling of capitalism, a relocation of accumulation centers [that does not affect] the [Western] logics of accumulation?" (Nederveen Pieterse 2008, 707), or whether it is something that introduces new organizational logics into the global economy? My claim is that the return of China is leading to a fundamental re-organization of global governance—economic and political—processes. In particular, the return of Orientalization alongside a declining but still strong Occidentalization, is leading to what can be called a new *postmodern* phase of globalization. I label it this precisely because we are now witnessing a new hybrid poly-civilizational form of globalization, as contemporary Orientalization operationalizes different organizing global principles to those of Occidentalization; and that such ordering principles either co-exist or compete in global space.

As we know, Occidentalization has sought to *culturally convert* societies across the world according to Western neo-liberal principles—typified by the lending policies of the International Monetary Fund and World Bank. And, of course, the World Trade Organization explicitly seeks to convert societies onto neoliberalism through the effecting of free trade convergence. All of which is summed up by the principles of the Washington Consensus, which emerged in the aftermath of the Eastern oil shocks. By contrast, the Chinese explicitly eschew the cultural conversion of societies according to a Chinese standard of civilization. Rather, the Beijing Consensus and the principles of co-existence explicitly allow for cultural heterogeneity in the world. In this sense China is returning to the principles that underpinned its historic tribute system (c. 100 BCE–1878 CE). Back then, China respected the cultural autonomy of the so-called vassal states as much as it does with respect to those states that it invests and trades with today. Nowhere is this clearer than in its relations with African states, where China cooperates with African states and seeks not to infringe upon their sovereignty, nor to impose conditionality—with the exception of China's condition that African states do not deal with Taiwan (see Jacques 2009; Alden 2006; Pere and Shelton 2006; Brautigam 2009). Overall, China is forging a new organizing principle of global politics/economics which seeks to provide an alternative to American-led hegemonialism. This has played a powerful role within Africa and the signs are that, unlike the failed Japanese proposal for an Asian Monetary Fund back in 1997, China is likely to be able to forge ahead in ways that Japan could not attain. The key question then becomes whether this will bring China into conflict with the U.S., with the latter viewing the former very much in terms of a threat. The paradox is that while China's rise has been peaceful and non-confrontational, the U.S. constructs this rise as the latest Yellow Peril scare. But I leave that issue aside here, preferring to conclude that we in some respects are now going back to the future of the world after 1450 when China led the way, witnessing not so much the rise of China but the return of China to the center of the global economy.

NOTES

1. Note that some Eurocentrics adopt an anti-paternalist Eurocentrism (e.g., Smith and Kant), or a defensive, anti-paternalist racism (e.g., Spencer and Sumner), both variants of which believe that Eastern societies will eventually develop into capitalism spontaneously in the absence of Western imperial intervention, even if this would take a very long time (see Hall and Hobson 2010; Hobson 2012, chs. 3 and 4).
2. See, for example, Frank and Gills (1996); Frank (1998); Hopkins (2002); Marks (2002); Gunn (2003); Hobson (2004); Nederveen Pieterse (2006); Flynn and Giráldez (2006).
3. See Goonatilake (1998); Pomeranz (2000); Goody (1996, 2004); Bala (2006); Ghazanfar (2006); Raju (2007); Goldstone (2008).
4. Note that Jerry Bentley (1993) locates the origins of globalization to the post-800 BCE Axial Age, while others trace it all the way back to Sumer in 3,500 BCE (e.g., Frank and Gills 1996; Goody 1996).
5. Actually the silver was transported on the Spanish Manila Galleons to the Philippines before it was imported into China on Chinese ships.

6. For example, Hobson (2004: ch. 8); Goody (2004); Bala (2006); Raju (2007); Ghazanfar (2006).

REFERENCES

Abernethy, David. 2002. *The Dynamics of Global Dominance*. New Haven: Yale University Press.

Abu-Lughod, Janet L. 1989. *Before European Hegemony*. Oxford: Oxford University Press.

Acharya, Amitav. 2005. "Why Is There No NATO in Asia? The Normative Origins of Asian Multilateralism." Wetherhead Center for International Affairs, Working Paper No. 05–05, Harvard University.

Alden, Chris. 2006. "China in Africa." *Survival* 47(3): 147–164.

Bala, Arun. 2006. *The Dialogue of Civilizations in the Birth of Modern Science*. Houndmills: Palgrave Macmillan.

Bentley, Jerry H. 1993. *Old World Encounters*. New York: Oxford University Press.

Blaut, James M. 1993. *The Colonizer's Model of the World*. London: Guilford.

Brautigam, Deborah 2009. *The Dragon's Gift*. Oxford: Oxford University Press.

Bromley, Simon. 1999. "Marxism and Globalisation." In *Marxism and Social Science*, edited by A. Gamble, D. Marsh, and T. Tant, 280–301. Basingstoke: Macmillan.

Bull, Hedley, and Adam Watson. 1984. "Conclusion." In *The Expansion of International Society*, edited by Bull and Watson, 425–435. Oxford: Oxford University Press.

Cox, Robert W. 1996. *Approaches to World Order*. Cambridge: Cambridge University Press.

Flynn, Dennis O., and Arturo Giráldez. 1994. "China and the Manila Galleons." In *Japanese Industrialization and the Asian Economy*, edited by A.J.H. Latham and H. Kawakatsu, 71–90. London: Routledge.

Flynn, Dennis O., and Arturo Giráldez. 2006. "Globalization Began in 1571." In *Globalization and Global History*, edited by B.K. Gills and William R. Thompson, 232–247. London: Routledge.

Frank, Andre Gunder. 1998. *ReOrient*. Berkeley: University of California Press.

Frank, Andre Gunder, and Barry K. Gills, eds. 1996. *The World System: Five Hundred or Five Thousand Years?* London: Routledge.

Friedman, Thomas L. 1999. *The Lexus and the Olive Tree*. London: Harper Collins.

Fukuyama, Francis 1992. *The End of History and the Last Man*. London: Hamish Hamilton.

Ghazanfar, S.M. 2006. *Islamic Civilization*. Lanham: Scarecrow Press.

Gill, Stephen. 1995. "Globalisation, Market Civilisation and Disciplinary Neoliberalism." *Millennium* 24(3): 399–423.

Gilroy, Paul. 1993. *The Black Atlantic*. Cambridge: Harvard University Press.

Goldstone, Jack. 2008. *Why Europe? The Rise of the West in World History, 1500–1850*. New York: McGraw-Hill Humanities.

Goody, Jack. 1996. *The East in the West*. Cambridge: Cambridge University Press.

Goody, Jack. 2004. *Islam in Europe*. Cambridge: Polity.

Goonatilake, Susanthe. 1998. *Toward a Global Science: Mining Civilizational Knowledge*. New Delhi: Vistaar.

Gunn, Geoffrey C. 2003. *First Exchange: The Eurasian Exchange, 1500–1800*. Lanham: Rowman & Littlefield.

Hall, Martin, and John M. Hobson. 2010. "Liberal International Theory: Eurocentric but Not Always Imperialist?" *International Theory* 2(2): 210–45.

Held, David, Anthony McGrew, David Goldblatt, and Jonathan Perraton. 1999. *Global Transformations*. Cambridge: Polity.
Hobson, John M. 2004. *The Eastern Origins of Western Civilisation*. Cambridge: Cambridge University Press.
Hobson, John M. 2007. "Is Critical Theory Always for the White West and for Western Imperialism? Beyond Westphilian towards a Post-Racist Critical International Relations." *Review of International Studies* 33(SI): 91–116.
Hobson, John M. 2012. *The Eurocentric Conception of World Politics: Western International Theory, 1760–2010*. Cambridge: Cambridge University Press.
Hodgson, Marshall G.S. 1974. *The Venture of Islam*, 3 vols. Chicago: Chicago University Press.
Hopkins, Anthony G. 2002. "The History of Globalization—and the Globalization of History?" In *Globalization in World History*, edited by A.G. Hopkins, 11–46. London: Pimlico.
Huntington, Samuel P. 1996. *The Clash of Civilizations and the Remaking of World Order*. London: Touchstone Books.
Jacques, Martin. 2009. *When China Rules the World*. London: Penguin.
Jones, Eric, Lionel Frost, and Colin White. 1993. *Coming Full Circle*. Boulder: Westview Press.
Landes, David. 1998. *The Wealth and Poverty of Nations*. Boston: Little, Brown & Co.
Marks, Robert B. 2002. *The Origins of the Modern World*. Lanham: Rowman & Littlefield.
Nederveen Pieterse, Jan. 1989. *Empire and Emancipation*. London: Pluto.
Nederveen Pieterse, Jan. 2006. "Oriental Globalization: Past and Present." In *Europe and Asia Beyond East and West*, edited by Gerard Delanty, 61–73. London: Routledge.
Nederveen Pieterse, Jan. 2008. "Globalization the Next Round: Sociological Perspectives." *Futures* 40(8): 707–720.
Nederveen Pieterse, Jan. 2009. *Globalization and Culture*. Lanham: Rowman & Littlefield.
Pere, Garth Le, and Garth Shelton. 2006. "Afro-Chinese Relations: An Evolving South-South Partnership." *South African Journal of International Affairs* 13(1): 33–53.
Pomeranz, Kenneth. 2000. *The Great Divergence*. Princeton: Princeton University Press.
Pratt, Mary Louise. 1992. *Imperial Eyes*. London: Routledge.
Raju, C.K. 2007. *Cultural Foundations of Mathematics*, 10(4): *History of Science, Philosophy and Culture in Indian Civilization*. New Delhi: Pearson Education.
Roberts, J.M. 1985. *The Triumph of the West*. London: BBC Books.
Stoddard, Lothrop. 1920. *The Rising Tide of Color against White World Supremacy*. New York: Charles Scribner's Sons.
Wallerstein, Immanuel. 1974. "The Rise and Future Demise of the World Capitalist System: Concepts for Comparative Analysis." *Comparative Studies in Society and History* 16(4): 387–415.
Wallerstein, Immanuel. 1984. *The Politics of the World-Economy*. Cambridge: Cambridge University Press.
Wink, André. 1990. *Al-Hind: The Making of the Indo-Islamic World*, Vol. I. Leiden: E.J. Brill.
Wolf, Eric R. 1982. *Europe and the People without History*. Berkeley: University of California Press.
Wolf, Martin. 2005. *Why Globalization Works*. New Haven: Yale University Press.

2 Global Rebalancing
Crisis and the East-South Turn

Jan Nederveen Pieterse[1]

The share of emerging markets in global gross domestic product (GDP) has risen from 21 percent in 1999 to 36 percent in 2010.[2] Emerging societies are rising in trade, multinational firms, finance, international influence, and cultural presence (Marber 1998; Prestowitz 2005; Agtmael 2007; Nederveen Pieterse 2008a; Magnus 2010). This unfolds under various headings such as the rise of the second world, the "rise of the rest" and the BRIC (Brazil, Russia, India, China). The BRIC, "the only developing economies with GDPs of more than $1 trillion per year . . . have provided 45 percent of economic growth worldwide since the financial crisis began in 2007." Together their foreign reserves are six times the assets of the International Monetary Fund (IMF).[3] Other categories are N-11 or the "next eleven nations" to emerge as major economies and systemically important countries (or BRIC plus Mexico, South Africa, Turkey, and South Korea).[4] Without a doubt these trends represent the "next big thing" in globalization and international development. Consider a sampling of recent headlines as writings on the wall:

"Why Brands Now Rise in the East"
"Consumption Starts to Shift to China, India and Brazil"
"Developing Economies Lead the Way in 2010 Forecast, While Rich Nations Lag"
"Developing Countries Underpin Boom in Advertising Spending"
"Architecture Firms Go East for Work"
"Bankers Sense Shift in Capital Flows"
"Emerging Market Debt Is the New Safe Haven"
"Emerging Economies Set to Play Leading Investment Role"
"Benchmark Expert Watches Market Weight Shift Eastwards"
"U.S. Cities Seek to Woo Chinese Investment"
"Chinese Investment Keeps Greece, Iceland and Others Afloat"
"The Deal Makers Who Matter Are Rising in the East"[5]

Geely has bought Volvo, Lenovo bought IBM's PC division, Tata bought Jaguar and Land Rover, Mittal bought Corus and other steel industries, Brazilian companies have bought Burger King and Anheuser Busch (brewer of the all-American Budweiser beer), Qatar Holdings bought Harrods, Qatar and Dubai investment companies bought 48 percent of the London Stock Exchange, emerging economies' sovereign wealth funds have made major investments in western financial houses, and in the luxury market Asian fashion houses have bought western companies such as S.C. Fang in Hong Kong which bought Pringle of Scotland. Sahara India Pariwar is making a $2 billion bid for the MGM movie studio.

Fukuyama's triumphalist account of the "end of history" to mark the end of the cold war now seems long past. In a case of political economy outflanking ideology and geopolitics, this narrative has been slowly overtaken by the rise of new industrializing economies.

Accounts of the new emerging equation range wildly. It is variously described as a flat world (T. Friedman 2005), a "spiked world" (Florida 2008), a condition of "globality" in which everyone competes with everyone (Sirkin et al. 2008), as the "rise of the rest" (Amsden 2001) and a "post-American world" (Zakaria 2008). The U.S. National Intelligence Council (2008) anticipates the end of American superpower by 2025.

Not too long ago it may have been sufficient for many purposes to view the world as split between North and South, core and periphery, developed and developing, industrial and agro-mineral economies. This is the classic international division of labor that goes back to colonial times. In the 1970s this began to change with multinational corporations investing in low-wage countries in Latin America, the Caribbean, and Asia, which was then termed the "new international division of labor." Dependency thinkers argued it was a fad, a fantasy; investors would flee once labor cost rose; dependent capitalist development brings only underdevelopment. A new branch of studies began to critically examine the semiperiphery as a formation in-between the core and periphery which acts as a periphery in relation to the core (exporting raw materials, adopting its cultural styles) and as a core in relation to the periphery (exporting finished products, setting cultural standards, acting as regional police). Wallerstein (1984) argued that the emergence of the semiperiphery gives the world-system a more stable structure; rather than the polarized North-South, rich-poor field, balancing forces in-between give the overall structure greater resilience. Table 2.1 summarizes the schema of the three way division.

Table 2.1 Three Worlds Revisited

North	*East and South*	*South*
Core	Semiperiphery	Periphery
Developed	Developed and developing	Developing
Industrial and post-industrial	Industrial and agro-mineral	Agro-mineral

In the 21st century the semiperiphery has come of age. "The noughties of the 21st century" notes Martin Wolf "now have the same fin-de-regime feeling as those of a century ago"[6] (when the British Empire went down). The 2008 crisis both reflects and accelerates this process. According to Robert Zoellick, president of the World Bank, "the developing world is becoming a driver of the global economy. Even though developing world imports are about half of the imports of high-income countries, they are growing at a much faster rate. As a result, they accounted for more than half of the increase in world import demand since 2000" (2010, 2). He adds,

> The world economy is rebalancing. Some of this is new. Some represents a restoration. According to Angus Maddison, Asia accounted for over half of world output for 18 of the last 20 centuries. We are witnessing a move towards multiple poles of growth as middle classes grow in developing countries, billions of people join the world economy, and new patterns of integration combine regional intensification with global openness. (Zoellick 2010, 2)

The thesis of "decoupling" or the world economy delinking from the American economy and recoupling to emerging economies finds growing confirmation. "The developing world's rapidly growing middle class, which includes about two billion people in a dozen emerging economies, spends $6.9 trillion a year. McKinsey research suggests that, during the next decade, their annual spending will rise to $20 trillion, a very big market indeed—twice current U.S. consumption, in fact" (McKinsey 2010).

What is at stake in these changes? First is "the rising influence of rising affluence."[7] This is where the new growth markets are so in business, finance, commodities, transport, advertising, technology, architecture; this is the big story, the next great frontier that inspires enthusiasm in business schools. New iconic buildings arise in Kuala Lumpur, Taipei, Seoul, Shanghai, Beijing, Dubai, Qatar; new museums; new biennales; new art markets; and record sales of luxury goods. Shanghai chic sets a new tone. Major retailers, global brands, diamond traders, wine merchants, architects, advertising agencies, universities, bankers, all head east. Major international cultural events—the Olympic Games, the World Cup, the World Expo—are drawn to emerging societies, beginning with the 1988 Olympic Games in Seoul. Maybe the refrain is simply "follow the money," but our global horizons are changing.

The avant-garde architect Jacques Herzog who designed Beijing's Bird's Nest Stadium, observes, "I think we may be able to learn from China, Brazil and India, to see how society is able to transform."[8] (However, the stadium now stands unused.) So what is also happening is a revitalization of modernity and the staging of new modernities (Nederveen Pieterse 2009b). With this come new spheres of cultural influence such as the "Korean Wave" (*Korea Herald* 2008), the popularity of Thai soaps in China and Turkish soaps in Saudi Arabia, and Brazil setting up TV broadcasting in Africa.

Third, it is a reconfiguration of the world economy. A "new geography of trade" has taken shape in relations between Asia, Latin America, the Middle East and Africa (Nederveen Pieterse 2008a). In development studies the talk is of "Asian drivers" of growth in developing countries (Kaplinksy and Messner 2008). Emerging societies are increasingly fulfilling core functions on the world stage—acting as development role models, providing stable markets, loans, aid, and security, with China as a leading force. Emerging societies don't just play this role in relation to developing countries; some of their model, creditor, and stabilizing functions unfold at a global level.

Fourth, the role of emerging economies in finance has been growing as well. Sovereign wealth funds from Asia and energy exporting countries provide credit on a world scale and to international financial institutions (Teslik 2009). "It was the emerging markets, most notably China, which pulled the world back from the brink of financial meltdown."[9] China's investments in Greece follow the older pattern of East Asian firms investing in Europe's deindustrializing regions. There has been a remarkable reversal of the creditor-debtor relation between the U.S. and Asia and Middle East oil exporters, remarkable because it unfolds in international finance, the central powerhouse of western influence and the sector through which the U.S. sought to shape emerging economies. Besides, finance is traditionally the terrain in which hegemons retain their lead when it fades in economic, political, and military domains (Arrighi 2007). There has been a reversal, too, of classic economic postures—the world's leading protagonists of free trade now are emerging markets, not the U.S.

Fifth, in time it will portend a reconfiguration of world order. So far this is only dimly visible on the horizon. The unipolar world is no more nor is the world of the big powers, as indicated in the shift from the Group of Eight (G8; Canada, France, Germany, Italy, Japan, the U.K., the U.S., and Russia), to the Group of Twenty (G20; the addition of Argentina, Australia, Brazil, China, the European Union [EU], India, Indonesia, Mexico, Saudi Arabia, South Africa, Republic of Korea, and Turkey) in the throes of the 2008 crisis (Altman 2009). Yet, even as hegemonic capacity isn't what it used to be, the institutions have barely changed and habits of hegemony and of following hegemony linger. Global governance is "still lost in the old Bretton Woods,"[10] the G20 may be a step back for it expands the rule of big countries over small[11] and it has transformed into an arena of contention over trade and currencies. Political transformations are more salient in regional developments such as the Shanghai Cooperation Organization, Association of Southeast Asian Nations and China, Japan, and South Korea (ASEAN+3), China's free trade agreement with ASEAN, and cross-regional cooperation such as between Brazil, Turkey, and Iran, and India, Brazil, and South Africa. The crisis does indicate that the North-South polarity has given way to a different fault line that runs between (trade and current account) surplus and deficit societies.

Taken together these trends signal a major tipping point in history. North-South relations have been dominant for some 200 years (1800–2000) and current trends see the onset of an East-South turn. The East in this shorthand language refers to the emerging societies—East because East Asia (ASEAN+3) is the leading cluster, but generally it refers to all newly industrialized countries; while the South refers to the global South, as shorthand for developing countries. There are now three sets of relations to consider. First, relations *within* semiperipheral countries between industrial and agro-mineral sectors, between urban and rural populations, and between rich and poor; second, between the core and semiperiphery, between old and new forces; and third, relations between the semiperiphery and periphery, East-South or South-South relations such as relations between China and Africa and Latin America, which is the theme of a growing literature. All are important; the first set is the theme of a recent volume (Nederveen Pieterse and Rehbein 2009). This discussion focuses mostly on the second theme.

Why is this theme important? The present juncture is an in-between condition. The old hegemony is no more, and its frailties pose growing risks; a new constellation isn't available yet although some contours are taking shape. Current trends can be read in two ways, toward recalibrating the old order or toward the emergence of new logics.

This can be simplified as a tale of three scripts. One is global plutocracy with Anglo-American capitalism and financial markets in the West back in the lead, emerging markets joining the club, and the G20 as the de facto governing board of the IMF. An instrument for achieving this is the discourse of "global rebalancing" which functions both as hegemonic ideology and policy framework. The second script is multipolarity, with new forces at the table but no new institutions, so a different but unstable situation. The third script, way on the other end of the continuum, is emancipatory multipolarity, considering that countries representing the majority of the world population have come to the global head table. This chapter argues that the rise of emerging societies is a major turn in globalization and asks whether this holds an emancipatory potential, which is highly contentious and controversial, but worth posing as a key question. Let us consider as a guiding image the global situation as a giant see-saw or teeter totter. The middle position is multipolarity—that is, not just New York, London, and Tokyo matter but also centers such as Beijing, New Delhi, Sao Paulo, Seoul, Istanbul, and so forth. Multipolarity is already a given and is noncontroversial; what is controversial are the *terms of multipolarity* and its extent and ramifications. As the middle position multipolarity is wobbly and unstable and constantly oscillating (see Table 2.2).

The first section of this chapter discusses global rebalancing according to the G20 and contrasts it with actual ongoing rebalancing and rebalancing

Table 2.2 Global Balance

Global Plutocracy	*Multipolarity*	*Emancipatory Multipolarity*
Anglo-American capitalism back in the lead, emerging markets join the club, G20 as governing board of IMF	Global rebalancing	Countries representing the majority of the world population come to the global head table

Note: G20 = Group of Twenty; IMF = International Monetary Fund.

from the viewpoint of new forces and new emerging multilateralism. The next sections discuss the scripts of global plutocracy, multipolarity and emancipatory multipolarity. A further section reviews the problematic of capitalism or capitalisms. The closing sections reflect on analytics and methods and argue for a multilevel analysis in which elements of both scripts combine.

GLOBAL REBALANCING

> Playbooks are not readily available when it comes to new systemic themes. This leads many to revert to backward-looking analytical models, the thrust of which is essentially to assume away the relevance of the new systemic phenomena. (Mohamed El-Erian 2010)

When in the early 2000s the U.S.'s trade and current account deficits grew ever larger, economists honed in on global imbalances (e.g., Roubini 2006; Feldstein 2008), and several argued that the imbalances were unsustainable and would produce either an orderly or a disorderly adjustment, either a soft or a hard landing. Gradually the perspective widened to include not just American deficits but also Asian surpluses, especially of China (El Erian 2008; Bagnai 2009; Okimoto 2009). A comment notes "global economic imbalances" are "code, as everyone knows, for the U.S. current account deficit and the Chinese surplus" (Stephens 2009).

The crisis of 2007–2009 brought the imbalances in trade and finance into the headlines. According to widely held view on Wall Street and in Washington, the "savings glut" in Asia prompted the crisis. According to Krishna Guha,

> the current crisis is in the strictest sense a crisis of globalization, fostered and transmitted by the rapid and deep integration of very different economies. Fast-growing developing countries with underdeveloped financial systems were exporting savings to the developed world for packaging and re-export to them in the forms of financial products . . . the claim that this was sustainable assumed core financial centres—above all New York

Figure 2.1 Mike Keefe cartoon—Obama Asia trip (The Denver Post and InToon.com).

> and London—could create the financial products efficiently and without blowing up. They could not. (Guha 2009)

Thus the culprit is the "savings glut" in Asia that overwhelms American financial institutions. This overlooks that three decades of deregulation had enhanced the vulnerability of these institutions and the Federal Reserve's low interest rates relayed these flows, creating a credit bubble society (Baker 2009; Phillips 2009).

The major post-crisis script discussed in G20 meetings, Davos, and business media is global rebalancing. If global imbalances are the underlying cause of crisis, managing crisis means addressing the imbalances. In the U.S., U.K., and EU—where this discourse has been dominant—rebalancing essentially means that China should appreciate its currency, the renminbi (RMB), and surplus countries (East Asia and oil exporters) should fund the IMF so the IMF resumes its role of managing world economic stability (e.g., Wolf 2010). Further prescriptions are that Asia should export less, save less, and consume more, and the U.S. should consume less, save more, and export more. Since the latter prescriptions involve not just policy changes but structural changes they are on the backburner. Protectionism is the threat behind this agenda. While the U.S. and EU put steady pressure on China to appreciate the RMB China accuses them of protectionism and "restricting China's development." The situation is reminiscent of the 1985 Plaza Accord in which the Group of Five (G5; U.S., U.K., Japan, Germany, and France) agreed on appreciation of the Japanese yen and devaluation of the U.S. dollar. Now, however, China has learned from the Japanese experience, the U.S. has less leverage and China, as the U.S.'s major creditor, expresses concern about American deficits and fiscal policies.

The argument of rebalancing presents several problems. It recycles a neoclassical idea of equilibrium and upholds an abstract model. The emphasis on *global* rebalancing diverts the attention from domestic reform. The dominant ideas of rebalancing reflect the perspectives of the advanced economies, several of which are now deficit countries; they seek to restore a balance that is unrecoverable and has been overtaken by economic trends. It also assumes more robust global governance than is realistic given the existing imbalances and the past record.

In economics there have been as many ideas of balance as there have been political and economic systems. Each political and economic transition is marked by a redefinition of balance. In neoclassical economics the price mechanism is supposed to balance supply and demand. Efficient market theory, the lead paradigm during recent decades, also assumes that markets are self-equilibrating. The 2008 crisis debunks this assumption. In Keynesian economics when demand falters the role of government is to rebalance the economy through demand management. Richard Nixon's adage "We're all Keynesians now" has made a comeback but takes on a different meaning in a global economy than in a national setting.

If equilibrium models don't apply in economies, generally they apply even less in the world economy. Imbalances such as the triangular trade, relations between colonial and colonized countries, and unequal exchange between manufactured goods exporters and suppliers of raw materials have been at the foundation of the contemporary world economy. This also holds for recent times. "The blunt fact is that at no point in the past century has there been anything resembling a global economic equilibrium. . . . When officials and economists today speak of correcting global imbalances, it is unclear what benchmark they have in mind" (Karabell 2009).

Besides, global imbalances are embedded in domestic imbalances. When during recent decades American consumption drove world economic growth, private consumption was 72 percent of U.S. GDP (comparative rates in 2005 were 57 percent in Europe, 51 percent in Asia, and 36 percent in China). As American consumption levels were rising, median wages did not, in part because American workers compete with low wage, no-union labor in the American South and with low-wage labor overseas (Nederveen Pieterse 2008b; Reich 2010). The combination of rising consumption, rising productivity, and stagnant wages was made possible by long working hours, two-earner households, imports of cheap Asian consumer goods, and a vast expansion of credit. Deferred payments, credit card debt, home equity financing, and adjustable rate and subprime mortgages were enabled by Federal Reserve low-interest policies and by external borrowing, which during the past decade absorbed 70 to 80 percent of world net savings. The financialization of the American economy and the credit bubble then primarily reflect the conjunction of rising consumption and growing inequality in the U.S., rather than global imbalances or a "savings glut" in Asia.

So balance has no precedent in the world economy, imbalance is common, and balance is a recurrent ideal. Global economic balance is a hegemonic utopia. Besides, the actual significance of an appreciation of the RMB is doubtful. It doesn't affect the American trade deficit, which stems from offshoring production capacity across borders where profit margins have been higher. An appreciation of the RMB will not fix America's import dependence; as Min Gong argues (see Chapter 8, this volume), the U.S. trade deficit would remain what it is and imports would be sourced from other Asian countries and Latin America. China's de-pegging the RMB from the U.S. dollar, begun in 2005 and resumed in June 2010, barely affects the Sino-U.S. trade imbalance. The *China Daily* notes, "It is the sovereign right of a country to decide the value of its currency. And it should not change to suit another country's need."[12] When in the run up to a G20 meeting in June 2010 China resumed its de-pegging of the RMB from the dollar (effectively appreciating the RMB by 0.53 percent), presumably to deflect tensions with the U.S. congress, American attention shifted to Germany with calls that it should adopt policies to stimulate demand, increase consumption, and cut exports and savings, which the German government promptly declined.

"Global rebalancing" is code for shifting the burden of reform on China and other surplus societies: keep the "free market" in the West courtesy of adjustments in the East and Germany. It implies there is little need for reforming American ways as long as there are external remedies. But in fact it shows that the global fault lines no longer run between North and South but between trade (and current account) deficit (such as U.S., U.K.) and surplus countries (notably East Asia, Germany along with energy exporting countries).

Actual ongoing global rebalancing means dynamic imbalance or transitions from one type of imbalance to another. Further features of actual global rebalancing are, first, the imbalances reflect long-term changes in the world economy, so beyond immediate effects we must consider long-term trends. Second, the 2008 crisis is not a cause of imbalances but a manifestation. Crisis is a prism through which global rebalancing is perceived and a process through which it takes place. The crisis then is not an "ordinary systemic crisis" and is more than a financial and banking crisis (the trigger is not the cause). Third, global rebalancing is multidimensional. Although it is primarily discussed in economic and financial terms it is as much a political, institutional, social and cultural process. Fourth, ideas of rebalancing depend on narratives of crisis, which are influenced by the nature of the recovery; what emerges as the dominant crisis narrative will affect the idea of balance. Fifth, what is needed is to compare narratives of crisis and imbalance and policies of rebalancing in societies located at different places on the spectrum of global imbalances. Thus rebalancing must be viewed not merely from the viewpoint of advanced societies but as much from the viewpoint of emerging societies and developing countries.

GLOBAL PLUTOCRACY?

Will there be a global convergence of capitalisms on the American model? Will American capitalism gobble up emerging markets, and will emerging societies join the club of big powers as franchises of western ways with different interior design? This is under discussion worldwide. I will present perspectives on both sides of the equation.

Martin Sorrell, chief executive of the British global marketing group WFF, expects adjustments and the end of the era of superconsumption, but the pendulum will swing back, albeit with a different geographic balance of power and a new capitalism with an Asian-Pacific, Latin American flavor.[13] The tenor is: let regulations come, they will fail again, incorporate the new capitalism and the London City will be back in business. Others observe a merger of elites, with business elites and ruling elites west and east forming a new global "superclass" (Rothkopf 2008). World-system analysis and the transnational capitalist class perspective (Sklair 2001) argue along similar lines.

Transnational capitalist cooperation occurs in institutions (World Trade Organization, IMF), intellectual property (patents, licensing), technology (industrial standards), transport, travel, and in firms, particularly in mining, energy, telecoms, and finance sectors. Governance and international law (United Nations, International Criminal Court [ICC]) are other domains of cooperation. The limits to such cooperation include national interests. Currency, interest rates, and sovereign wealth funds are jealously guarded national agendas. Security, logistics, trade routes, strategic resources, energy and metals, sensitive technology, and foreign investments are closely watched as well. In 2006 the U.S. congress resisted Dubai Ports World's bid to buy the British firm P&O and take over the management of many U.S. port facilities. U.S. regulators rejected China's National Offshore Oil Corporation's bid to buy the U.S. oil company Unocal and Huawei's offer to buy 2wire, an internet software unit of Motorola. Australia rejected the attempt of Chinalco, China's state-owned metals group, to invest $19 billion in Rio Tinto. Western companies complain of restrictions they face in China, and China complains about restrictions on technology transfer. While transnational enterprises, migrants, and "new argonauts" straddle regions and combine technologies and resources (Saxenian 2006) this doesn't rule out differences across countries and zones and in fact may reinforce them. Many firms practice institutional arbitrage, juggling different arrangements between countries and zones (tax laws, labor rights, environmental regulations, special economic zones) so their actions are conditioned by and condition institutional differences (Ong 2006). Thus, processes are layered and include transnational cooperation as well as competition and corporate and national, regional, and local agendas. Layered processes, then, produce layered outcomes—with different and combined patterns of transnational, regional, national, and local cooperation, so diverse scripts coexist at different levels.

Another perspective holds that the most advanced form of capitalism, which is taken to be neoliberalism, predominates. David Harvey, Mike Davis, Patrick Bond, and others tend to equate contemporary capitalism and neoliberalism and thus take differences in capitalist organization to be marginal (e.g., Harvey 2005; Petras 2009; Westra 2010).We can term this the "neoliberalism everywhere" thesis; I come back to this in the section on capitalisms. Let's note that scholars who in the 1980s argued that the semiperiphery wouldn't fly such as Samir Amin (1997) and James Petras, now typically dismiss emerging societies as neoliberal economies; in other words, theirs is a script in which western capitalism always wins. But scripts are contingent—contingent on paradigms, ideologies, politics, institutions, data sets, and expectations of continuity and risk. The main elements of contention are narratives of crisis, frontiers of regulation, and developments in emerging societies.

In American elite views, the crisis is a systemic failure, no one's fault, and Wall Street wizards are needed to unwind the mess.[14] If the crisis has been brought about by a "savings glut" in Asia, remedies are to cut savings in Asia and borrow less in the U.S. To the extent that financial excess and deregulation in the West are contributing factors, the remedy is to regulate banks. Then, a broad (though not uniform) expectation on Wall Street and in London is that rebalancing will converge on dominant institutions and will restore the balance that existed prior to crisis.

Nigel Lawson, former Chancellor of the Exchequer, asks "Will capitalism need to change in the future?" "The lesson of history is that the answer is 'not really'. The economic cycle is endemic and inescapable, and everyone . . . has always known this. What the current cycle does underline, however, is that a cyclical downturn associated with a collapse of the banking system is by an order of magnitude worse than a normal cyclical downturn," so we need to re-install the separation between commercial and investment banking that was eliminated under the Clinton administration.[15] That is the extent of reform required.

Regulation is on the table and reform is inevitable, but there is ample pushback on the frontiers of regulation. Over the past decade bank lobbyists spent almost $370 million in Washington on lobbying and campaign donations to ward off tighter regulation.[16] Gary Becker of the Chicago school cautions that the "cure" should not destroy capitalism, and a recession isn't the right time to change the rules of the economic game (and the healthcare bill is flawed and voters will go back to limiting government).[17] Wall Street voices claim that derivatives are necessary, insider trading makes markets function more smoothly, speculation is crucial to the functioning of financial markets, robo-trading is functional, and "government control" is a nightmare that haunts investors.[18] Business fights back "in defense of free enterprise" by pointing out the problems and cost of government control, the mistaken idea that the recession has been purely a failure of markets, and that market failures are readily overcome by government solutions.[19] Tory historians such as Niall Ferguson counsel against creating yet another layer of government regulation.[20]

Reforms, then, should not go too far. The rise of emerging markets takes time, and for all their shortcomings western institutions and financial markets are best placed to manage the transition. Globalization is moving at Mach speed and the financial crisis is just a small cloud fleeting over the road of rapid global innovation (Easterbrook 2009). Across the world the

Figure 2.2 AUTH ©2009 The Philadelphia Inquirer. Reprinted with permission of UNIVERSAL UCLICK.

tide has turned in favor of regulation but "the skyscrapers are high and the regulators are far."[21] Institutions are resilient, paradigms are slow to give way, market forces are swinging back, herd behavior hasn't ended, the rewards of discipline are unclear, and the reforms are relatively marginal.

Thus, if a return to normal is likely in the short run it comes with continuing economic frailty and financial instability. The new normal anticipated in financial markets is slow growth in the West, more regulation, and rising risk of sovereign debt (El Erian 2009).

If the emerging societies are the next big thing, the "other big thing" is finance and its sheer magnitude. In the U.S. the FIRE sector (finance insurance real estate) employs 20 percent of the workforce, the largest sector of employment. "In 1995, the assets of the six largest banks were equivalent to 17 percent of GDP; now they amount to 63 percent of GDP."[22] In 2002 finance generated 41 percent of U.S. corporate profits. The pay rate in the finance sector is 181 percent of median pay. In 2007 American households spent on average 20 percent of their disposable income on finance charges. In the U.S. and U.K. it is a story of "banks gone wild" and "a financial sector that turned away from the business sector, then caused its self-destruction, and a business sector beset by short-termism."[23] When during the U.S. Senate hearing of Goldman Sachs a senator exclaimed "this is gambling!" it elicited a swift, indignant response from the Las Vegas casino industry: "the comparison is insulting, for our industry, unlike theirs, is highly regulated; here a pit boss knows exactly what is going on, but they have no clue." Susan Strange's (1986) "casino capitalism" that was once a daring critique has now long been overtaken by (citing the business press) toxic finance, death-wish finance, and doomsday finance.

Several rebalancing policies are contradictory. While trying to fix domestic imbalances they add to global imbalances, or while fixing one problem they create another. (While U.S. stimulus spending remedies recession it increases imports and thus the external deficit. The 2009 "cash for clunkers" program increased sales of cars of foreign manufacturers rather than cars made in Detroit.) Most accounts deal with financial crisis and gloss over *economic* crisis. They treat crisis as a liquidity crisis, a credit squeeze triggered by external circumstances, and overlook the deeper *solvency* crisis (Morris 2008), which in the U.S. is far more serious than in Europe and Japan. In the U.S. the deeper problem is decades of underinvestment in productive capacities. According to a trenchant diagnosis, "bankruptcy could be good for America" for bankruptcy focuses the mind.[24]

In sum, the weaknesses of the global plutocracy script are several: the Anglo-American financial sector is vast, politically embedded, and out of control. Because of decades of deregulation and structural deficits the Anglo-American institutions are crisis-prone, and the appeal of western institutions has been receding. Anglo-American institutions can possibly co-opt part of the emerging societies' elites but not all and not the majority of the population. Economic and financial surplus has shifted and international institutions, too, must adopt a more balanced course. Luke Johnson explains "why I fear the west's luck has run out" and offers a dark and mournful evocation of global rebalancing:

> It is clear that as a society we must learn something painful and radical—how to live within our means—because the credit just is not there anymore. The easy money is all gone, and there will be no more for a long time. . . . The growth game is over. . . . So why should industrious Asians earn a tiny fraction of what citizens in the West earn? Especially when they have so much of the cash and productive resources, while we have deficits, high costs and poor demographics. Prepare for a wrenching, unstoppable redistribution of resources—and I am not talking about domestic taxes.[25]

MULTIPOLARITY: GLOBAL REBALANCING PLAN B

So we turn to scripts of multipolarity. In Asia and the global South, global rebalancing holds different meanings. Thus according to Ronnie Chan, a banker in Hong Kong, it entails:

- A shift in moral authority in which the West no longer holds the moral high ground

- A shift in decision making in the world economy in which emerging societies carry greater weight (as in the expansion of voting rights in IMF and World Bank)
- A shift in the center of gravity of the world economy from the Atlantic to the Pacific
- A gradual shift away from the U.S. dollar as world reserve currency in favor of a basket of currencies and bilateral currency deals
- A shift toward growing East-South or South-South economic cooperation.[26]

Since in Asia the new normal means shrinking demand and rising protectionism in the West, free trade agreements in Asia have been rapidly expanding,[27] and trade relations between Asia, Latin America, Africa, and the Middle East have been growing steadily as well. Part of this is the "new silk roads" between Asia and the Middle East (Simpfendorfer 2009). Because western markets are shrinking, emerging societies must adjust their export-led models to domestic, regional, and global south demand. Just as import dependence is unsustainable for the U.S., so is export dependence for Asia: "If the import-and-consume business model is dead, so too is export-and-save."[28]

Measured in financial assets emerging markets, including the Middle East and Eastern Europe, add up to about $25 trillion, the U.S. about $54 trillion, the EU $42 trillion, and Japan $26 trillion, so their total assets are less than those of Japan and of course more disparate and dispersed. From the viewpoint of western institutions emerging economies and their financial markets are too small to manage and absorb major investments. The other side of the equation is that although the large financial markets are in the West, the surplus is increasingly in emerging societies, and this is where economic trends are turning. Emerging markets have had a "good crisis," their high growth has resumed, their domestic and regional markets are growing, they borrow at cheap rates, their currencies are rising against the dollar, and they have mostly young populations. In mergers and acquisitions and in bankers' "call sheets" (the list of potential buyers contacted when a company is put up for sale) the trend is clear:

> In 2010, the player at the edge of the frame has now moved to its center: Asia. The change has been building for nearly a decade. It's finally here. From Tokyo, west to Seoul, to Beijing, south to Hong Kong, and west again to Mumbai, Asian companies and governments are asserting themselves as the deal makers who matter. Asian acquirers—not including Australia and Japan—have been behind one of every six deal-making dollars globally in 2010 and are on pace for the biggest year ever . . . much as the United States [after World War II] was left to rebuild a devastated world in its own image, so today are hale Asian companies filling a vacuum that the West occupied before the financial crisis.[29]

The idea that western financial markets can absorb the emerging economies underestimates the growing gap between financial institutions in the West and financial surplus in emerging markets. According to Martin Wolf, "Go east! That is the advice one would give an ambitious financier. This will change the nature of the financial industry. It will also change the philosophy of finance: for most emerging and developing countries, the financial industry exists to push the economy along a development path broadly determined by the state."[30] Another report notes, "within 15 years half of capitalization will be in emerging markets and asset allocation will reflect that."[31] According to the president of the World Bank, "Asia's share of the global economy in purchasing power parity terms has risen steadily from 7 percent in 1980 to 21 percent in 2008. Asia's stock markets now account for 32 percent of global market capitalization, ahead of the United States at 30 percent and Europe at 25 percent" (Zoellick 2010).

In portraying the crisis as a global system crisis, the U.S. and U.K. seek a tripling of IMF funds while the IMF expands emerging societies' voting quotas (G20 2009). China, Saudi Arabia, and other surplus societies are called upon to contribute funds to enable the IMF to act as crisis manager. Emerging societies have stepped into the breach with provisional arrangements such as the IMF issuing bonds rather than their granting loans. Additional Special Drawing Rights may function as a channel through which surplus countries can offload unwanted U.S. dollars without upsetting the applecart. Such arrangements signal an unstable interregnum. Surplus countries are underrepresented in international institutions and are yet supposed to carry a major burden of global economic recovery while the benefits accrue to hegemonic countries whose institutions have been the agents of financial shipwreck. It stands to reason that significant changes in the global power structure are in the cards, including the status of the U.S. dollar as global reserve currency. Several signals point to the gradual onset of a multi-currency world. The oil-dollar system has been eroding for some time. Russia, China, and an international panel convened by the United Nations call for alternatives to the U.S. dollar as reserve currency, and in 2009 Asian central banks cut their accumulation of dollar reserves to less than 30 percent.[32]

EMANCIPATORY MULTIPOLARITY?

If economic and financial multipolarity then is not in question, let us consider its emancipatory or democratic potential. Is the rise of emerging societies mainly a matter of their "joining the club" or does it imply genuine advances for the majority of the population? There are general, transnational, and domestic components to this question, and the domestic are the most important.

First, the general threshold is low. Two hundred years of North-South relations have been framed by Anglo-American hegemony and its frontiers such as imperial rivalries, the cold war, and the vanity wars of American hegemony in Iraq and Afghanistan. In the big picture development aid has had little effect. It has often been a disciplinary exercise (as in IMF conditionalities), a matter of "aid-in-reverse," or grandstanding with targets that are habitually unmet such as the Millennium Development Goals. Far more important has been the interdependence between deindustrializing/post-industrial societies and new industrializing societies. Second, the East-South turn represents a comeback of oriental globalization and global history returning to its "normal" mode (Nederveen Pieterse 2006).

Next are the dynamics of the East-South turn in global political economy. When during the postwar boom (1950–1970) industrial countries in the West and Japan were drivers of world economic growth, commodity prices were high, commodity exporting countries prospered, and it was a period of relatively equalizing growth globally. The period 1980–2000 when postindustrial consumer societies propelled, the world economy was marked by unequal, polarizing growth in and between countries. With industrializing economies again driving the world economy, rising commodity prices, as in the commodities boom since 2003, enable relatively equalizing growth globally, a pattern that is structurally similar to the period 1950–1970. Thus the East-South turn again redirects the overall pattern toward global redistributive growth.

Zoellick notes, "The developing world's share of global GDP in purchasing power parity terms has increased from 33.7 percent in 1980 to 43.4 percent in 2010. Developing countries are likely to show robust growth rates over the next five years and beyond. Sub-Saharan Africa could grow by an average of over 6 percent to 2015 while South Asia, where half the world's poor live, could grow by as much as 7 percent a year over the same period" (Zoellick 2010). Such figures were inconceivable in the eighties and nineties; a different pattern has set in.

Because they are also developing countries and share colonial experiences and frictions with institutions of the North, emerging societies have greater affinity with other developing countries and are less burdened by stereotypes. A case in point is the role Brazil, South Africa, India, and China played in the World Trade Organization negotiations of the Doha round in Cancún, taking the position that "no deal is better than a bad deal" and acting in sync with the Group of 77 (G77) developing countries. Even so, emerging markets also compete with one another and with light industries in developing countries. Thus, Chinese garment exports have had a devastating impact on textile industries in Bangladesh, Kenya, South Africa, and other developing countries; China's shoe exports have eliminated Pakistan's shoe industry. East-South relations are not exempt from unequal exchange, the reproduction of an old type of international division of labor, big power aspirations, and regional hegemony, although challenges to hegemony are growing.[33]

If emerging societies opt for broad-based development rather than for polarizing growth their development is likely to be more sustainable, according to classic human development perspectives (Haq 1995) and recent assessments (Jomo and Baudot 2007; Wilkinson and Pickett 2009; Nederveen Pieterse 2010). If the overall choice is for narrow growth the likelihood of capitalisms converging toward a Davos-style transnational capitalism and global plutocracy (now more centered in the east) is greater but will pose risks of wider international instability over time. In addition, if social inequality is addressed it is likely that addressing political and ecological constraints will follow suit; policies with regard to inequality are also an indicator of wider dynamics. Third, as emerging societies step onto the world stage their problems will increasingly become global problems. Fourth, an inclusive development approach in the domestic sphere will also inform emerging societies' relations with developing countries.

But the major frontiers of emancipation are the domestic dynamics. Emerging societies' transnational role could never improve on their domestic policies. This is far too large and complex to address here; this chapter can only offer general considerations. To the extent that the rise of emerging societies is based on industrialization they face the main challenge of modernization: how to incorporate the peasant majority. Past answers to this challenge have been fascism, Nazism, Soviet communism, and Maoism, so the stakes are momentous. Japan, South Korea, and Taiwan have been able to integrate the rural majority into modernity through land reform, balanced investments in agriculture and industry, and broad-based educational and social policies, in marked contrast to Latin America and most of Asia (Kay 2009).

The monumental numbers of GDP growth in emerging societies cannot be taken at face value because the prices of labor, land and environment have been kept artificially low. Rural sacrifice has been the flipside of emerging societies' growth. Since economic development involves technological changes, strategic interest groups, multinational corporations, global value chains and global finance, inequality is a variable in competition and new inequalities are being generated.

Due to shrinking demand in the West, emerging societies' exports will increasingly go to regional markets and to the global south. When export-led growth makes place for growing domestic consumption and domestic demand-led investment it may enhance opportunities for broad-based social development, but this is a complex path. While there are strong political and social pressures toward inclusion, inequality is deeply embedded and culturally encoded, so this needs to be empirically examined (Nederveen Pieterse and Rehbein 2009; Akram-Lodhi and Kay 2009; Thompson 2010).

Inequality is the crucial variable. China's constraints include growing inequality, a construction and housing bubble, a gradually aging population, and tough equations of development and ecology. In response to major social and political unrest, China abandoned fast-track polarizing growth and adopted the "harmonious society" framework in 2003. The 12th five-year plan (2011–2015) embarks on a new development stage (see Chapter 7, this volume). Labor protests in 2010 produced significant wage increases, possibly enabled by the Labor Contract Law that went into effect in 2008 and strengthens worker rights.[34] India is at a difficult crossroads with growing crises of rural and urban poverty and mounting challenges from Naxalites, dalits, and Adivasis. Because the emerging societies are also developing countries for economic (human skills, domestic market), political (stability), and social reasons (cohesion), broad-based development and inclusive policies are likely over time. It was on these grounds that apartheid came to an end in South Africa. It isn't possible to industrialize with the majority of the population dispossessed and excluded. However, the sobering realities of post-1994 South Africa indicate the limits of this general reasoning.

CAPITALISMS?

A fundamental conceptual dimension to assessing current trends is whether they are viewed through the lens of capitalism or capitalisms. The rise of emerging societies could simply be understood in terms of the "rise and decline of nations within the world-system" (E. Friedman 1982) and as a reshuffling within the bounds of western capitalism. Yet, whether or not they unfold within the sphere of western capitalism is not a given but part of the problem to be examined. The 2008 crisis highlights the variation in capitalisms. While the impact of crisis is global, it is not uniform. Societies across the world are affected but are affected in markedly different ways. Crisis is a threat for some and an opportunity for others.

During the 1997–1998 Asian crisis, Anglo-American capitalism was upheld as the sole viable model. The 2008 crisis, however, shatters the headquarters of the erstwhile exemplar. Several after-crisis assessments now reclaim the paradigm of a single, standard-bearing capitalism (in relation to which also west Europe is an outlier). But the 2008 crisis exposes the frailties of Anglo-American capitalism on all levels—as ideology (laissez-faire), as paradigm (efficient market theory), as economics (shareholder short-termism, financialization), as policy (deregulation, liberalization), institutions (accounting, rating agencies, regulators), as methodology (financial mathematics, quantitative investments), and as culture (bonus culture, predatory CEOs). The 2008 crisis is part of a series from the American bank crises in the early 1990s, the bailout of LTCM, the collapse of Enron and other corporations to the subprime mortgage crisis, and the Goldman episode. The shareholder principle fosters short-termism (boost quarterly earnings numbers to ensure high stock ratings and dividends), and with financialization comes a disconnect between finance and economics (Dore 2000).

For decades the Washington consensus lorded over the developing world; now the lecturing has changed direction and emerging societies "talk back." From Europe to China, critical comments about American capitalism now come not just from backrooms but from official podiums. The tables have turned, and there is a different refrain in the air: the West must learn from the Asian crisis and must learn economic prudence from Asia (Mahbubani 2009).

Various indices (such as the "economic freedom" and "competitiveness" index) typically assume a single model of capitalism. However, the 2008 crisis again shows the absence of a general growth model or script for the relations between state, capital, and civil society (cf. Hall and Soskice 2001; Stiglitz 2010). This variation is central to rebalancing processes. Institutions matter as part of economic imbalances and as part of rebalancing. Certain institutions prove to be crisis-prone and others crisis-resistant. Since institutions are political formations analyzing this involves, besides institutional economics, politics and ideology. There is no general benchmark by which to measure and evaluate institutional change. Yet most perspectives, explicitly or implicitly, treat capitalism in the aggregate. This holds for mainstream views in media and economics as well as for neo-Marxist views such as world-system theory and transnational capitalist class perspectives. Crisis, then, becomes a crisis of capitalism period, not of a particular type of capitalism. The main variation this view acknowledges is historical, between stages of accumulation and phases of capitalism, between early and latecomers to industrialization and modernity. In treating capitalism in the singular, unilinear theories of capitalism, from Marx to world-system theory, view variation mainly as variation over time (with "dependent capitalism" as the main outlier). This perspective is unsuited to examining regional variation because, like postwar modernization theory, it tends to assimilate regional variation into historical patterns (such as "lagging behind" or "catching up"). Thus while much current discussion focuses on the "future of capitalism," a more productive question is "the future of capitalisms." Capitalism survives thanks to the diversity of capitalisms: "the flexibility of capitalism derives from *capitalisms* and regional variation" (Nederveen Pieterse 2004, 146). Diversity is not disappearing, but the terms of diversity are changing, and what is at issue is the realignment of capitalisms. Now, far more than in the past, this involves regions outside the old metropoles, the emerging societies from Asia to Latin America and the Middle East.

The idea that emerging societies can be incorporated in Anglo-American capitalism underestimates their different ways of organizing capitalism amid the political and social pressures they face. With the lead model imploding under corporate scandals, toxic finance, feeble institutions, inept governance, aging populations, mammoth fiscal debt, massive sovereign debt, and government eviscerated by tax cuts, the developmental state capitalisms in the east and south emerge as more dynamic and, in some respects, more sustainable. The Asian crisis was attributed to "crony capitalism"; now "permissive capitalism" turns out to be a much greater weakness while the robust public sector in most emerging societies emerges as a source of strength, at any rate as long as it is accompanied by competent policies. This isn't simply a matter of state or market; what matters is what *kind* of state. The concentration of wealth and power in the U.S. combined with free market ideology has contributed to an "anti-state state" (MacLennan 1997).

ANALYTICS

Let us pause for general considerations. First, let us be wary of totalizing scripts, whether they come from Davos or Porto Alegre, from the World Economic Forum or the World Social Forum. For the sake of argument I have presented extreme scripts; but either/or outcomes are too simple. As mentioned before, layered processes produce *layered* outcomes—with different and combined patterns of transnational, regional, national, and local cooperation. Regional entities such as the EU, the Gulf Cooperation Council and ASEAN follow dynamics of their own. Then there is local variation, say between China's Pearl River Delta and Harbin in the north. Hence capitalist convergence and divergence occur at the same time. Elites and business classes in different countries cooperate *and* follow their own ways; which brings us back to the classic thesis of combined and uneven development.

A parallel in cultural studies is that while many expect globalization to produce cultural standardization and McDonaldization, this happens but only in some spheres and to some extent; regional, national, and local variations continue with dynamics of their own, combine with transnational cultural assemblages, and generate new patchworks of difference, which may be described as "global multiculture" (Nederveen Pieterse 2007).

This chapter combines variables wide apart (in the vein of global studies), examines their interaction from the viewpoint of development studies, sets forth scenarios, and discusses their probabilities. While the variables in these probabilities are fairly straightforward, their interaction is contentious and the outcomes depend to a large extent on political processes. After all, everything is a matter of political struggle. It is a fiction that economic models can script societal change. As Polanyi observed, markets are embedded; they are embedded in institutions and political formations, so markets are ultimately political. In contrast to the principle "enter economism, exit politics" (Teivanen 2002) what is at issue now is taking the economism out of economics and putting politics back in: enter politics, exit economism. While there are overall patterns and trends, changing political tides alter equations. It's impossible to take politics out of the equation, and with politics *in* the equation the outcomes are unpredictable.

Then there is the fallacy of units. We speak of "China" and "the U.S." because that is how economic data pile up, but what matters are classes, strata, and regions within and across these units. This is a two-way street: because technological, business, and communication interweaving is growing, national units are of limited purchase; yet nations are units of political decision making and forums of social reflexivity. In each country there is a continuously shifting balance between multiple factions, also in response to international trends. Thus in China, the new right (neoliberal), the new left (social and green), the old left (Maoist), and the old right (nationalist, Confucian) vie for influence, each with different shades of nationalism.

We must also factor in ideological noise. There are gaps between the actual economic policies and practices in various settings and the way they are represented in international media, which are socialized in and biased toward dominant paradigms and underrate institutional variation (Nederveen Pieterse 2009a).

METHODS

Several points of methodological caution follow. Arguing continuity is easier than arguing trend breaks. Trend breaks invite the autopilot response: you're exaggerating; changes aren't nearly as large as you suggest. New data are not readily shared, and once a different future door opens there is no playbook, so resistance is considerable.

Therefore assessing the degree of change is crucial. The usual recourse is to metrics. If you can't count it, does it count? But metrics follow paradigms—in Hazel Henderson's words, people measure what they treasure. Data are theory-dependent; hence the problem of indicators. Indicators such as GDP measure economic activity from limited assumptions (Stiglitz 2010).[35] Metrics matter but because measurements reflect limited assumptions quantitative data are often qualitative assessments in disguise. When it concerns system change, assessing the degree of transformation is difficult because the *criteria* of assessment are contingent and are different when viewed from within or outside the box.

A possible remedy is to supplement the approach to global dynamics by global multi-sited ethnography as a way to get past macroeconomics and to ground our understandings in everyday experience in different parts of the world. In brief, this seeks to enter the social tissue of transformation more deeply by looking at different panels of global coexistence, comparing societies and strata placed differently on the spectrum of global imbalance, not just in metrics and generalizing judgments but also in experiential terms. Nevertheless, methodological finesse will not deliver without theoretical finesse.

NOTES

1. An earlier version of this chapter appeared in *Development and Change* (2011, Vol. 42, No. 1: 22–48). It has since undergone major changes. The arguments have been presented at various universities (Institute of Social Studies, The Hague, Maastricht University, Transnational Institute, Amsterdam, Pusan National University, Shanghai University, and Xiamen University in 2010; Goldsmiths College, London, Zhejiang University, Hangzhou, and Fudan University, Shanghai in 2011). I am indebted to responses, to Andrew Lee and Jeb Sprague for references, and to comments of referees and of Jongtae Kim. The cartoons are reprinted with permission.
2. Estimate by Morgan Stanley, *New York Times*, January 10, 2010.
3. "The BRICs: The Trillion-Dollar Club," *The Economist,* April 15, 2010.
4. D. Oakley, "Different Strokes for Different Folks?" *Financial Times,* December 1, 2008: 17.

5. Cited in J. Gapper, *Financial Times,* April 23, 2009; E. Rigby, *Financial Times,* April 21, 2010: 3; G. Silverman, *Financial Times*, October 24, 2005; B. Davis, *Wall Street Journal*, January 27, 2010: A9; M.W. Sadovi, *Wall Street Journal*, October 21, 2008: C8; G. Tett, *Financial Times*, January 22, 2010: 6; J. Booth, *Financial Times*, August 29, 2007: 22; A. Wood, *Financial Times*, August 4, 2008: 4; M. Mobius, *Financial Times*, November 6, 2009: 24; K. Chen, *Wall Street Journal*, April 6, 2010: A6; Liu Jie, *Shanghai Daily,* July 1, 2010: A6. D.K. Berman, *Wall Street Journal*, September 21, 2010: C1, respectively.
6. M. Wolf, "How the Noughties Proved To Be a Hinge of History," *Financial Times,* December 24, 2009: 9.
7. *Wall Street Journal,* December 6, 2009.
8. E. Heathcote, "Practice Makes Perfect: Interview," *Financial Times*, March 13–14, 2010: 3.
9. D. Oakley, "Building Success," *Financial Times,* November 9, 2009: 4.
10. "Still Lost in the Old Bretton Woods," *Financial Times*, December 28, 2009.
11. A. Aslund, *Financial Times,* November 16, 2009; R. Sally, "The Quest for a Global Solution Is Misguided," *Financial Times*, March 19, 2009.
12. "Editorial, Currency Confusion," *China Daily*, June 26–27, 2010: 5.
13. Martin Sorrell, "The Pendulum Will Swing Back," *Financial Times*, April 8, 2009: 9.
14. U.S. Congressman Barney Frank, quoted in C. Freeland, "Top Dogs Remain in Denial Over Public Anger," *Financial Times*, March 27, 2009: 2.
15. Nigel Lawson, "Capitalism Needs a Revived Glass-Steagall," *Financial Times*, March 16, 2009: 9.
16. E. Luce, "Subprime Groups Spent $370M to Fight Regulation," *Financial Times*, May 6, 2009: 1. See also the "Report on The Future of Finance: Fixing Global Finance," *Wall Street Journal*, December 14, 2009: R1–9.
17. G. Becker and K. Murphy, "Do Not Let the 'Cure' Destroy Capitalism," *Financial Times*, March 20, 2009: 9; G.S. Becker, S.J. Davis, and K. M. Murphy, "Uncertainty and the Slow Recovery," *Wall Street Journal*, January 4, 2010: A17; P. Robinson, "Weekend Interview with Gary Becker," *Wall Street Journal*, March 27–28, 2010: A13.
18. J. Quinlan, "The Nightmare of Government Control That Haunts Investors," *Financial Times,* October 21 2009: 22; D. Boudreaux, "Learning to Love Inside Trading," *Wall Street Journal,* October 24–25, 2009: W1–2; P. Murphy, "The Truth About Speculators: They Are Doing God's Work," *Financial Times*, March 13–14, 2010: 9.
19. This occurs particularly on the editorial pages of the *Wall Street Journal.* K.A. Strassel, "The Weekend Interview with Tom Donohue (President of the Chamber of Commerce)," *Wall Street Journal,* October 24–25, 2009: A13.
20. N. Ferguson and T. Forstmann, "Back to Basics on Financial Reform," *Wall Street Journal*, April 23, 2010: A19.
21. F. Guerrera, "The Skyscrapers Are High and the Regulators Are Far Away," *Financial Times*, March 27–28, 2010.
22. *New York Times*, April 21, 2010.
23. E. Phelps, "Uncertainty Bedevils the Best System," *Financial Times*, April 15, 2009: 9.
24. G. Rachman, "Bankruptcy Could Be Good for America," *Financial Times*, January 12, 2010: 9.
25. Luke Johnson, "Why I Fear the West's Luck Has Run Out," *Financial Times*, January 28, 2009.
26. Ronnie Chan, "The West's Preaching to the East Must Stop," *Financial Times*, January 4, 2010: 11.

27. P. Stein, "West Is Wary, so Asia Seeks Free Trade within," *Wall Street Journal*, March 22, 2010: C7.
28. "Editorial: America's Fate Is Not in Its Hands," *Financial Times,* April 16, 2009: 8.
29. D.K. Berman, "The Deal Makers Who Matter Are Rising in the East," *Wall Street Journal*, September 21, 2010: C1.
30. M. Wolf, "New Dynamics, *Financial Times* Report on the Future of Finance," November 9, 2009: 3.
31. B. Bollen, "A New Economic Leadership Stirs," *Financial Times,* April 7, 2008: 14.
32. D. Roman, "Asian central bankers say it with gold," *Wall Street Journal,* December 28, 2009: C10.
33. Reviewing debates and social movements in India and China, Manoranjan Mohanty (2009) finds that "the probable scenario is the simultaneous unfolding of both these trends—the rise of India, China and some other countries and their entry to the big power club and those policies being increasingly challenged at various levels and the demand for democratization growing in strength. . . . The ideology of domination is under attack everywhere . . . Today not only global hegemons are under challenge; regional hegemons are under even greater challenge. In South Asia, for example, not only Pakistan but even smaller countries like Nepal, Bangladesh would not accept any form of domination by India."
34. Dan Harris and Brad Luo, "The Impact of China's Labor Contract Law," *China Law Blog*, posted September 2008, accessed August 29, 2010 from www.chinalawblog.com/2008/. . ./the_impact_of_chinas_labor_con.html.
35. The Stiglitz Commission Report (2009) commissioned by the French government, critiques GDP as measure of economic performance, accessed from www.stiglitz-sen-fitoussi.fr.

REFERENCES

Agtmael, Antoine van. 2007. *The Emerging Markets Century*. New York: Free Press.

Akram-Lodhi, A.H., and C. Kay, eds. 2009. *Peasants and Globalisation: Political Economy, Rural Transformation and the Agrarian Question*. London: Routledge.

Altman, Roger C. 2009. "The Great Crash, 2008: A Geopolitical Setback for the West." *Foreign Affairs* 88(1): 2–14.

Amin, Samir. 1997. *Capitalism in the Age of Globalization*. London: Zed.

Amsden, A.H. 2001. *The Rise of 'The Rest': Challenges to the West from Late-Industrializing Economies*. New York: Oxford University Press.

Arrighi, Giovanni. 2007. *Adam Smith in Beijing*. London: Verso.

Bagnai, A. 2009. "The Role of China in Global External Imbalances: Some Further Evidence." *China Economic Review* 20(3): 508–526.

Baker, Dean. 2009. *Plunder and Blunder: The Rise and Fall of the Bubble Economy*. Sausalito: PoliPoint.

Dore, R.P. 2000. *Stock Market Capitalism / Welfare Capitalism: Japan and Germany versus the Anglo-Saxons*. Oxford: Oxford University Press.

Easterbrook, Gregg. 2009. *Sonic Boom: Globalization at Mach Speed*. New York: Random House.

El Erian, Mohamed A. 2008. *When Markets Collide: Investment Strategies for the Age of Global Economic Change*. New York: McGraw-Hill Professional.

El Erian, Mohamed A. 2009. "The New Normal." *Business Week*, June 1: 73–74.

El Erian, Mohamed A. 2010. "How to Handle the Sovereign Debt Explosion." *Financial Times,* March 11: 9.

Feldstein, Martin. 2008. "The U.S. Trade Deficit: Resolving the Global Imbalance: The Dollar and the U.S. Saving Rate." *Journal of Economic Perspectives* 22(3): 13–25.
Florida, Richard. 2008. *Who's Your City?* New York: Basic Books.
Friedman, E., ed. 1982. *Ascent and Decline in the World-System*. London: Sage.
Friedman, Thomas L. 2005. *The World Is Flat*. New York: Farrar Straus and Giroux.
G20. 2009. *Pittsburgh Meeting*. London: Newsdesk Publications.
Guha, K. 2009. "Imbalances Imply a Trouble Well beyond Risky Banking." *Financial Times*, March 10: 9.
Hall, P.A., and D. Soskice, eds. 2001. *Varieties of Capitalism: The Institutional Foundations of Comparative Advantage*. Oxford: Oxford University Press.
Harvey, David. 2005. *A Brief History of Neoliberalism*. New York: Oxford University Press.
Haq, M. ul. 1995. *Reflections on Human Development*. New York: Oxford University Press.
Jomo, K.S., and J. Baudot, eds. 2007. *Flat World, Big Gaps: Economic Liberalization, Globalization, Poverty and Inequality*. London: Zed.
Kaplinsky, R., and D. Messner. 2008. "Introduction: The Impact of Asian Drivers on the Developing World." *World Development* 36(2): 197–209.
Karabell, Zachary. 2009. "The 'Global Imbalances' Myth." *Wall Street Journal*, December 21: A21.
Kay, Cristóbal. 2009. "Development Strategies and Rural Development: Exploring Synergies, Eradicating Poverty." *Journal of Peasant Studies* 36(1): 103–137.
Korea Herald, ed. 2008. *Korean Wave*. Paju: Jimoondang.
MacLennan, Carol A. 1997. "Democracy under the Influence: Cost-Benefit Analysis in the United States." In *Meanings of the Market: The Free Market in Western Culture*, edited by James G. Carrier, 195–224. Oxford: Berg.
Magnus, George. 2010. *Uprising: Will Emerging Markets Shape or Shake the World Economy?* New York: Wiley.
Mahbubani, Kishore. 2009. *The New Asian Hemisphere: The Irresistible Shift of Global Power to the East*. Reading: Perseus.
Marber, Peter. 1998. *From Third World to World Class: The Future of Emerging Markets in the Global Economy*. Reading: Perseus.
McKinsey Quarterly. 2010. *Chart Focus Newsletter*, September.
Mohanty, Manoranjan. 2009. "China and India: Competing Hegemonies or Civilisational Forces of Swaraj and Jiefang." Siler Forum lecture, unpublished paper.
Morris, Charles R. 2008. *The Two Trillion Dollar Meltdown*. New York: Public Affairs.
National Intelligence Council. 2008. *Global Trends 2025*. Washington, DC: National Intelligence Council.
Nederveen Pieterse, J. 2004. *Globalization or Empire?* New York: Routledge.
Nederveen Pieterse, J. 2006. "Oriental Globalization: Past and Present." In *Europe and Asia beyond East and West: Towards a New Cosmopolitanism*, edited by Gerard Delanty, 61–73. London: Routledge.
Nederveen Pieterse, J. 2007. *Ethnicities and Global Multiculture: Pants for an Octopus*. Lanham: Rowman & Littlefield.
Nederveen Pieterse, J. 2008a. "Globalization the Next Round: Sociological Perspectives." *Futures* 40(8): 707–720.
Nederveen Pieterse, J. 2008b. *Is There Hope for Uncle Sam? Beyond the American Bubble*. London: Zed.
Nederveen Pieterse, J. 2009a. "Media and Global Divides: Representing the Rise of the Rest as Threat." *Global Media and Communication* 5(2): 1–17.
Nederveen Pieterse, J. 2009b. "Multipolarity Means Thinking Plural: Modernities." *Protosociology* 26: 19–35.

Nederveen Pieterse, J. 2010. *Development Theory: Deconstructions/ Reconstructions*, 2nd ed. London: Sage.
Nederveen Pieterse, J., and Boike Rehbein, eds. 2009. *Globalization and Emerging Societies: Development and Inequality*. London: Palgrave Macmillan.
Okimoto, D.I. 2009. "The Financial Crisis and America's Capital Dependency on Japan and China." *Asia-Pacific Review* 16(1): 37–55.
Ong, Aihwa. 2006. *Neoliberalism as Exception: Mutations in Sovereignty and Citizenship*. Durham: Duke University Press.
Petras, James. 2009. *Global Depression and Regional Wars*. Atlanta: Clarity Press.
Phillips, Kevin. 2009. *Bad Money: Reckless Finance, Failed Politics and the Global Crisis of American Capitalism*, rev. ed. New York: Penguin.
Prestowitz, Clyde. 2005. *Three Billion New Capitalists: The Great Shift of Wealth and Power to the East*. New York: Basic Books.
Reich, Robert. 2010. *Aftershock: The Next Economy and America's Future*. New York: Knopf.
Rothkopf, David. 2008. *Superclass: The Global Power Elite and the World They Are Making*. New York: Farrar Strauss and Giroux.
Roubini, Nouriel. 2006. "The Unsustainability of the U.S. Twin Deficits." *CATO Journal* 26(2): 343–356.
Saxenian, Annalee. 2006. *The New Argonauts: Regional Advantage in a Global Economy*. Cambridge: Harvard University Press.
Simpfendorfer, Ben. 2009. *The New Silk Road*. London: Palgrave Macmillan.
Sirkin, H.L., J.W. Hemerling, and A.K. Bhattacharya. 2008. *Globality: Competing with Everyone from Everywhere for Everything*. New York: Business Plus.
Sklair, L. 2001. *The Transnational Capitalist Class*. Oxford: Blackwell.
Stephens, P. 2009. "Co-ordination Falls Away as the Global Crisis Abates." *Financial Times*, June 26: 9.
Stiglitz, Joseph E. 2010. *Freefall: America, Free Markets and the Sinking of the World Economy*. New York: Norton.
Strange, Susan. 1986. *Casino Capitalism*. Oxford: Blackwell.
Teivanen, Teivo. 2002. *Enter Economism, Exit Politics: Experts, Economic Policy and the Damage to Democracy*. London: Zed Books.
Teslik, Lee H. 2009. "Sovereign Wealth Funds." Council on Foreign Relations. Accessed February 27, 2012 from http://www.cfr.org/international-finance/sovereign-wealth-funds/p15251.
Thompson, Mark. 2010. "The Dialectic of 'Good Governance' and Democracy in Southeast Asia." In *New Asias: Global Futures of World Regions*, edited by H.-C. Lim, W. Schäfer, and S.-M. Hwang, 175–208. Seoul: Seoul National University Press.
Wallerstein, I.M. 1984. *The Politics of the World Economy*. Cambridge: Cambridge University Press.
Westra, Richard, ed. 2010. *Confronting Global Neoliberalism: Third World Resistance and Development Strategies*. Atlanta: Clarity Press.
Wilkinson, Richard, and Kate Pickett. 2009. *The Spirit Level: Why More Equal Societies Almost Always Do Better*. London: Allen Lane.
Wolf, Martin. 2010. *Fixing Global Finance*, updated ed. New Haven: Yale University Press.
Zakaria, Fareed. 2008. *The Post-American World*. New York: Norton.
Zoellick, Robert B. 2010. *The End of the Third World? Modernizing Multilateralism for a Multipolar World*. Washington, DC: World Bank.

3 Profit, People, Planet, and Global Rebalancing

The Environmental Implications of Development in Japan, South Korea, China, and India

Lynne Ciochetto

INTRODUCTION

Japan was the first of the Asian nations to industrialize—in the 1960s—followed by Korea a decade later. In the 1980s China and then India began to open up to international capitalism, and economic liberalization was gradually introduced into societies that still remain relatively regulated and closed. Some feudal features persist in all of the JKCI countries (Japan, South Korea—"Korea," China, and India), along with cultural values that include a high value placed on education, frugality and saving, and honoring traditions that have been in place for millennia. They also have strong and distinctive perceptions of national identity (Kim 2011). The economic systems in these countries cover a range of approaches to capitalism as well as sharing more similarities than they do with western capitalist economies. Attitudes to modernization and development vary between these countries. The Koreans strove to maintain rapid economic development toward *seonjinguk* (advanced country) and enthusiastically embraced the western neo-liberal model, while the Japanese had a stronger sense of their own "uniqueness" (*nihonjinron*) and saw their own rapid economic development and high standards of living as a reflection of that uniqueness (Kim 2011). The colonial and neo-colonial experiences of these nations also differ. Both Japan and Korea have had close contact with the Americans. India shrugged off centuries of British colonialism in 1947 but retains many institutional legacies of the British, including the judicial system and parliamentary democracy. Having experienced colonial aggressions from the European powers and the Japanese, China followed a rigorous path of isolationist socialism from 1950 until the 1980s, aiming for "revolutionary modernity" combining nationalism, socialism, and developmental ism (ibid.).

This chapter explores those countries—Japan, Korea, China, and India—in terms of their economic, social, and environmental profiles (profit, people, and planet) and assesses the environmental implications of the projected growth and development scenarios in the next decades. The conclusion explores the implications of reprioritization: planet, people, and profit. The main criticism is directed at the "business-as-usual" approach of neo-liberal economics with its fixation on growth rates, ignoring social and environmental costs and the impact of growth on the planet and its population. What emerges is the necessity to change the tools of analysis as well as the methods of production and modes of consumption in the contemporary capitalist system. Instead of treating the environment as an invisible and infinite resource, the real costs and benefits of development and growth need to be incorporated into analysis. Rethinking profits and pricing to reflect real, sustainable costs of resources and production will play a key role in reducing levels of consumption. It is also necessary to change the types of products that are consumed and the way they are produced. Along with these changes we need to address the major humanitarian issue of our time: the development of sustainable strategies to meet the basic needs of the world's poor the "bottom billion" (Collier 2007)—actually the 1.2 billion people, who live on less than $1 per day (Brown 2006, 8), and 22 percent of whom live in India (CIA 2011a). Stiglitz's (2009) later figure is even higher at 1.4 billion people.

GLOBALIZATION

The recent decades of globalization have been driven by the international expansion of global corporations and the spread of the industrialized capitalist system, what Nederveen Pieterse (2011) calls the "global plutocracy." The philosophy underpinning the system is the neo-liberal economic model of capitalism, focusing on growth and development and based on the particular historical characteristics of industrialized countries, most notably the U.S. This model has dominated American political thinking in recent decades and has been exported throughout the world. In promoting the free market and deregulation the American government reinforced its own international political and economic goal, especially the expansion of international business. The model also underpins the policies and practices of global institutions such as World Bank, the International Monetary Fund (IMF), and The World Trade Organization (WTO). The IMF serves the interests of its financial backers, whereas the WTO serves commercial interests (Stiglitz 2002, 216). "There is not just one market model" (Stiglitz 2002, 217), and pure, free-market fundamentalism in reality has never existed in any society ("Eric Hobsbawm . . . A Conversation" 2011). Many of the countries that staunchly promote the model actually protect agriculture and other key sectors of their own economies.

The uncritical use of growth rates as an analytical tool can be misleading, but as they are one of the standard tools used in contemporary economics and mainstream media they are still useful as an indicator of economic trends. My main criticism is that by omitting environmental and human costs they distort reality. Economists would argue that it is not their task to provide a comprehensive picture of reality, but as these models are used to make policy the omission of key variables results in distorted policies. Growth models need to incorporate all key variables if they are to continue to be used as the primary tool to assess trends, including globalization. The environmental implications of business practices need to be reflected in growth models as a variable and one that embodies important risks.

The advent of digital communications during the 1980s enabled instantaneous financial transactions and global communication, facilitating the accelerated expansion of global business. During this time markets were starting to flatten in the industrialized economies, and corporations began moving their production to "developing countries" to reduce costs by hiring cheaper labor and to avoid tougher labor and environmental regulations. "Incentives" were offered by destination countries, which included establishing special "export processing zones" and offering tax exemptions. This process generated a "race to the bottom," where countries competed with each other to secure foreign companies. It also brought economic hardship, low wages for workers and environmental degradation (Klein 2000, 196–228). The transfer of finance and technology did stimulate the economies of destination countries, though the countries that did not embrace the "Washington Consensus" neo-liberal model (including Japan, South Korea, and China) and which made social equity a higher priority, fared better than those who relied on the "trickle-down" model (Stiglitz 2002, 79). During the 1990s many of these countries, now termed "emerging economies," began to experience growth. With the expansion of consumption and the growth of internal markets the middle classes expanded. China was one of the most prominent of these "emerging economies"; and in the last 15 years growth and development began to accelerate in India.

As Hobsbawm points out, it is useful to see the capitalist system as a family of systems with some common features but with individual systems also having unique profiles and characteristics ("Eric Hobsbawm. . . A Conversation" 2011). Thus European welfare capitalism differed from American free-market corporate capitalism, and both differ from the variants of capitalism as they evolved in Asia, first in Japan and then in the "tiger economies" of Taiwan, Singapore, Hong Kong, and South Korea. Japan was one of first Asian economies to industrialize as part of the rebuilding process after World War II, and by 1968 it was the second largest economy in the world. Japan's development in the period after 1945 was assisted by not having a military budget (one of the terms of the armistice) and driven by a strong sense of national identity that was recovering from the humiliation of defeat. Economic success and high standards of living became an important source of national pride, leading to feelings of superiority toward the West (Kim 2011). High levels of personal savings also provided capital for industrial growth at this time.

South Korea's economy began to expand in the 1970s, and the country also benefited from significant American aid and finance. South Korea embraced the western development model and neoliberalism and strove to become a fully developed country (*seonjinguk*; Kim 2011). The economic systems of South Korea and Japan share similarities. Companies are somewhat like fiefdoms, demanding total employee allegiance. Jobs have been for life and many worker benefits are supplied by the employer. Economic growth in both countries was preceded by a decline in population growth; Japan cut population growth in half between 1950 and 1958, and South Korea soon followed (Brown 2009, 185).

European welfare capitalism has been the version of capitalism that best served the interests of the majority of citizens. This system worked well in western industrialized nations from the 1950s until the 1980s when both welfare and corporate capitalism changed significantly. In western industrialized nations, under the influence of neo-liberal politics and the transition to an era of deregulation and market-led growth, welfare capitalism evolved into finance capitalism. Digital technology accelerated the speed and capacity of conducting global financial transactions, and the deregulated financial institutions invented new ways of re-bundling and on-selling assets, such as loans and mortgages and commodity trading ("Eric Hobsbawm . . . A Conversation" 2011). By 2002 finance generated 41 percent of the corporate profits of the U.S. (Nederveen Pieterse 2011). Another major variant of capitalism has evolved since the 1980s in the form of "market socialism," epitomized in the introduction of capitalism by China's communist leadership.

The political and economic events unfolding in "emerging" economies were also part of the process of globalization. Ever since the "development decades" of the 1960s, leaders in emerging economies had borrowed money from international banks and organizations to "develop" their industries, usually behind protective tariffs and import taxes. During the 1980s and 1990s many of these countries had difficulties repaying these loans. Financial assistance from the World Bank or the IMF came with the requirement to implement structural readjustment policies, including opening the economies to foreign business, reducing tariffs and taxes, and cutting social welfare spending. This is what happened in India when the economy was on the verge of bankruptcy. India's finance minister, who recently returned from working at the World Bank, introduced liberalization policies after 1991, a decade after China.

GLOBALIZATION AND GLOBAL REBALANCING

Deregulation in a number of Asian economies in the 1990s had encouraged financial speculation which eventually led to financial crises. Such a crisis developed in South Korea in 1998, a result of reliance on extensive short-term foreign borrowing. As part of the recovery process Korea opened its economy to more foreign investment and imports. From 2003 to 2007 growth averaged between 4 percent and 5 percent annually (CIA 2011d). After three decades of strong growth Japan also suffered an economic downturn in the 1990s, brought on by inefficient investing and an asset price bubble (CIA 2011c). The government responded by focusing on export-led growth, which was successful for nearly a decade. The economic dependence on exports caused growth to plummet a decade later during the western financial crisis. Japan then suffered an earthquake and subsequent tsunami in 2011. The economic effects of this crisis will be substantial and long term. Predicted growth for 2011 was already low and has been further reduced, from 1.6 percent to 1.4 percent. Predictions for 2012 have increased from 1.4 percent to 1.5 percent because the economy will get some impetus from rebuilding (The Economic Intelligence Unit 2011). As the economies of India and China were only gradually liberalizing in the 1990s, their economies were still relatively closed, which protected them from being hit by the economic crisis experienced in other Asian economies. China joined the WTO in 2001, which has led to further deregulation. China's economy, like Japan's, is export-led and was also affected by the western financial crisis in 2008–2009. When export markets contracted, 10 million migrant workers lost their jobs in China (BBC World Newsb 2010). The government is now focusing on developing internal markets to avoid such crises in the future. Growth and development in China are ahead of India by about 10 years, and India now is experiencing similar increases in growth to those in China in the 1990s.

Since the 1980s China has benefitted from embracing the role of "factory of the world" as foreign companies moved their production to China to take advantage of low wages and a weak regulatory environment. China's export-driven growth has enabled an economic transformation. China is in the position of being a major world creditor helped by the low value of the yuan. Since 2001 there has been a significant growth in the balance of payment deficit with the U.S. Now that China owns so much American debt it has a major stake in the American economy staying solvent. The U.S. Government claims that the yuan is "artificially low" but American consumers like China's cheap products. The prices of many products in the industrialized world have gone down in the last two decades, which has further stimulated consumerism and overconsumption. Though India and China were relatively resilient throughout the "Asian financial crisis" in the 1990s, they suffered setbacks in the recent financial crisis. Growth rates dropped a couple of percentage points in both countries but still stayed high and are again increasing (Appendix 4), while western industrialized countries are struggling to recover.

Financial strength is at the heart of the changing balance of world geopolitical power that has intensified since the 2008–2009 financial crisis. The crisis reinforced a realignment of the balance of international economic power and undermined the economic hegemony of western industrialized economies—and called into question the philosophical underpinnings of the whole neo-liberalist, free-market model ("Eric Hobsbawm . . . A Conversation" 2011). The western industrialized countries that had embraced financial deregulation, including the U.S. and European Union countries, were hardest hit when the repercussions of the sub-prime mortgage fiasco in the U.S. rippled quickly through the international economy. When the "house of cards" fell, banks failed, finance dried up, western industrialized economies contracted, unemployment went up, and growth plummeted. Recovery will take a long time. Growth in the Organisation for Economic Co-operation and Development countries in 2011 is predicted to be 1.5 percent compared to 6.5 percent in emerging economies (The Economist Intelligence Unit 2011). The Asian export economies were all affected by the contracting markets for consumer goods in western countries. Japan's economy was out of balance even before it had to endure a series of crises. In 2010 when growth was 3 percent the deficit had reached 200 percent of gross domestic product (CIA 2011c). The South Korean economy recovered from the downturn quite quickly and is already growing once more. The size of internal markets softened the blow for India and China when export markets contracted between 2008 and 2009, but they have yet to achieve the growth rates of 2007. The size of these potential internal markets is a source of future economic security for these two countries. In the 12th Five Year Plan in 2010 the Chinese Government reinforced its 2004 commitment to raise standards of living (*The Economist* October 21, 2010). Growth predictions for 2011 for China and India are higher than the average for emerging economies, 8.5 to 9.0 percent for India and 11.5 percent for China in 2011, an increase over the 10.2 percent in 2010 (The Economist Intelligence Unit 2011).

Though rarely done, it is fundamentally sound business practice and basic risk analysis to include the future implications of climate change and sustainability into economic assessment, planning, and growth models (Stern 2010). By ignoring these variables growth projections appear healthier than is realistic, and this optimism flows over into economic and political policy. Corporate vested interests have gained enormous power over the American electorate and politicians. The U.S. is one of the few countries to have signed but not ratified the Kyoto Protocols and therefore has made no commitment to meeting them. Ignoring environmental issues rather than planning accordingly is likely to intensify the process of global rebalancing and further marginalize the U.S. both economically and politically, while India and China are planning to address the causes of climate change. In assessing this process of rebalancing I now want to explore each of these four countries in terms of "profit, people, and planet."

PROFIT: THE ECONOMIC PROFILES OF JKCI

> A country must maintain and improve growth conditions in order to achieve its potential. (O'Neill and Stupnytska, 2009, 17)

The very different political and economic histories of Japan, Korea, China, and India are reflected in the diversity of their present-day challenges. Japan has been an industrial economy for half a century. It experienced nearly three decades of strong economic growth from the 1960s until the late 1980s, based on steel, shipbuilding, automobile, and consumer electronics industries. During the 1970s and 1980s Japan had one of the highest standards of living in the world and was one of the largest consumer markets. Only recently, in 2010, was Japan overtaken by China as the world's second largest economy. Japan has few natural resources so it relies on importing most of its industrial raw materials and much of its food. Japan is therefore vulnerable to fluctuations in supply, especially as resources become scarcer. The strength of Japan's economy has been concentrated on adding value to products, based on the strength of its technological excellence. Growth throughout the 1990s was slower than in previous decades, but picked up again after 2000 when more emphasis was put on export-led growth. This growth was affected by the international economic crisis in 2008 and dropped back significantly (CIA 2011c), and now it is dealing with the aftermath of the 2011 earthquake and tsunami. Japan, along with American automobile makers, is looking at the expanding, middle-class, Chinese market to expand future sales ("Fire Recall Dents Toyota's Chinese Plans" 2009). The recent crisis in Japan is likely to shorten the time before India overtakes Japan as the third largest economy. One resource Japan does have is timber, but a political decision was made to import most of its wood requirements (70 percent). Japan has a poor history of exploiting the resources of the Third World, investing in projects which quickly deplete non-renewable resources and cause major damage to ecosystems (The World Guide 2007, 299).

South Korea's recent history has been influenced by its location and the strategic role it plays in the U.S. global defense strategy. Like Japan, South Korea has few natural resources, a shortage of fertile land and has to import most of its raw materials. Korea's economy began to take off a decade after the Japanese economy and grew steadily from the late 1960s to the late 1990s. South Korea is one of the most industrialized economies in Asia and was one of the few industrialized countries to avoid a severe recession from the recent economic crisis. South Korea has been identified as one of the N-11, the next 11 "emerging economies" that will continue to develop and have growth rates (O'Neill and Stupnytska 2009).

In the last decade India and China have had some of the highest growth rates in the world. China's economy grew steadily at an average of 9 percent from 1975–2000 (Brown 2006, 123), and continued to climb. Growth reached 13 percent in 2007 and slowed to 9.1 percent in 2009 with the contraction of export markets (CIA 2010c). Indian industrial development has been more recent. Yearly economic growth averaged over 7 percent from 1997–2010 (CIA 2010d). The governments in both India and China are focusing on economic growth and high levels of employment. Future development in these countries is only partially dependent on selling to industrialized markets. In the near future development they will focus on expanding internal markets and increasing disposable income levels. There are still major discrepancies in the standards of living between China and India and industrialized nations. Per capita incomes in the U.S. are nearly 12 times higher ($41,733) than in China ($3,567). Though the total size of China's economy could overtake that of the U.S. by 2027, per capita income would remain much lower than in the U.S. (O'Neill cited in "China Set for Prolonged Spending Boom" 2010). Continuing to export to industrialized countries and developing internal markets at current levels are ultimately unsustainable.

India and China are undertaking major programs of city building and infrastructure development. This expansion is consuming enormous amounts of raw materials and energy, especially oil and electricity. Most of China's electricity generation is produced by coal-fired power stations, which account for a large proportion of its carbon emissions and high pollution levels. China overtook the U.S. in 2007 as the world's largest carbon emitter (Vidal and Adam 2007). How China deals with current and future growth in emissions will have major implications for global climate change. It is equally necessary for the U.S. to take action to reduce emissions, as it is still the second largest emitter, and per capita emission levels are much higher than China's. Individuals urgently need to cut their personal consumption and modify their lifestyles, starting in industrialized nations. Most countries have signed up for the United Nations Millennium Goals (Appendix 5), but social, humanitarian, and environmental goals usually get displaced by economic priorities and the focus on measures for achieving economic growth. Social justice and sustainability, discussed in the next sections, need to be included in measures that evaluate and measure societies' wellbeing.

PEOPLE

The consumption of products links people, the economy, and the environment and is part of a global interlocking chain. Economic development needs to be linked to social and environmental justice to be sustainable. Japan and South Korea became industrialized after the 1960s and 1970s, and this was accompanied by high standards of living. More recently, as the economies in India and China expanded, new jobs and new business opportunities also helped raise income levels, but nowhere near those of Japan and South Korea. China has conducted the greatest victory over poverty in history since 1949, and incomes have risen 400 percent since 1980 (Brown 2006, 165). The numbers of people living in poverty in China dropped from 685 million in 1990 to 213 million in 2007 (Brown 2009, 169), though the criteria for the poverty line is very low (CIA 2011a). India has had some success in reducing poverty, but 270 million still live in poverty (CIA 2011b).

According to the CIA "World Factbook," poverty rates in Japan and South Korea are quite similar to those in China. Poverty levels in 2007 were 15.7 percent in Japan (CIA 2011c) and 15 percent in South Korea (CIA 2011d), compared to 16 percent in China (Brown 2009, 169). Of the four countries, India has by far the highest percentage of people living in poverty—25 percent (Appendix 6). The total number living in poverty in JKCI countries is 509 million or roughly half the "bottom billion."

Despite the reduction in poverty in India and China only a minority of people have experienced significant benefits from growth in the last two decades and could be seen as having a "middle class" lifestyle. There is a big gap between living above the poverty line and the excessive consumption of the West. Most of the people lifted out of poverty do not have a consumption lifestyle remotely approximating that of the industrialized societies. Average per capita income in China in 2010 was $3,567 compared to the U.S. where it was $41,733. Given the size of the population there is enormous potential for expansion in China ("China Set for Prolonged Spending Boom" 2010) as well as in India. The size of the middle classes in India was estimated to be 5 percent (55 million) in 2007 (Dragusanu and Wilson 2008), and 15 percent in China (195 million; Doctoroff 2008), which means the number of people yet to join the middle classes in those countries is 2.3 billion. Because such a large proportion of India's population is young people, and its population growth is more rapid than China's, the growth potential of India's market is even larger than that of China.

Economic growth does not benefit all sectors of the population equally. The expansion of western business and finance into emerging economies in recent decades, including South Korea, China, and India, also stimulated growing inequalities within those societies (Stiglitz 2002). A good measure of social inequality is the profile of income distribution, the proportion of national income received by the top 10 percent of the population compared to that of the bottom 10 percent (United Nations Development Programme 2011). China comes out the most equal of the JKCI countries and India the least equal. Japan scores well, with the bottom 10 percent earning 4.8 percent, while in India the bottom 10 percent earns 3.6 percent; China 3.5 percent. In South Korea the bottom 10 percent earns the lowest (2.7 percent) of the four countries. In India the top 10 percent get a significant 31.1 percent of national income; South Korea 24.2 percent; Japan 21.7 percent, and China 15 percent (Appendix 7).

The management of economic development needs to encompass equity and issues of social justice. There have been changes in perceptions about responsibilities. "We recognize today that there is a 'social contract' that binds citizens together, and with their government" (Stiglitz 2002, 78), and this extends to preserving the environment for future generations. Nations that signed the Millennium Goals (United Nations 2011) have extended this contract to include the world's poor. The very poor have the least resources to improve their standards of living and are the most affected by changes in climate resulting from industrialization that produces rising standards of living for other people. The potential increases in standards of living of large numbers of people in India and China, and the processes of urbanization and industrialization that will accompany those changes, will impact on the global environment and increase competition for the diminishing resources of the planet.

PLANET

The environmental implications of future growth in the JKCI economies are potentially disastrous. In the last 50 years growth rates have been spectacular in all the JKCI economies; first in Japan, followed by South Korea, and more recently by China and India. The impact of that growth has been from industrial production as well as the rising levels of consumption of millions of people. Risk analysis tends to be omitted from growth projections that concentrate on financial criteria. The benefits of growth are obvious when standards of living rise, but if human and environmental costs were factored into growth models and adjustments were made for social justice and sustainability then figures would be much lower, prices would be higher, and patterns of consumption would change. Growth figures present a distorted image of reality and ignore the negative aspects of economic development and industrialization. The major "threats" or "risks" to ongoing growth are the finite resources of the planet and the effects of climate change. Continued consumption at current levels cannot be sustained, let alone any expansion in those levels. Industrialization is accelerating climate change, which is already having a significant economic impact (International Panel on Climate Change 2007). Future growth in "emerging" or newly "emerged" economies will accelerate these processes. Other environmental effects of that growth, including species extinction and destruction of habitats, have a non-quantifiable intrinsic value, along with increasing hardship for the world's poor.

The environmental impact of nations on the planet is quantified in the national per capita ecological footprints, which reflect the hectares of land currently required to provide for the population, while the national bio-capacity figures assess the resources that a nation has to draw on (Appendix 3). All of the JKCI countries are in resource deficit. A state of bio-capacity deficit means they are dependent on imports from other countries. Japan and Korea are both high-income nations with significant resource deficits. In 2007 Japan's per capita footprint was 4.7 hectares, while Korea's was 4.9 hectares. Both Japan and South Korea had a relatively high bio-capacity deficits (–4.1) hectares in Japan, (–4.5) hectares in Korea. The population giants have much lower per capita footprints, India's is 0.8 hectare and China's is 1.8 hectares; however this advantage is neutralized by the size of their populations. Their national ecological reserves in 2007 had recently moved into deficit, (–0.4) hectare for India and (–1.0) hectare for China. With rising standards of living, these deficits are likely to increase significantly in the next decades. In comparison the U.S. has the highest level of consumption, with a per capita footprint of 8 hectares, and its bio-capacity is in deficit (–4.1) hectares.

Population increase, rising standards of living, and changing patterns of consumption in the JKCI economies will have a major impact on future global resources. The populations of India and China are currently not the world's major consumers on a per capita basis, and there is still a major disjunction in the contemporary global context between the relatively small percentage of people (1.1 billion) in high-income nations who consume resources at a far higher level than is required to fulfill their basic needs and the majority of the world's population who consume much less. The balance of people in JKCI who have still not reached middle-class income levels is 2.2 billion (Appendix 1). The current levels of consumption of the middle classes in Japan and South Korea are important, along with the future expansion of the middle classes in China and India. As standards of living rise, general consumption patterns change, including "moving up the food chain" (Brown 2006, 176). Food consumption increases and the types of food consumed change to more resource intensive foods such as meat and dairy products.

There has been a massive expansion in world food production since the 1950s, resulting from changes that are unlikely to be replicated on such a scale: the expansion into new territories and the increased productivity through use of mechanization, fertilizers, and irrigation. Significant increases in world population (from 2.5 billion in 1950 to 6.6 billion in 2010) have also increased levels of demand for food. World meat consumption is rising twice as fast as population growth, as increased meat intake seems to always accompany rising levels of income (Brown 2006, 176). The population of China consumes the largest quantities of meat on the planet, and consumption has been rising steadily since 1978 (Brown 2009, 230). An increasing proportion of the world's grain harvest is also being used for meat production. Meat production is very energy and water intensive and a wasteful use of scarce food and water resources and diverting food from the poor. Growth in meat consumption in India and China will contribute to future global food scarcity. The biofuel industry is also contributing to global food scarcity by competing for agricultural products as the global demand for energy increases (Stiglitz 2002, 130–131).

When countries move up the value chain and standards of living rise, energy consumption also increases, mostly oil and electricity, both of which increase global carbon emissions and accelerate climate change. Car ownership is another dream of many middle class consumers and is borne out by the rising levels of car ownership in India and China. Even small increases in car ownership percentages in China and India will have major ecological impacts. The automobile manufacturers in industrialized countries, including Japan, Korea, Europe, and the U.S., are all looking to the expanding demand in China as their future lifeline ("Recession Boosts Status of Emerging Markets" 2010). In 2010, for the first time Chrysler sold more cars in China than in the U.S. (*The Economist* 2011).

The economies of China and India, and to a lesser extent South Korea, remained relatively strong during the recent economic downturn. China and India have continued to be driven by ongoing infrastructure development and consumption. Awareness is increasing that ongoing growth has to be managed differently, and that "business as usual" is not environmentally sustainable and may not even be possible. In both countries politicians acknowledge that if ongoing growth and rising standards of living are paralleled by the expansion of carbon emissions the pace of climate change will intensify. At the time that India recently overtook Japan as the third highest carbon emitter in the world India's environmental minister stated clearly that India was committed to a high growth, low carbon, development model (Sharma 2010). The Chinese Government has recently made a huge effort to address environmental issues and has started planning for a different economic and environmental future. China is targeting a 40–45 percent reduction in greenhouse gas emissions as a proportion of gross domestic product by 2020 (Macfie 2010). The central issue is finding a replacement source of energy needs, 70 percent of which are still being met by coal (Yang 2010).

THE PROBLEM OF RESPONSIBILITY

The "fossil fuel based, car-centered and disposable" western economic industrial model won't work for India and China (Brown 2009, 243), nor will it meet the needs of the "bottom billion." There are not enough resources on the planet even for China to achieve a middle-class, high-income lifestyle when the world is currently consuming resources at 1.5 times the rate they are being replenished (Global Footprint Network 2010a). Developed industrialized economies cannot continue with their high-income lifestyles. It is the industrialized nations that have had the major historical impact on the environment and continue to do so (International Panel on Climate Change 2007). China is still a poor country with low average per capita income levels (BBC World News 2010a). Conditions are worse in India. While ongoing development in the JKCI economies will have an accelerating environmental impact, it is necessary for the industrialized countries, including Japan and Korea, to control their carbon emissions and consumption as soon as possible. In recent years dramatic climatic events in industrialized nations have stimulated renewed international awareness about climate change. Inter-governmental attempts to take concrete action to implement policies have been paralyzed by politics since the 1980s, examples include The World Commission on Environment and Development, which released Our Common Future in 1987; the UN Conference on Environment and Development in Rio de Janeiro in 1992, which adopted "Agenda 21, a Blueprint for Sustainable Development"; the 1997 Kyoto Protocols, which strengthened the mandate of the 1992 Climate Change Convention, with industrialized countries pledging to reduce their CO_2 emissions by 6–8 percent by 2012 (Worldwatch Institute 2004); and the recent UN Climate Change Conference in Copenhagen 2009. The follow-up conference in Cancun in 2010 has made progress in achieving international agreement but that process is so slow it will be difficult to avoid significant increases in world temperatures. Even the two degrees of sea-level temperature increase proposed by the European Union will cause the sea level to rise many meters this century (Hansen and Sato 2011).

CONCLUSION: PLANET, PEOPLE, PROFIT

> The two defining challenges of the 21st century are the battle against poverty and the management of climate change. If we fail on one, we will fail on the other. (Stern 2010)

The winners in the next century will be those who embrace these realities and start planning for a sustainable future where the priority is on sustainability and social justice rather than profit and conflict.

Planet: The planet will survive the current environmental crisis, and climate changes that occurred in the past could be replicated relatively rapidly if the human effects on climate change are ignored and we continue with BAU or "business as usual," which could result in three to six degrees Celsius increase in temperatures (Hansen and Sato 2011). Embracing the environmental sustainability of the planet is an issue to do with survival of any semblance of the life as we know it today. Saving the planet and dealing with environmental sustainability involves changing the patterns of consumption in "developed societies" and among the middle classes in "emerging societies." In his Plan B.4, Lester Brown (2009, 263–264) estimated the costs of environmental sustainability to be $110 billion, much lower than world military expenditure in 2008 of $1.464 billion. Cost is not the issue. The key requirements are the political will at national and global levels, the support of business interests, and popular individual support. Political leadership on environmental issues from China, and to a lesser extent India, will further change the international balance of political power, as it has already changed the balance of economic power.

People: Social justice is a moral and ethical issue for humanity, part of what Stiglitz has called the "social contract." All nations that signed the United Nations Millennium Goals have made a commitment to achieving those goals, similar to the social goals of Lester Brown's Plan B, which he estimated as costing $77 billion, and thus easily achievable. Social goals are dwarfed by the politics and power that drives the "military-industrial complex" especially in the western industrialized countries (Hartung 2011).

Profit: The winners in the next century will be those who embrace environmental realities and start planning for a sustainable future. Whatever governments say, their overwhelming preoccupation is with economic growth and retaining political power. The market with its fixation on growth rates ignores the ecological costs of depleting resources and the subsidies and trade barriers that protect wealthy economies; where free trade does not mean equality of access to markets and where prices paid for products do not reflect workers being paid living wages. This focus is a distortion that is depleting the planet of resources and accelerating climate change. It is necessary to change the criteria of assessment and adopt a new model of contemporary society and develop different tools to incorporate the environment in economic calculations.

The challenges presented by ending world poverty and dealing with environmental sustainability are vastly different challenges, and dealing with world poverty is a much easier task than dealing with the environment which involves a complete change in the way the middle classes, mainly in industrialized economies, conduct their lives. The key goals of society need to be the cutting of carbon emissions to prevent global warming and climate change and the sustainable procurement and use of resources and mitigating all the effects of the use of those resources. Social justice and fair trade are fundamental goals that would be easily implemented if there was the political will. The cost of meeting social goals is only a fraction of yearly military expenditure.

Implementing such changes is likely to intensify the current rebalancing of the global economy, which is in turn changing the political balance of power. China is the most dynamic and the largest of the global emerging economies. It has both the weight of population and economic strength. It has made significant progress toward poverty reduction and is committed to ongoing reduction of social inequalities. India is trying to address the same issues. The environmental impact of China's growth has been devastating, and the government realizes the need to find an alternative path. The Indian environment minister recently also made a commitment to carbon-less economic growth (Sharma 2010). The U.S. has yet to commit to the Kyoto Protocols and is losing international credibility as a leader in environmental issues and climate change. The global financial rebalancing of power could well be replicated politically as leadership shifts to those who will take action on environmental issues, climate change and poverty elimination, for one cannot be achieved without the other. If China and India unite in this goal, hopefully joined by Japan and South Korea—and the European Union—it will change the balance of global power. The countries that take action, even on the pragmatic economic grounds of risk avoidance, will be the survivors of the next century. Consumption links people with the environment. The market needs to tell the ecological truth or there will not be a market.

APPENDIX 1: JKCI POPULATION PROFILES 2003, 2010, 2050

2003

Japan = 127.3 million
South Korea = 47.6 million
India = 1 billion
China = 1.28 billion

Total = 2.454 billion (39 percent of the world's population of 6.3 billion)

2010

Japan = 127.4 million
South Korea = 48 million
India = 1.1 billion
China = 1.3 billion
Total = 1.8 billion (27 percent of the world's population of 6.6 billion)

2050

Japan = 93.6 million
South Korea = 43.3 million
China = 1.303 billion
India = 1.656 billion

Total = 3.059 billion (33 percent of the world's population of 9.2 billion)
U.S. Bureau of the Census. (2011) International Database.

APPENDIX 2: JKCI 2010 GROSS DOMESTIC PRODUCT

Japan = $4.338 trillion (CIA 2011c)
South Korea = $1.467 trillion (CIA 2011d)
China $10.9 trillion (CIA 2011a).
India $4.06 trillion (CIA 2011b)

Total = $20.765

APPENDIX 3: JKCI ENVIRONMENTAL PROFILES 2007

Japan = high income nation
Per capita footprint = 4.7 hectares
Per capita bio-capacity= (−4.1) hectares

Korea = high income nation
Per capita footprint = 4.9 hectares
Per capita bio-capacity = (−4.5) hectares

China = middle income nation
Per capita footprint = 2.2 hectares
Per capita bio-capacity= (–1.2) hectares

India = low income country
Per capita footprint = 0.9 hectare
Per capita bio-capacity = (–0.4) hectare
Global Footprint Network. (October 13 2010b) Ecological Footprint and Biocapacity, 2007. Accessed January 16 2011 from www.footprintnetwork.org.

APPENDIX 4: JKCI 2009 AND 2010 GROWTH PROFILES

2009 Growth Rates

Japan =–5.2 percent (CIA 2011c)
Korea = 0.2 percent (CIA 2011d)
China = 9.1 percent (CIA 2011a)
India = 7.4 percent (CIA 2011b)

2010 Growth Rates

Japan = 3 percent (CIA 2011c)
Korea = 6.1 percent (CIA 2011d)
China = 10.3 percent (CIA 2011b)
India = 8.3 percent (CIA 2011a)

APPENDIX 5: THE MILLENNIUM DEVELOPMENT GOALS

Goal 1: Eradicate extreme poverty and hunger.
Goal 2: Achieve universal primary education.
Goal 3: Promote gender equality and empower women.
Goal 4: Reduce child mortality.
Goal 5: Improve maternal health.
Goal 6: Combat HIV/AIDS, malaria, and other diseases.
Goal 7: Ensure environmental sustainability.
Goal 8: Develop a global partnership for development.
(Resolution adopted by the General Assembly, United Nations, September 8, 2000)

APPENDIX 6: JKCI POVERTY LEVELS

Japan = 15.7 percent (2007; CIA 2011c)
Korea = 15 percent (2006; CIA 2011d)

India = 25 percent (2007; CIA 2011b)
China = 16 percent (2007; Brown 2009, 169)

APPENDIX 7: JKCI INEQUALITY LEVELS (CIA 2011A, 2011B, 2011C, 2011D)

Japan lowest 10 percent = 4.8 percent; highest 10 percent = 21.7 percent (figures for 1993!)
Korea lowest 10 percent = 2.7 percent; highest 10 percent = 24.2 percent (figures 2007)
China lowest 10 percent = 3.5 percent; highest 10 percent = 15 percent (figures 2008, urban households only)
India lowest 10 percent = 3.6 percent; highest 10 percent = 31.1 percent (figures for 2005)

REFERENCES

BBC World News. 2010a. "Hard Talk: Former Vice-Chairman of the 10th National People's Congress Standing Committee Cheng Siwei." September 13.

BBC World News. 2010b. "World Business Report." April 23.

Brown, Lester R. 2006. *Plan B 2.0: Rescuing a Planet under Stress and a Civilization in Trouble.* New York: W.W. Norton & Company.

Brown, Lester R. 2009. *Plan B: 4: Mobilizing to Save Civilization.* New York: W.W. Norton & Company.

"China Set for Prolonged Spending Boom." 2010. August 18. Accessed September 10, 2010 from http://www.warc.com/News/TopNews.asp?ID=27123.

CIA. 2011a. "World Factbook China." Updated March 8. Accessed March 15, 2011 from http://www.cia.gov.

CIA. 2011b. "World Factbook India." Updated March 8. Accessed March 15, 2011 from http://www.cia.gov.

CIA. 2011c. "World Factbook Japan." Updated March 8. Accessed March 15, 2011 from http:www.cia.gov.

CIA. 2011d. "World Factbook Korea." Updated March 8. Accessed March 15, 2011 from http:www.cia.gov.

Collier, P. 2007. *The Bottom Billion: Why the Poorest Countries Are Failing and What Can Be Done.* Oxford: Oxford University Press.

Doctoroff, T. 2008. "Chinese Consumers, Brands and the MNC Learning Curve." *Market Leader,* 41.

Dragusanu, R., and D. Wilson. 2008. "The Expanding Middle Class: The Exploding World Middle Class and Falling Global Inequality." Goldman Sachs, Global Economics Paper No. 170. Accessed October 6, 2010 from https:///360.gs.com.

The Economist. 2010. "China's Economy: A New Epic. China's New Five-Year Plan Is at Odds With Itself." October 21. Accessed October 22, 2010 from http://www.economist.com/node17314578.

The Economist. 2011. "Business This Week 22–28 January 2011." January 28. Accessed January 28, 2011 from http://www.The_Economist-business-admin@news.economist.com.

The Economist Intelligence Unit. 2011. "The World in 2010–2011." January 27. Accessed January 28, 2011 from http://www.economist-online-newsletters-admin@news.economist.com.

"Eric Hobsbawm: A Conversation . . . About Marx, Student Riots, the New Left and the Millibands". 2011. Interview with Tristrum Hunt, January 16. Accessed January 21, 2011 from http://www.guardian.co.uk/books/2011/jan/16/eric-hobsbawm-tristram-hunt-marx.

"Fire Recall Dents Toyota's Chinese Plans." 2009. "Data Sourced from The Times; Additional Content by Warc Staff." August 25. Accessed August 17, 2010 from http://www.warc.com /News/PrintNewsItem.asp?NID=25579.

Global Footprint Network. (2010a) Living Planet Report. 2010. Accessed December 16, 2010 from http://www.footprintnetwork.org/en/index.php/GFN/page/2010_living_planet_report/.

Global Footprint Network. (October 13 2010b) Ecological Footprint and Biocapacity, 2007. Accessed January 16 2011 from www.footprintnetwork.org.

Hansen, J.E., and M. Sato. 2011. "Paleoclimate Implications for Human-Made Climate Change." NASA Goddard Institute for Space Studies and Columbia University Earth Institute, New York. Accessed June 11, 2011 from http://www.columbia.edu/~jeh1/mailings/2011/20110118_MilankovicPaper.pdf.

Hartung, W.D. 2011. *The Prophets of War: Lockheed Martin and the Making of the Military Industrial Complex*. New York: Nation Books.

International Panel on Climate Change. 2007. "Climate Change Report." Accessed January 21, 2009 from http://www.picc.ch.

Kim, J. 2011. "The West and National Identities: A Comparison of the Discourses of Korean Seonjinguk, Japanese Nihonjinron, and Chinese New Nationalism." *Sahoe Gwahak Yeongu* [Social Science Studies] 19(2): 8–37.

Klein, N. 2000. *No Logo: Taking Aim at the Brand Bullies*. New York: Picador.

Macfie, R. 2010. "The Greening of the Monster." *New Zealand Listener,* July 10: 26–33.

Nederveen Pieterse, J. (2011) "Global rebalancing: crisis and the east-south turn," *Development and Change*, 42(1): 22–48.

O'Neill, J., and A. Stupnytska. 2009."The Long-Term Outlook for the Brics and the N-11 Post-Crisis." Goldman Sachs Global Economics, Commodities and Strategy Research. Global Economics Paper 192 (December 4). Accessed October 10, 2010 from https://360.gs.com.

"Recession Boosts Status of Emerging Markets." 2010. Data Sourced from Bloomberg; Additional Material from Warc Staff (September 15). Accessed September 16, 2010 from http://www.warc.com/News/PrintNewsItem.asp? NID=27243.

Sharma, G. 2010. "India Says Is Now Third Highest Carbon Emitter." Accessed February 10, 2011 from http://www.reuters.com/article/2010/10/04/us-india-climate-idU.S.TRE6932PE20101004.

Stern, N. 2010. "Managing Climate Change and Promoting Development: Risks, Scale and Values." Lecture 1, Sir Douglas Robb Lectures, The University of Auckland. Accessed November 2010 from http://www.auckland.ac.nz/webdav/site/central/shared/about/news-events-notices/events/2010-events/2010%20Robb%20Lecture%201%20Lord%20Stern.pdf.

Stiglitz, J.E. 2002. *Globalization and Its Discontents*. London: Penguin.

Stiglitz, J.E. 2009. "Wall Street's Toxic Message." *Truthout*. Accessed from http://www.globalpolicy.org/social-and-economic-policy/the-world-economic-crisis/47930.htm.

United Nations. (2011) Millenium Development Goals. Accessed February 13 2012 from http://www.un.org/milleniumgoals/bkgd.shtml.

United Nations Human Development Programme (2011) United Nations Human Development Report. Accessed February 14 2012 from http://hdr.undp.org/en/reports/global/hdr2011/.

United States Bureau of the Census. 2011. "International Database Online." Accessed March 15, 2011 from http://www.census.gov/ipc/www/idb/rank.php.

Vidal, J., and D. Adam. 2007. "China Overtakes U.S. as World's Biggest CO2 Emitter." Accessed November 25, 2010 from http://www.guardian.co.uk/environment/2007/jun/19/china.usnews/print.

The World Guide. 2007. 11th edition. Oxford: New Internationalist.

Worldwatch Institute. 2004. "Environmental Milestones." Accessed March 15, 2011 from http://www.worldwatch.org/brain/features/timeline/timeline.htm.

Yang, Ailun. 2010. "China's Contribution to Solving Global Climate Challenges." Victoria University of Wellington, Policy Studies: Seminar Series.

4 The West and East Asian National Identities

A Comparison of the Discourses of Korean *Seonjinguk*, Japanese *Nihonjinron*, and Chinese New Nationalism[1]

Jongtae Kim

INTRODUCTION

In East Asia, countries' dominant ways of interpreting and responding to globalization vary from country to country. In South Korea, for instance, globalization tends to be considered by a wide range of elite groups as a universal trend. Opinion leaders vociferously promote globalization as something to embrace in order for Korea to win global competitiveness and ultimately become a fully advanced country. Even during the recent Kim Dae-Jung and Roh Moo-Hyun administrations, which were considered as "progressive" political powers in the Korean context, the need to follow the trend of globalization was widely promulgated by political leaders as a historical necessity. As S. Kim (2000, 16) notes, "For Kim Dae Jung, globalization is conflated with 'universal globalism,' which he described as resting on universal values such as 'freedom, human rights, justice, peace and efficiency.'"

In Japan, the universal disguise of globalization is notably contested by the ruling elites. In an article entitled "Japan must shake off U.S.-style globalization," Yukio Hatoyama (2009), the head of the Democratic Party of Japan, argued that "in the post-cold war period, Japan has been continually buffeted by the winds of market fundamentalism in a U.S.-led movement that is more usually called globalization." As for the effect of globalization, he insisted that:

> The recent worldwide economic crisis resulted from a way of thinking based on the principle that American-style free-market economics represents a universal and ideal economic order—and that all countries should modify the traditions and regulations governing their own economy in order to reform the structure of their economic society in line with global standards (or rather American standards). (ibid.)

As such, Japanese attitudes toward globalization are somewhat cautious. Rather than willingly accept globalization, they often see it reflecting American or western interests and, thus, conflicting with their own national interests. In this regard, Grimes (2000, 55) points out that "there seems to be an emerging consensus in contemporary Japan that globalization is changing Japan, and not necessarily in welcome ways."

The Chinese show another trait in regard to globalization. Their interests in globalization, above all, are relatively weak compared with Koreans and Japanese. For them, globalization is somewhat limitedly interpreted as a sort of economic phenomenon characterized by the expansion of multi-national corporations. Globalization is regarded as an externally given condition that needs to be addressed in their pursuit of a strong socialist country with Chinese characteristics. In this respect, the Chinese approach to globalization is somewhat limited and strategic. Globalization does not have enough discursive power to affect their pursuit of national goal and identity. As Moore (2000, 106) notes, "globalization remains surprisingly underconceptualized by Chinese leaders, bureaucrats, and strategic analysts alike."

Given those different attitudes toward globalization, this chapter attends to the countries' contrasting national identities in relation to the West. Neoliberal globalization has been widely promoted by major western countries in recent decades, for example, the U.S. and Britain. While we are in an epochal point where the "East-South turn" in globalization is notable (Nederveen Pieterse 2011), the West has been the most significant other for many non-western countries in their modernization processes. In this respect, countries' responses to globalization are related to their national identity constructions vis-à-vis the West.

National identity is a nationally popular process of boundary making between "us" and "them." A dominant national identity is generally promoted by certain circles of national elites with a wide range of support from the general public. According to Dittmer and Kim (1993, 13), it is understood "as an ongoing process or journey rather than a fixed set of boundaries, a relationship rather than a free-standing entity or attribute." Thus, a group of significant others, a "reference group," plays important roles in the process of identity construction. In this regard, there can be two types of reference groups: one is positive reference groups with which "a state desires to associate itself," and the other is negative reference groups "whose opposition serves to dramatize the importance of defending the values of 'us' against 'them'" (Dittmer and Kim 1993, 16).

Korea, China, and Japan share in common that their onsets of early modernization projects were promoted by external shock, that is, western countries' expansion in the "age of empire" (Hobsbawm 1987). Encountering the threat from outside, they were desperate for strengthening their economic and military powers in order not to be taken over by the "barbarians." Their modernization processes can be regarded as those which were provoked by "a sudden external threat" (Therborn 1995). They suddenly faced a paradoxical situation in which they had to participate in the game set by the West in order to resist it (Sakai 1989). In this historical context, the West has played crucial roles as a reference group for those countries in their modernization processes in either positive or negative ways. In regard to this, they have constructed their own images of the West in relation to the representations of their national selves.

It is interesting to see that there have appeared three conspicuous discourses on national identity in East Asia in recent decades: that is, the discourses of Korean *seonjinguk*, Japanese *nihonjinron*, and Chinese new nationalism. Each discourse has its own images of national self and the West, which reflect each country's distinguished collective sentiments. While the discourse of *seonjinguk* is a developmental discourse, *nihonjinron* is a cultural one, and Chinese new nationalism an ideological type of discourse. Despite these differences, they have been one of the most dominant discourses on national identity in those countries with variations in different historical circumstances. They have been widely promoted by certain circles of national elites with a notable degree of popularity in the general public.

As an attempt to comparatively understand noticeable nationalistic sentiments appearing in East Asia, this chapter examines different national identities and worldviews reflected in those discourses. In particular, this chapter focuses on the ways of those discourses' constructing national selves and the images of the West, and evaluating their modernization processes. Analyzing commonalities and differences in the imaginations of national self and the West, it intends to broaden a comparative understanding of notable collective sentiments appearing in those countries.

This chapter is organized in four main sections. The first section examines the historical backgrounds of the rise of the discourses of *seonjinguk*, *nihonjinron*, and new nationalism, and their characteristics in general. The second section investigates the commonalities and differences in the perception of the West reflected in those discourses. The third section focuses on the three discourses' different constructions of national self. And the last section explores their subjectivities of self modernities.

THE DISCOURSES OF *SEONJINGUK*, *NIHONJINRON*, AND NEW NATIONALISM IN HISTORICAL CONTEXTS

The discourse of *seonjinguk* is a system of knowledge that is constructed around the concepts of *seonjinguk* (advanced country) and *hujinguk* (backward country; J. Kim 2011a). One of its most notable characteristics is a hierarchical distinction between *seonjinguk* and *hujinguk*, in which the former assumes the latter as its alienated other. Naturalizing the hierarchy between the two central concepts, it has historically given justification to

Korea's efforts to "catch up" with *seonjinguk*. In this way, it has played a crucial role in supporting Korean developmental regime. It has also provided the dominant interpretive frameworks of national identities and worldviews for South Koreans in their national developmental processes.

The distinction between *seonjinguk* and *hujinguk* is akin to the Eurocentric developmental distinction between the "developed" and "developing" (or "underdeveloped") (Sachs 1992; Escobar 1995; Nederveen Pieterse 2009). Virtually referring to western countries as *seonjinguk*, the discourse takes a strong Eurocentric bearing. Given that discourse is a structural formation in which objects and subjects of knowledge are constructed in a certain way (Foucault 1976), the discourse of *seonjinguk* can be understood as South Koreans' own construction reflecting the specificity of their historical developmental experiences, rather than a faithful reflection of reality "out there." In fact, Koreans have projected their positive and negative developmental values into the concepts of *seonjinguk* and *hujinguk*, respectively, in the process of national development. As an ideal image, *seonjinguk* has played central roles in guiding the transformation of the Korean society, as an urgent national goal, an important reference point, and so forth.

The formation of the *seonjinguk* discourse was accompanied by the rise of the Park Chung-Hee regime in the early 1960s. Seizing power through a military coup d'etat, the Park regime sought for its legitimacy from the achievement of "*joguk geundaehwa*" (the modernization of motherland). As South Korea actively embraced the global discourse of development in the process of its national development, which put much focus on the development of the "underdeveloped" in the Cold War context, the discourse of *seonjinguk* arose dominant in supportive of the South Korean developmental regime. The Park regime's pursuit of aggressive modernization and rapid economic growth was justified by the discourse of *seonjinguk*, as it supposed a somewhat linear universal path of development with *seonjinguk* ahead and Korea (*hujinguk*) behind.

In the discourse, the West as *seonjinguk* plays the role of a major positive referent with which Korea should catch up in the near future. The discourse tends to assume various social, cultural, and political economic ideas and practices of the West as advanced and universal, and, thus, directly applicable to Korean situations. They are frequently considered as what Korea has to adopt to become *seonjinguk*. Korea's neoliberal reformations in various fields in recent years, which were promoted under such slogans as *seonjinhwa* (achieving advancement) and *segyehwa* (globalization), well demonstrate its willingness to embrace the global neoliberal trend led by major western countries in its pursuit of *seonjinguk* (J. Kim 2011b).

In comparison, *nihonjinron* (theories of Japaneseness) encompasses a variety of ideas and theories on Japanese national identity, which reflect Japanese deep-rooted awareness of "uniqueness" and "difference." As Befu (2001, 2) notes, the whole genre of *nihonjinron* deals with "Japan's identity, attempting to establish Japan's uniqueness and to differentiate Japan from other cultures." It is based upon some mythical notions claiming to the uniqueness and homogeneity of Japan. For instance, imagining an abstractly enclosed community within the national boundary, it asserts that "the Japanese people are a homogeneous 'race' and possess a homogeneous culture" (ibid., 68). Japanese uniqueness is considered as deeply related to their homogeneity, and thus "Japaneseness" is assumed as inherent in people, culture, language, and land in itself. In this way, it tries to create an essentialistic link between the supposed national characteristics and cultural and geographical conditions of Japan. It argues, for instance, that "the Japanese language is natively spoken only by Japanese in Japan" (ibid., 35).

Japanese identity constructions have wide historical variations. While the *kokugaku* (national learning) school in the Tokugawa period promoted the "uniqueness" of Japan vis-à-vis China, then the most significant other, the discourse of *nihonjinron* appeared mainly as a response to western cultural hegemony. For a while after World War II, Japan had to struggle with identity confusion associated with "symbolic vacuum" as formerly absolutized national symbols lost their legitimacy and authority in the wake of defeat in the war. As Befu (2001, 87) notes, "With defeat, Japan was no longer able to exploit effectively the most important symbols expressing national identity and nationalism," such as "the imperial institution, the 'national' flag, the 'national' anthem, the 'national' emblem, and national monuments and state rituals." In this situation, the Japanese re-experienced a certain degree of "inferior complex" in relation to the West, as they did in front of the western expansion in the late 19th century.

Japanese identity has alternated between positive and negative ones according to the changes of geo-political economic factors. That is to say, when such factors were considered as favorable to Japan, positive cultural nationalism prevailed and vice-versa (Befu 2001). Compensating for the Japanese identity confusion in the postwar period, the *nihonjinron* discourse revived positive national identity, reflecting their economic prosperity in the 1960s and 1970s. With the rise of *nihonjinron*, the Japanese began to promote their self-confidence again and went further to argue that Japanese society and culture were not only unique and different from those of the West but also even superior to them.

Regardless of its ultra-ethnocentric implications, *nihonjinron* has been one of the most prominent discourses on Japanese national identity in the postwar period. In the political context, it has served for Japanese conservative ruling elites as a discourse for the management of nation, society, and organizations by appropriating the values of collectivity, loyalty, and harmony. In this respect, *nihonjinron* has played the role of a "kind of ideology" associated with the "interests of the ruling social class or stratum" (Yoshino 1992, 185).

Unlike the capitalist development of the two neighboring countries, China chose a totally different path of socialist one. In Lin's (2006) terms,

China took "revolutionary modernity" that combined nationalism, socialism, and developmentalism at the same time. With regard to this, she notes that "nationalism denotes national unity, sovereignty, and autonomy; socialism stands for equality and social justice; and developmentalism implies a determination to overcome backwardness" (Lin 2006, 60).

Ever since China's encounter with the imperial expansion of the West, one of the most important goals of China has been to establish a "strong nation," as is expressed in the term "*qiangguomeng*" (the dream of strong China; Zhao 1997). Chinese intellectuals' nationalistic "quest for national greatness" is based upon the "recollections of ancient grandeur combined with outrage at China's humiliation" (Zhao 1997, 725). Remembering the glory of the Central Kingdom in the past, the Chinese tend to consider that modern Chinese history was studded with humiliation mainly brought by western powers. While Chinese nationalists' aspiration for a strong nation is common across diverse political sectors, there is a discrepancy among them in regard to the ways of achieving it. For instance, they divide in the perception of the self and the West in their endeavors for a strong nation. A notable trend among Chinese intellectuals in the 1980s was anti-traditionalism (*fanchuantong zhuyi*), which was popularized with the launch of Deng Xiaoping's reform and opening policies. Reflected in the term "western learning fever" (*xixue re*), the anti-traditional trend regarded the West as an ideal, and argued for the reformation of the society modeling after it.

This intellectual trend, yet, was challenged in the 1990s under different domestic and international circumstances, by the rise of the new strand of nationalism. As for "Chinese problems," the new nationalism argued that the western-oriented modernization promoted by anti-traditional reformers brought about various crises in China, such as "the decline of national identity, the decline in traditional values and in Marxist or Maoist faith" (Zheng 1999, 47). To redress them, the new nationalism developed alternative arguments emphasizing the need for a strong centralized government and the promotion of "Chineseness," the recognition of the importance of Chinese traditions and cultural heritages, as well as the reevaluation of Mao Zedong. It denounced the liberal modernization process during the 1980s as a kind of westernization that would eventually endanger China. Witnessing the disintegration of the Soviet Union, the advocates of new nationalism argued that "a strong State is crucial for China to survive as a unified nation-state" and that modernization should be based upon nationalism (Zheng 1999, 44). Many of the advocates came from the so-called "New Left" (distinguished from the Mao's Left in the pre-reform period), who reemphasized the importance of Chinese socialist identity. In this context, the New Left promoted new conservatism and new authoritarianism, and came to be familiar with anti-western ideas.

The rise of the Chinese new nationalism reflects the change of international circumstances around China. As Zhao (1997, 738) notes, it "coincided with the end of the Cold War and China's rapid economic growth [in the 1990s]." This is related to a perspective that the Soviet Union did not achieve a strong nation by adopting the western model but collapsed just because of it. The Chinese mistrust to the West is interlinked with their gaining of confidence in the nation's rapid economic growth, which is putatively in contrast with the fate of their rival country in the socialist race.

THE PERCEPTIONS OF THE WEST

The discourse of *seonjinguk* is a convergence theory premised upon a belief in the linear universal path of development. On this development path, *seonjinguk* is represented as the foregoer having advanced social systems while *hujinguk* as the follower. As western countries are referred to as *seonjinguk*, they are conceived of as having desirable social, political, economic, and cultural forms, as well as the prototypes of modernity that other societies are to catch up. The rise of the West is mainly attributed to endogenous factors, such as the development of human reason, while its historical expansions accompanied by the unprecedented levels of physical and mental violence are generally overlooked.

As an idealized being, *seonjinguk* is regarded as having various aspects that Korea has to emulate. The relationships between Korea and *seonjinguk* are basically assumed as reciprocal and, thus, the increase of interactions with it is justified. As modernization theory tends to consider the West as a benevolent helper of the development of the underdeveloped, the West in the discourse of *seonjinguk* is basically regarded as the cooperator of the development of Korea.

As a convergence theory, the discourse of *seonjinguk* does not much take into account the historicity of each society's modernity. Western countries are frequently homogenized into *seonjinguk*, and the diversity and heterogeneity of social and political economic systems among them are overlooked. The social, cultural, and political economic characteristics of western societies tend to be conceived of as universal and, thus, directly comparable and applicable to Korean society.

It is interesting to see that the discursive authority of *seonjinguk* is rarely challenged in Korea. For instance, even "progressive" political groups, which have relatively critical attitudes toward the West, do not dispute that the U.S., for instance, is *seonjinguk* and it has a better social system than that of Korea. Their criticisms of the U.S. for certain issues occur in different discursive frameworks, such as imperialism, neoliberalism, and so forth. The authority of the discourse of *seonjinguk* was intact even during the recent "progressive" Kim Dae-Jung and Roh Moo-Hyun administrations, as one of their important national policies was to achieve the status of *seonjinguk*. Thus, we can say that the basic assumptions of the discourse of *seonjinguk* are widely accepted in Korea, even by "progressive" political groups.

In the hierarchical discursive framework, Korea is generally considered as "near *seonjinguk*" but not full-fledged *seonjinguk* yet and, thus, there is a clear epistemic hierarchy between Korea and the West. In this respect, many aspects of Korean society are criticized and even stigmatized in comparison with western societies, which justifies the western-oriented transformation of Korean society. In regard to this, the concept of *seonjinguk* plays diverse roles in Korean society by presenting a point of direction, a standard of comparison, a desirable model, a trend to follow, a criterion of normality, and so forth.

In the discourse of *nihonjinron*, in contrast, the image of the West becomes less attractive. In this discourse, the West is perceived as lacking many of what Japan uniquely has. It is considered that the West has achieved economic prosperity but not social harmony, while Japan has both of them. Japanese uniqueness supposedly inherent in diverse aspects of Japanese culture and society is regarded as the secret for the Japanese successful achievement of both economic prosperity and social harmony. This becomes the basis of the assumption that Japan is, in many aspects, superior to the West.

Yet, this does not necessarily mean that the West is ignored in *nihonjinron*. Rather, the Japanese have been very aware of the West as the most significant other throughout their modern history. There were historical periods when the Japanese sense of inferiority was relatively strong vis-a-vis the West, such as the late 19th century and the mid-20th century. The discourse of *nihonjinron* has appeared as a response to western hegemony and, therefore, many aspects of Japanese uniqueness proposed by *nihonjinron* are virtually meaningful only in relation to the West (Befu 2001). That is to say, what is assumed to be unique in Japan is actually what the West is not assumed to have. As Befu (2001, 7) notes, "It is only because Japan and the West happen to share a similar kinship system (including monogamy), share a materialistic orientation, and lack a caste system that these phenomena are not at issue in the modern *Nihonjinron*." In a similar vein, he adds that "*Nihonjinron* would probably concern itself with Japan's monogamous marriage system" if the Islamic world or India, instead of the West, happened to be Japan's reference group (ibid.).

Japanese perceptions of the West have been closely related to how they perceive the status of their country. The degree of Japanese self-confidence vis-à-vis the West has been reflected on the degree of positive attitude toward their national self. When they had confidence over the West, they saw their national self in a positive way and vice versa (Befu 1993). In this respect, *nihonjinron* reflects the Japanese recovery of self-confidence from the identity problem in the postwar period. With the excessive level of self-assurance, *nihonjinron* issued a serious challenge to the assumption of universal history and western cultural hegemony.

In Chinese new nationalism, the West appears primarily as a hostile competitor. Historically, it was western imperial powers that forced the Chinese to get out of the imagined castle of the Central Kingdom. In this respect, the Chinese imagination of their national self and the world has also been deeply affected by the image of the West. In this regard, Wang (1998, 11) notes that modernization has been conventionally understood as a "process of reevaluating their society and tradition against the yardstick of western society and its cultures and values." For instance, Mao Zedong stressed a need for narrowing the economic gap with the West by arguing for "catching up to Great Britain and the United States" (Zhao 1997, 726).

The image of the West for the Chinese has varied according to changing domestic and global circumstances. In the 1980s, when China launched economic reform and opening policies, the West tended to be idealized especially by anti-traditional liberal intellectuals. Being critical of Chinese socialism for the nation's economic backwardness, those intellectuals asked for political economic reforms by modeling after the West. The western-learning mood was high in this context as was expressed in such phrases as "cultural fever" (*wenhua re*) and the "new enlightenment movement" during the 1980s (Zhao 1997; Wang 1998). This intellectual trend regarded western societies as important references for Chinese modernity in terms of such aspects as "the establishment of autonomy and freedom in the economic, political, legal, and cultural spheres" (Wang 1998, 19). In this vein, they were generally critical of state authoritarianism and Chinese tradition.

The new nationalistic discourse arose from a sense of crisis about Chinese identity caused by the anti-traditional atmosphere. Criticizing the previous intellectual trend for blindly romanticizing the West without much knowledge of it, the new discourse promoted the "de-romanticization of the West" (Zhao 1997). The previous discrepancy between the Chinese Communist Party and the general public in the interpretation of the West disappeared when it came to the new nationalistic discourse in the 1990s. The West in the new discourse was portrayed basically as a hostile entity that had an intention of tackling China's bid for a strong country.

Attributing the collapse of the Soviet Union to western conspiracy to some extent, the new nationalism strongly supported the centralized power structure of the Chinese Communist Party in order to "maintain social stability and economic development" (Zhao 1997, 732). The new nationalistic discourse argued that the Chinese should realize the true nature of the West. Nationalistic publications charged with anti-western and anti-American sentiments, such as *Zhongguo keri shuo bu* (The China That Can Say No), made bestsellers in this intellectual mood. In relation to this, the state-led patriotic education campaign was launched in 1993, which "laid out patriotism as a guiding principle for China's educational reform" (Zhao 2004, 218). Asian values, which were disregarded by the "cultural fever" intellectuals, were reevaluated in this period in terms of China's socio-economic development.

In the new nationalistic discourse, the West tends to be conceived of as having affluent economy, yet, with poor culture. It is suspected as hiding imperial intentions somewhat similar to those in the colonial era and as creating unfair game rules to China by using its economic and military powers. Global conflicts are often blamed upon the conflictive and binary worldviews of the West. Upon this, new nationalist discourses raise a need for enhancing harmonious Chinese cultural heritages and emphasize China's role in building a better world. In this context, as Zheng (1999, 80) notes, new nationalists argue that "it is time to change the rule of game-playing produced by the western civilization."

THE PERCEPTIONS OF NATIONAL SELF

In the hierarchical framework of the discourse of *seonjinguk*, Koreans' national identity is based upon a sense of lacking over *seonjinguk* and that of advancement over *hujinguk*. For Koreans, the former can be considered as an important positive reference group and the latter as negative one in their construction of national identity. On the supposed universal path of development, Korea is considered as having moved from the status of *hujinguk* toward that of *seonjinguk*. It is now frequently considered as almost *seonjinguk* or "on the threshold of *seonjinguk*" (*seonjinguk munteok*).

Koreans experienced a dramatic identity transition from *munmyeong-guk* (civilized country) in a spiritual sense to *hujinguk*, as the previously dominant discourse of *munmyeong* (civilization) was replaced by the discourse of *seonjinguk*. Under the influence of modernization theory in the Cold War context, Korea's early developmental regime defined their nation as *hujinguk* and sought for their legitimacy from the vigorous efforts for escaping from it. It is during the 1970s that Korean developmental elites began to perceive their country as having escaped from the status of *hujinguk*. When it came to the late 1970s, they began to designate their country as in top-tier of *jungjinguk* (developing country between *seonjinguk* and *hujinguk*) or being close to the rank of *seonjinguk*.

Koreans' self-identification as being short of full-fledged *seonjinguk* incurs both pride and shame for them. On the one hand, Koreans feel a great sense of pride in their achievement of the status of "almost *seonjinguk*" in such a short period, for which the West is assumed to have taken hundreds of years. Developmental elites tend to argue that this is due to the previous generations' blood, sweat, and tears, and that it is our generations' responsibility to make the nation a full-fledged *seonjinguk*. In a similar vein, they also insist that Korea should not fall back into the status of *hujinguk* by maintaining its competitiveness in today's competitive globalized circumstances.

On the other hand, Koreans' national identity of being short of *seonjinguk* creates a ground for their tendency of self-orientalization. In the hierarchical framework, Koreans often perceive many aspects of their country as somewhat irrational, immature, and abnormal in comparison with rational, mature, and normal *seonjinguk*. In this regard, Mora (2009, 418) refers to "internalized Orientalism" as an attitude that "the East represents and expresses itself from the eyes of the West and with the image which the West fictionalized for it." By continuously comparing their country with idealized *seonjinguk*, Koreans show a certain degree of "inferiority complex" and "double consciousness," which are typical social psychological phenomena for colonized or marginalized people (Fanon 1967; Du Bois 1994). In the hierarchical relationship between Korea and *seonjinguk*, the former tends to remain as the lacking unauthentic copy of the sufficient authentic latter.

In the discourse of *nihonjinron*, the Japanese national self appears as different vis-a-vis the West, but the difference is considered as the source of Japan's strengths and merits. In this respect, it is rather closer to an Occidentalistic attitude, than to Orientalistic one, in which the West is constructed insufficient in relation to the East. The Japanese sense of uniqueness about their national self appears in virtually every field of the country from ecology, social structure, economy, to language (Befu 2001). For instance, Japanese geographical conditions for wet rice cultivation are considered as the ecological source of "*amae*," the Japanese propensity for psychological interdependence, and of the unique ties of kinship (ibid.). This goes further to argue that the Japanese wet rice-based subsistence economy is in contrast with the pastoral economy of the West that is a material condition for the rise of monotheism and related conflictive worldviews (ibid.). As such, *nihonjinron* sees Japanese uniqueness inherent in their material and cultural lives. In this discourse, the Japanese national self is represented as homogeneous, harmonious, and inherent in Japan's geographic conditions, which takes on excessive ethnocentric implications.

The sense of uniqueness reflected in *nihonjinron* is based upon confidence that they have already achieved what the West has, for example, economic prosperity. In contrast, the West appears to struggle with various social problems such as social conflict, high crime rate, extreme individualism, and so forth. *Nihonjinron* theorists emphasize Japanese strengths in what the West does not have yet, such as social harmony. As for the Japanese "economic miracle," for instance, *nihonjinron* emphasizes the distinguished Japanese management style that is characterized by "permanent employment, seniority, and enterprise unionism" (Befu 2001, 24). Thus, what is considered as "different" is in no way an obstacle to Japan's development. Rather, as Befu (2001, 68) notes, it is argued that "Japan became an economic giant because of what Japan is."

In a historical sense, the national self constructed in *nihonjinron* reflects the Japanese desire to overcome its sense of lacking vis-a-vis the West, which was prevalent in the previous identity confusion period in the wake of defeat in the war. In Befu's (2001) words, it shows the "return of positive identity" from the previous period of "postwar auto-Orientalism." In this respect, *nihonjinron* can be understood as a self-conscious nationalistic discourse aimed to overcome western cultural hegemony, in the process of which Japanese uniqueness is overtly highlighted.

Through the economic recession in the 1990s, the Japanese seemed to have lost some of the confidence in their uniqueness. In this regard, P.-D. Kim (2007) points out that there came out various criticisms of Japanese values from the Japanese themselves amidst Japan's economic struggles in the 1990s. However, as P.-D. Kim also mentions the perpetuity of Japanese values, it may be inappropriate to consider that the Japanese values promoted by *nihonjinron* disappeared during the 1990s. Rather, deeply rooted in Japanese consciousness, *nihonjinron* still plays as major national identity discourses widely circulating in the elites as well as the public. In this regard, Befu (2001, 15) says that "it is likely to continue to be a long-run publishing industry in Japan."

The Chinese new nationalistic discourse puts their national self mainly in a position to compete with the West, which is suspected as an interrupter of the Chinese project for building a strong nation. Like Japanese *nihonjinron*, the new nationalism arose in reaction to the previous anti-traditional pro-western discursive movement that showed a certain degree of "internalized Orientalism" by assuming China's lacking position vis-à-vis the idealized West. The anti-traditional trend of "cultural fever" in the 1980s was based upon the "criticism of traditional Chinese culture and criticism of Chinese national character" (Zhao 1997). In contrast, the new nationalism asserts that China has pursued a different path of socialist development, incorporating Chinese tradition and culture into it. It emphasizes that China can build a stronger, wealthier, and more harmonious country with socialist characteristics than western capitalist countries. For new nationalism, the Chinese started a different game from the one set by the West, by choosing a socialist path to development. In this respect, China is in competition with the West in a multi-forked developmental race.

In fact, socialism with Chinese characteristics and Chinese rich cultural heritages are the two most important grounds for the construction of Chinese national self in new nationalism. As for the former, the new nationalism aims for the fast growing economy with more equal and distributive socio-economic systems that can replace exploitative capitalist systems. It argues that western societies have already exposed weaknesses in many aspects, especially in their conflictive, exploitative, and unequal social and political economic relationships. In this regard, the new nationalism perceives Chinese national self as being responsible for developing alternative political socio-economic models globally as well as domestically. The "Mao fever" of the 1990s reflected this intellectual atmosphere. Reevaluating Mao's socialist values, the New Left emphasized his role for economic growth by saying, for instance, that "Maoism's contribution to China's economic growth lies in its collectivism" (Zheng 1999, 62).

Unlike the previous anti-traditional trend, the new nationalism pays much attention to the usefulness of China's cultural heritages in its building of a harmonious country. For new nationalism, Chinese cultural heritages are not a detrimental factor but, rather, a precious element for their country's advancement. In this respect, the new nationalistic discourses are cautious about the encroachment of Chinese culture by others. Chinese pride in their cultural legacy has become a basis for their "cultural nationalism," which often warns that "the dominance of western culture in international cultural exchanges was threatening the cultures of . . . China" (Zhao 1997, 735). With the rise of cultural nationalism, "western learning fever" (*xixue re*) in the 1980s was replaced by "Chinese/Confucius learning fever" (*guoxue re*) in their search for "Chineseness" (ibid.).

THE SUBJECTIVITIES OF MODERNITIES AND POSTMODERNITIES

In terms of modernity, the discourse of *seonjinguk* still follows the basic assumptions of modernization theory by assuming a universal linear path to modernity in the singular. In this framework, the modernity of *seonjinguk* is considered as the archetype that all societies have to achieve regardless of their different historical and cultural backgrounds. In this respect, the discourse of *seonjinguk* does not much appreciate the diversity of societies and modernities and even considers the various forms of modernities as somewhat aberrant from the normal path to modernity.

In the framework of binary distinction between *seonjinguk* and *hujinguk*, the former is assumed to monopolize modernity. Thus, Korea's modernity tends to be considered as being short of western modernity. It is not appreciated as a specific form of modernity reflecting its own historical and cultural backgrounds that are different from those of western societies. As such, the discourse of *seonjinguk* rather maintains the conventional Eurocentric ideas of modernity in which the West possesses its archetype. Despite the widespread criticisms of the Eurocentric singular notion of modernity, it rarely recognizes the possibility of the plural types of modernity, that is, "modernities."

In comparison, two perspectives are notable for Japanese discourses on modernity: one tends to understand Japanese modernity with the concept of "non-modernity" and the other with "postmodernity" (Miyoshi and Harootunian 1989; Clammer 1995; McCormack and Sugimoto 1988). They share in common the assumption that Japanese society has achieved what is regarded by westerners as modernity through different or unique social, cultural processes. As a result, it is assumed that Japanese society is hard to be understood with the conventional Eurocentric concepts of modernity and modernization. In these conceptualizations, Japanese modernity is not only located outside of Eurocentric historiography, but often assumed better than western modernities. In this regard, Clammer (2001, 39) notes that "not only was Japan a postmodern society, but that it was also the only one yet to emerge (and as such the pioneer, well ahead of the West)." He goes further to argue that Japan is "the one society which has passed directly from pre-modernity to postmodernity without passing through modernity at all" (ibid., 50). As such, the Eurocentric periodization distinguishing the premodern, the modern, and the postmodern becomes ambiguous in the conceptualizations of Japanese modernity.

In fact, many Japanese scholars have consciously refused to locate their historical experiences within the Eurocentric periodical framework. Takeuchi Yoshimi, for instance, argues that "modernity is the self-recognition of Europe, the recognition of Europe's modern self as distinct from her feudal self" (cited in Sakai 1989). To include Japan in history imagined by the West means consigning Japan to be a "perpetually incomplete version of the West" (Tanaka 1993, 45). Therefore, rather than trying to fit the Japanese case into the western periodization, they choose to emphasize its "uniqueness" and "difference" of modern experiences vis-à-vis the West. In relation to this, *nihonjinron* can be understood as a kind of "nationalistic sentiments calling for the recovery of Japan's 'true identity' supposedly erased by the process of modernization/westernization" (Iida 2002, 205).

In regard to Japanese modernity, the discourses on postmodernity (or non-modernity) and *nihonjinron* share much in common. They gained popularity around the same time in the 1980s. Despite the fundamental difference between the decentralizing, heterogenizing postmodern discourses and the centralizing, homogenizing *nihonjinron*, both of them highlight the difference and uniqueness of Japanese society from the West. While postmodern discourses interpret Japanese society as "postmodern" with an awareness of western theorizations, *nihonjinron* construes it with the ethnocentric notion of "intrinsic uniqueness." As for this, Iida (2002, 200) notes that "although *nihonjinron* discourse runs seemingly counter to these latter trends [of postmodernism], it also has 'postmodern' components." The 1980s witnessed the discourses of Japanese uniqueness and postmodernity at the peak. As McCormack and Sugimoto (1988, 13) notes, "Japan in the 1980s is embarking on the path toward a postmodern society."

The Chinese discourse of new nationalism reflects their notion of "alternative modernity." This is based upon the assumption that China has undergone an "alternative path" to Eurocentric modernity through "socialism with Chinese characteristics." In this way, the Chinese refuse to identify modernity with capitalism. Furthermore, they argue for building a better societal system upon the recognition of the limitations of western capitalist modernity.

In the new nationalism, the capitalist form of modernity contains conflictive, discriminative, and exploitative relationships among people as well as between people and nature. In this regard, Sheng Hong, a representative new nationalistic theorist, argues for the superiority of Chinese culture, saying that "[because] each religion in [western civilization] worshipped only one god, war and competition were inevitable" (Zhao 1997, 737–738). He goes further to argue that "in the context of religious conflict and competition, social Darwinism was developed," and thus "western culture [would] lead humanity into catastrophe" (ibid., 738). Thus, the new nationalism argues that Chinese modernization should aim for an equal, distributive, and harmonious society. Pursuing alternative development models, the new nationalism insists that the Chinese have to effectively combine socialist reforms with traditional cultural values. As for the importance of Chinese cultural heritage, Sheng Hong argues that "Confucian respect for universal harmony and collectivism in Chinese culture should be especially instrument for world peace and development" (ibid.).

The concept of modernity for the new nationalism does not just mean economic prosperity and high technology, but encompasses harmonious and egalitarian Chinese cultural values. The discussions of Asian development models no longer see Asian values, such as Confucianism, as an obstacle to economic development, but a vital factor for it. In this regard, the new nationalism also believes that "traditional culture could play an important role in robust economic growth" (Zhao 1997, 739).

In those respects, the Chinese concept of modernity is in competition with the Eurocentric notion of modernity. For their different path to modernity, the Chinese have tried various experimental ideas such as "new collectivism" and "the theory of rural enterprise-led modernization" (Wang 1998). In these experiments, they put emphasis not just on "efficiency," which is the central theme of western modernity, but also on the values of political participation, economic equality, and the protection of the environment (ibid.).

The new nationalist understanding of Chinese modernity reflects Chinese ambition to restore the "glory of the Chinese past." It is assumed that achieving a harmonious socialist country with national wealth and strength is an ultimate way to win the competition with western capitalist modernity. In this regard, Tian (2005b, 3) argues for the adoption of "market socialism" in which "the market is the means for developing a productive force, and the goal is to build socialism." Reflecting his confidence and optimism in the Chinese path, Tian (2005a, 298) also argues that there is a difference between Chinese alternative modernity and western liberal modernity in the sense that "the former is more universal and more thoroughgoing than the latter." Thus, the new nationalist concept of modernity poses a serious challenge to the Eurocentric notion of modernity.

CONCLUSION

This chapter has comparatively examined the constructions of national self and the West and the subjectivities of modernities reflected in the discourses of Korean *seonjinguk*, Japanese *nihonjinron*, and Chinese new nationalism. It has shown that the three Asian countries' dominant discourses on modern self and the world are based upon different conceptual frameworks despite their regional proximity (see Table 4.1).

Table 4.1 Korea, Japan, and China's Perceptions of the West and National Self and Concepts for Self Modernity

	The West	*Self*	*Concepts for Self Modernity*
Korea	Advanced	Lacking	Eurocentric modernity
Japan	Lacking	Unique	Non-modernity; postmodernity
China	Hostile	Alternative	Alternative modernity

In terms of the perception of the West, the *seonjinguk* discourse considers it mainly as an advanced being, which Korea and other societies are to emulate. With the dualistic distinction between *seonjinguk* and *hujinguk*, it gives a respect to the West by designating it as *seonjinguk* in general. On a presumed universal path of development from *hujinguk* to *seonjinguk*, Korea is frequently posited on the threshold of the rank of *seonjinguk*, which renders both positive and negative self-identity for Koreans. In terms of the perception of modernity, the Korean discourse generally remains within the conventional Eurocentric notion of modernity by assuming the archetypal modernity of *seonjinguk*.

The Japanese discourse of *nihonjinron*, in contrast, shows strong self-confidence. In this discourse, the West is represented as having many weaknesses in their societies and lacking many positive aspects of Japanese society. Interpreting the superiority of Japanese society as deriving from Japanese intrinsic uniqueness, *nihonjinron* makes an effort to enhance Japanese national identity. In this context, it refuses to posit Japanese society within the Eurocentric conceptual framework of modernity. Rather, it tends to interpret Japanese society as non-modern or postmodern, which has many superior aspects over the West. In those respects, the Japanese *nihonjinron* discourse offers a serious challenge to European cultural hegemony.

Arguing that Chinese identity was eroded by the liberals' blind pursuit of western-style modernity, the new nationalism aims to reemphasize Chinese socialist values as well as their cultural heritages. It recognizes the insufficiency of Chinese economy, which raises a need for the adoption of the market economy for productive forces, but is also aware of the merits of their cultural values in building a better society in comparison with the West. Reflecting that the Chinese has long pursued "alternative modernity" through socialism with Chinese characteristics, the new nationalism asserts that the Chinese has gone on the right track of modernity. As for this, it argues that Chinese alternative modernity is closer to true universal values, such as equality and harmony, compared with exploitative western capitalist modernities.

In terms of self national identity vis-à-vis the West, it can be generally said that Koreans stick to the notion of "catch-up," the Japanese to "uniqueness," and the Chinese to "alternative." In the discourse of *seonjinguk*, Koreans express a strong willingness to accommodate the characteristics of western societies by setting them as the models of *seonjinguk*. In contrast, the Chinese and the Japanese tend to maintain a distance from the West in their identity formation by perceiving it as a kind of lacking "other" to their self-identities.

As for globalization, it is interesting to see that Korea, with a more compliant attitude toward the West, is more likely to embrace globalization as a universal trend to follow. In comparison, China and Japan, which have more self-conscious national identities in relation to the West, show more strategic and cautious approaches to globalization.

NOTES

1. Most of this chapter has appeared in a Korean journal *Sahoe Gwahak Yeongu* [Social Science Studies], Vol. 19, No. 2 (2011): 8–37. I deeply thank Prof. Jan Nederveen Pieterse for his support and comments for this research, and would also like to thank the anonymous reviewers of *Sahoe Gwahak Yeongu* for their valuable comments.

REFERENCES

Befu, Harumi. 1993. "Nationalism and *Nihonjinron*." In *Cultural Nationalism in East Asia: Representation and Identity*, edited by Harumi Befu, 107–135. Berkeley: University of California Press.

Befu, Harumi. 2001. *Hegemony of Homogeneity: An Anthropological Analysis of Nihonjinron*. Melbourne: Trans Pacific Press.

Clammer, John. 1995. *Difference and Modernity: Social Theory and Contemporary Japanese Society*. London: Kegan Paul International.

Clammer, John. 2001. *Japan and Its Others: Globalization, Difference and the Critique of Modernity*. Melbourne: Trans Pacific Press.

Dittmer, Lowell, and Samuel S. Kim. 1993. "In Search of a Theory of National Identity." In *China's Quest for National Identity*, edited by Lowell Dittmer and Samuel S. Kim, 1–31. Ithaca: Cornell University Press.

Du Bois, W.E.B. 1994. *The Souls of Black Folk*. New York: Gramercy Books.

Escobar, Arturo. 1995. *Encountering Development: The Making and Unmaking of the Third World*. Princeton: Princeton University Press.

Fanon, Frantz. 1967. *Black Skin, White Masks*, translated by Charles Lam Markmann. New York: Grove Press.

Foucault, Michel. 1976. *The Archaeology of Knowledge*. New York: Harper Colophon Books.

Grimes, William W. 2000."Japan and Globalization: From Opportunity to Restraint." In *East Asia and Globalization*, edited by Samuel S. Kim, 55–79. Lanham: Rowman & Littlefield.

Hatoyama, Yukio. 2009. "Japan Must Shake Off U.S.-style Globalization." *The Christian Science Monitor*, August 19. Accessed October 31, 2010 from http://www.csmonitor.com/Commentary/Opinion/2009/0819/p09s07-coop.html.

Hobsbawm, E.J. 1987. *The Age of Empire 1875–1914*. New York: Pantheon Books.

Iida, Yumiko. 2002. *Rethinking Identity in Modern Japan: Nationalism as Aesthetics*. London: Routledge.

Kim, Jongtae. 2011a. "The Discourse of *Sŏnjin'guk*: South Korea's Eurocentric Modern Identities and Worldviews." Ph.D. diss, University of Illinois at Urbana Champaign.

Kim, Jongtae. 2011b. "South Korea's Historical Constructions of 'Advanced Country': The Discourse of *Seonjinguk* from the 1980s to the Present." *Sahoewa Iron* [Society and Theory] 18(1): 315–351.
Kim, Pil-Dong. 2007. *Ilbon.Ilboninron-ui Jaebalgyeon* [The Rediscovery of Japan and Nihonjinron]. Seoul: JNC.
Kim, Samuel S. 2000. "East Asia and Globalization: Challenges and Responses." In *East Asia and Globalization*, edited by Samuel S. Kim, 1–29. Lanham: Rowman & Littlefield.
Lin, Chun. 2006. *The Transformation of Chinese Socialism*. Durham: Duke University Press.
McCormack, Gavan, and Yoshio Sugimoto. 1988. "Introduction." In *The Japanese Trajectory: Modernization and Beyond*, edited by Gavan McCormack and Yoshio Sugimoto, 1–14. Cambridge: Cambridge University Press.
Miyoshi, Masao, and H.D. Harootunian. 1989. "Introduction." In *Postmodernism and Japan*, edited by Masao Miyoshi and H.D. Harootunian, vii–xix. Durham: Duke University Press.
Moore, Thomas G. 2000. "China and Globalization." In *East Asia and Globalization*, edited by Samuel S. Kim, 105–131. Lanham: Rowman & Littlefield.
Mora, Necla. 2009. "Orientalist Discourse in Media Texts." *International Journal of Human Sciences* 6(2): 418–428. Accessed October 31, 2010 from http://www.insanbilimleri.com/en.
Nederveen Pieterse, Jan. 2009. *Development Theory*, 2nd ed. London: Sage.
Nederveen Pieterse, Jan. 2011. "Global Rebalancing: Crisis and the East-South Turn." *Development and Change* 42(1): 22–48.
Sachs, Wolfgang. 1992. "Introduction." In *The Development Dictionary: A Guide to Knowledge as Power*, edited by Wolfgang Sachs, 1–5. London: Zed Books.
Sakai, Naoki. 1989. "Modernity and Its Critique: The Problem of Universalism and Particularism." In *Postmodernism and Japan*, edited by Masao Miyoshi and H.D. Harootunian, 93–122. Durham: Duke University Press.
Tanaka, Stefan. 1993. *Japan's Orient: Rendering Pasts into History*. Berkeley: University of California Press.
Therborn, Göran. 1995. "Routes to/through Modernity." In *Global Modernities*, edited by Mike Featherstone, Scott Lash, and Roland Robertson, 124–139. London: Sage.
Tian, Yu Cao. 2005a. "Conclusion: The Theory and Practice of the Chinese Model." In *The Chinese Model of Modern Development*, edited by Tian Yu Cao, 293–317. London: Routledge.
Tian, Yu Cao. 2005b. "Introduction: Modernization, Globalization and the Chinese Path." In *The Chinese Model of Modern Development*, edited by Tian Yu Cao, 1–5. London: Routledge.
Wang, Hui. 1998. "Contemporary Chinese Thought and the Question of Modernity." *Social Text* 16(2): 9–44.
Yoshino, Kosaku. 1992. *Cultural Nationalism in Contemporary Japan: A Sociological Enquiry*. New York: Routledge.
Zhao, Suisheng. 1997. "Chinese Intellectuals' Quest for National Greatness and Nationalistic Writing in the 1990s." *The China Quarterly* no. 152 (December): 725–745.
Zhao, Suisheng. 2004. *A Nation-State by Construction: Dynamics of Modern Chinese Nationalism*. Stanford: Stanford University Press.
Zheng, Yongnian. 1999. *Discovering Chinese Nationalism in China: Modernization, Identity, and International Relations*. Cambridge: Cambridge University Press.

5 East Asian Community as Hybridization

A Quest for East Asianism

Seung Kuk Kim

INTRODUCTION

East Asian Community[1] and a Self-Fulfilling Prophecy[2]

East Asian Community (hereafter referred to as "EAC") is a dream as well as a reality. It is, on the one hand, an ongoing process or a multidimensional project. The Association of Southeast Asian Nations (ASEAN; Brunei, Cambodia, Indonesia, Laos, Malaysia, Myanmar, the Philippines, Singapore, Thailand, and Vietnam) +3 (South Korea, Japan, and China) as "the most elaborated form of regionalism" (Evans 2002, 137) organized and composed only by East Asian countries, has played significant roles for the last 20 years. Furthermore many political, economic, and cultural leaders continue to stress the desirability and necessity of building EAC. Two years ago in 2009 when former Japanese Prime Minister Hatoyama announced the policy of EAC, East Asians were greatly encouraged, expecting the earlier coming of EAC. With the strengthening of economic and cultural exchanges and ties among East Asian countries, EAC is becoming more and more a possible reality.

On the other hand, however, the prospect for realizing EAC in the near future is clouded with a lot of historical and structural obstacles. Recently the national boundary disputes between Japan and Korea, Japan and China, and China and Vietnam have seriously escalated. The fast growing nationalist zeal in China is becoming a potential threat to the peaceful coexistence in East Asia. China's pro-North Korean support in managing the nuclear crisis caused mainly by North Korea might shatter the whole efforts to build an East Asia of no more wars, forcing both South Korea and Japan to ally with and rely on the U.S. In this context, EAC is disappearing from any realistic horizon.

Paradoxically, however, the nuclear crisis and the warring state between two Koreas may provide a politically very sensitive but rich ground for initiating and consolidating the quest for EAC, since "Korea's division is the linchpin of regional division, and Korean reconciliation (though not unification) might bring forward a new era of interdependence in East Asia" (Cummings 2002, 175).

In facing with this contradictory situation, I would like to remember the not-so-easy history of European Union (EU),[3] which has been once called a great success, but now is increasingly regarded an unstable regional solidarity.[4] In 1950s when the idea of EU was first proposed, nobody believed it would be ever fulfilled, though only a few supported its visions and wished that its dreams would come true in the future. The lesson from EU provides one clear message to us. That is, the quest for EAC is neither a mission impossible nor an easy way to some kind of utopian world. It is a mission possible in the sense that some of its goals are already achieved and some are achievable. It should be clear from the start that EAC will be unable to realize a utopia without injustice and unhappiness. A minimum but most urgent aim of EAC is to prevent any war in East Asia.

These days, East Asian countries fully recognize that the interaction among East Asia increases rapidly, and the need to coordinate their individual interests is required. They cannot solve without close cooperation such transnational issues as the spread of drugs, diseases like AIDS, organized crimes, air contamination like Yellow Sand Winds, and toxic foods.

I am an optimist of dreaming and expecting that the establishment of EAC will bring us, East Asians at least the world of no wars and a peaceful multicultural world where we can work, trade, and think with others without defeating and without obeying. I am keenly aware that the formation of EAC is a long and difficult way to go, overcoming many unforeseen as well as predicted barriers generated from anti-global nationalist forces. Nonetheless, the dice for EAC is cast. As our proverb says, "well begun is half done." I can be an optimist because I assume that EAC has begun well enough for us to believe its sustainable future, and I judge that there is no other way to improve the risky and violent conditions of East Asia other than EAC.

In this historical context, the idea of East Asia is "a self-fulfilling prophecy" (Kim 2005, 2006) through which we can mobilize our sociological imaginations on and political strategies for the accomplishment of an alternative society.[5] EAC, like discourses on civil society, thus represents a system of solidarity, both a normative and real concept (Alexander 2006).

EAC AND HYBRIDIZATION

It is very crucial here to comprehend precisely that, with the acceleration of globalization and networking, we are rapidly entering into the world of hybridization. The fields where hybridization occurs have proliferated over time and space. Politically and economically, China is a hybrid system of market socialism, while many capitalist countries are in fact based on the practices of state capitalism rather than pure market economy. Ideologically, the distinction between socialism and capitalism becomes more and more blurred and overlapped. Culturally, we are already living in hybrid societies in which our everyday lives are, very much normally, surrounded with hybrid cars, fusion dishes, racially mixed marriage and families, all kinds of artistic inter-mixtures, and so forth. It is no exaggeration to say that "nowadays there's no end to the travel and spread of hybridity" (Nederveen Pieterse 2001, 223).

Hybridization, together with the tides of glocalization and nomadism, occurs in all spheres of social life. Even in the religious field as the last symbol of purification, recently meaningful dialogues instead of uncompromising animosity between major religious establishments have been attempted. Especially in China, Japan, and Korea where Christianity does not prevail dominantly, religious hybridization such as mutual respect and peaceful coexistence, though very preliminary and limited, is not a rare case but often tried project. The so-called but still controversial postmodern turn in the 21st century has propelled the global rise of hybrid society. Analytically speaking, there is a triangular circle of reinforcing linkage between hybridization, globalization, and networking (by information technologies), which is a historical-structural formation of our present world.

As a quite natural and functional social fact, hybridization has long been an unavoidable and indispensible process from the beginning of human history, since humans as inborn nomad, that is, Homo Nomad (Attali 2003) have always crossed their territories and boundaries and met different peoples with different values and lifestyles, thus creating everywhere hybrid forms of social life by mixing the native and endogenous with the foreign and exogenous. Because no man in the world is the same but he or she has to live with other man, he or she has to accommodate the difference of the other in any way and to some degree. That is the very reason why human societies cannot avoid the forceful necessity of hybridization. As recent post-colonialist cultural studies show interestingly, the colonized powerless can develop their own way of adapting to the rule of the colonizing power by transforming it in terms of their strategic interests of survival.

PURPOSE AND CONTENTS OF THE STUDY

An accurate approach to EAC, therefore, must be placed in this historical context of hybridization. Without carefully incorporating the degree and strength of increasing power of hybridization, the analysis of EAC will be misled to an empty world of rhetoric. Based on this premise, this study aims to analyze the building of EAC in terms of hybridization, utilizing the concept of East Asianism. East Asianism is introduced to explain five hybridizing functions of EAC which are assumed to become the catalyst for hybridization between the West and the East. EAC as hybridization requires, first of all, the Easternization[6] of Westernized East Asia. Then, I expect a second round hybridization between the West (recently a bit becoming Easternized) and the (Easternizing) East Asia, since our world thus far has long been too much dominated by the modernization or Westernization. This study begins with these critical reflections that we East Asians have to correct the continuing myth of Orientalism in the name of liberating Easternization or East Asianism.

To fulfill these aims, this study will first review theoretically both the concept of hybridization and discourses on EAC, and then introduce the idea of East Asianism. I will also briefly outline a hybrid history of EAC and identify five (politically, economically, socially, culturally, and religiously) hybridizing functions of East Asianism which shape EAC as a hybridizing force. Finally, some concluding words, with the outlook for a cosmopolitan EAC, that is, a project identity, will be offered. My major arguments are that EAC as both normative and real project identity can become an alternative or a better society where five hybridizing functions of East Asianism as the post-modern spirit or value orientation of EAC is able to Easternize the excessively Westernized East and finally balance the power of the East and the West.

THEORETICAL REVIEW

East Asian Community

Two types of approach to EAC are distinguishable. One is the pessimist view whose main concerns are given to the negative and unfavorable factors which may hinder and block the way to EAC. The pessimists usually compare the historical condition of EAC with EU, stressing very different political and cultural traditions; historical animosities of East Asian countries (China and Korea in particular) toward the Japanese colonial rule; no real and official repentance and compensations for the victims from Japan; ongoing historical distortions made by the ultra-right wing nationalists in Japan; the enormous gaps between the advanced economy and underdeveloped economy in East Asia; the worsening territorial disputes between China and Japan/Vietnam, China and South Korea, and between Thailand and Cambodia; and finally the increasing nuclear crisis caused by North Korea and a state of war in Korean peninsula.

All these conflicts and crises are assumed to justify the pessimistic view. Their judgment is persuasive as well as factual. But the currently negative conditions may be mitigated or turned into positive ones in the future. Moreover we may hypothesize reversely that some unfavorable factors may contribute to the integration of EAC. For instance, difference or gap and segmentation or discontinuity in this post-modern time is no longer the symptom of social fragmentation but a desired condition of self-organizing diverse society. A homogenous and one-dimensional society is likely to be more fragile to external shocks and internal cleavages. A loosely coupled organization is stable and sustainable. In this light I cannot wholly agree with the pessimistic view.

Another is the optimistic approach which often reminds us of the initial stage of EU when its prospect was almost closed, since nobody except a creative few believed its realization. EU has, anyhow, been established. The optimists, while acknowledging the difficulties and obstacles on the way to EAC, tend to emphasize that many substantial progresses have been already made for the institutionalization of EAC.

In fact, there are growing signs of East Asian solidarity and identity such as the expanding role of ASEAN+3 as a preliminary form of EAC, increasing intra-economic trades and cultural exchanges among East Asian countries, and revival of the Confucian and Buddhist (or perhaps Taoist) legacy. Besides, in order to survive in this era of regionalization such as EU, North American Free Trade Agreement (NAFTA), Asia-Pacific Economic Cooperation (APEC), Asia–Europe Meeting (ASEM), and so on, and to avoid another war in East Asia, the optimists point out the necessity of building EAC. To them, necessity makes anything possible. Given their visionary ambition toward a better society, optimists certainly provide a plausible picture of EAC.

What, then, is my position between pessimism and optimism? Quite naturally, mine is a hybrid with 49 percent pessimism and 51 percent optimism.

Hybridization

Many studies with different but unique perspectives have discussed the concept and empirical process of hybridization. I will identify five approaches that have influenced this study significantly.

Homi Bhabha and Cultural Hybridization

Bhabha (1994), a post-colonialist, has persuasively shown the strategic power of hybridization such as mimicry, sly civility, interstice, and the third space. To him, the powerless people utilized the skill of hybridizing their local lives with the demands of the colonialist, thus achieving simultaneously both adaptation to and resistance to colonial power. Bhabha (1994, 127) employs the concept of hybridity to overcome the essentialist binarism. Instead of proposing some explicit strategies of destroying class and gender inequalities, he emphasizes both the interdependence and negotiability between the divided groups by colonialist line (or by gender and by class). Bhabha's (1994, 18) positive recognition of hybridity is itself a recognition of community, or deep desires for social solidarity.

Antonio Negri and Politico-Economic Hybridization

Negri, a post-Marxist, regards hybridization as a principle of the becoming being in opposition to the bio-power or the contemporary capitalist empire. He provides much more powerful and liberating potentialities to hybridization than Bhabha, since Negri (2002) seems to believe that hybridization, if successful, could lead us to the kingdom of freedom for direct democracy. As historically well shown, hybridization can destabilize the existing hegemonic establishments which are characteristic of essentialist orientations, usually claiming to be the guard of purity.

To Negri (Hardt and Negri 2000), hybridization is, first of all, a political and normative discourse. He warns us that the Empire, with its unlimited controlling power, is skillful and clever enough to make use of the hybridization process itself and produce a lot of easily manageable hybrid identities and subjectivities. However, very fortunately, the creative potential of hybridization, whose transforming and destroying "posse" (Spinoza's potentia) does not fit structurally with the Empire, is able to generate the multitude or the militant who are opposing against the Empire.

Jan Nederveen Pieterse and Social Hybridization

According to Nederveen Pieterse (2001, 221), hybridization is "deeply rooted in history and quite ordinary." The evolution of human species or humanity, our history, and technological advances are all a mix, a collage, that is, a hybrid. Globalization is, therefore, hybridization (1995). Like Bhabha and Negri, Nederveen Pieterse also explains hybridization in terms of power relations. Powerful interests are invested in boundaries and borders. Since boundaries are set mainly by the powerful, hybridization as an act of crossing over them means either adaptation to the powerful boundaries or resistance to them. Boundaries will be continuously built again as far as the power relations in our society continue. As old boundaries wane, some remain, new ones are established. Thus hybridization keeps on going. Nederveen Pieterse (2001, 238–239), while acknowledging the postmodern, post-structuralist linkage with hybridization, stresses the critical and deconstructionist awareness of the unequal power structure of our times.

Hwa Yol Jung and Hybridization as a Transversal Middle Path

Jung (2010) explores a non-polar middle way between the global and the local, escaping from both abstract universalism and ethnocentric universalism, seeking for a transversal or cross-cultural world that hybridizes variant cultures and ethnicities. He criticizes Eurocentrism as the legacy of modernity. The division between the superior West and the inferior East has thus swept through the world. Transversality as a middle way between the universal tendency by Eurocentric modernists and the particularist tendency by de-centering post-modernists reaches "a world of hybridizations and hyphernations" (Jung 2010, 96) where everything is related to and influenced by everything. Jung warns us of the perils of essentialization like Easternizing the East or Koreanizing Korea.[7] Following Jung's transversality, we may envision EAC as hybridizing or middling force[8] as well as cosmopolitan orientation.

Theories of Both Yin/Yang and Five Ways and Ontological/Existential Hybridization

In my Easternized view, many crucial points of the previous four theoretical discussions may be derived from the classical East Asian explanation of cosmological principles offered by Logic of Yin/Yang and Five Ways. According to this wisdom, the structural logic governing human life as a part of cosmic world can be understood in two interrelated and hybrid relationships. First, Yin and Yang are contradictory with each other and antagonistic to each other while they also are reciprocal and complementary with each other. In short, they are reciprocal as well as conflicting. Our human existence or everyday life thus is viewed as nothing but a series of multiple hybrid combinations of Yin and Yang. The Yin/Yang as a hybridizing force or principle tells us that everything in the world represents a hybrid manifestation of Yin and Yang.

Theories of Five Ways as the specific functional dimension of Yin/Yang structure are also based on the same logic of both reciprocity and contradiction. These dual relationships among five ways constitute an undisputable chain of hybrid functions required to maintain social/individual existence of human life. Following but extending the Parsonian model of four functional requisites, that is, AGIL(adaptation, goal attainment, integration, latency), I propose, according to Five Ways, five functional dimensions of Yin/Yang combination system such as political, economic, social, cultural, and (a newly added) religious functions.[9] Unlike AGIL scheme, my five hybrid functions are causally and one-directionally but circularly linked in a negative as well as positive way, composing an endless hybrid functional network.

The principle of Yin/Yang and Five Ways has certainly shown great explanatory power and philosophical insights. It gives this study specifically the following three guidelines:

1. Everything changes because of the imbalance between Yin and Yang: hybridization occurs because of unequal or imbalanced power relations.
2. We must try to achieve and keep the balance: hybridization aims to balance the difference by mixing.
3. However, the balance is destined to be broken because of the cyclical movements of Yin/Yang or the change itself: hybridization continues as long as power relations exist.

In short, hybridization is a balancing force or a changing power to achieve a temporary balance which is going to be broken and to be rebalanced, repeating this chain of inevitable change.[10]

According to these three premises, we can reinterpret the theoretical implications of hybridization. Negri's Empire, on the one hand, is being built by the global hybridization of capitalist world system, while, on the other hand, the controlling power or to put it differently, the balancing power of the Empire is eroding from the another hybridization between old proletariats and newly emerging radical mass, or the formation of militant multitude. Nederveen Pieterse's view of the incessant process of hybridization and the construction/deconstruction of boundaries follows exactly the same logic of the endless circulation of Yin/Yang combination: no Yin/Yang structure, no power relation, or vice versa.

EAST ASIANISM FOR EAC

Hybrid Evolvement of EAC and Identity Conflict

The history of EAC itself is a hybrid formation. First, in its early pioneering stage of development during the imperialist/colonialist domination of East Asia, a quest for EAC was made by imperialists[11] as well as Anarchists[12] and Marxists.[13] The current conflicting ideas on EAC show the ideologically hybridized origin of EAC. Imperialists, of course, used EAC to legitimize the Japanese colonialist empire, while anarchists and Marxists were eager to build an anti-imperialist solidarity beyond nationalist boundaries.

The second stage of EAC, from the end of the World War Two until now, is also characteristic of hybrid constitution and influences. ASEAN as the preliminary but first institutionalization of EAC has been mainly an economically oriented system though its rhetoric is always covered with political co-operations. With the rise of Japan, South Korea, and China, ASEAN was expanded into ASEAN+3 and transformed into a hybrid terrain of competing politico-economic interests of Japan and China in particular. Japan's pro-U.S. policy, South Korea's ambivalent attitude between the U.S. and China, and China's counter-U.S. tendency are causing an identity crisis of EAC which has been hybridized continuously by internal and external interest conflicts and power shifts among member countries.

The future developmental stage of EAC too will be unable to escape from its history of hybridization. Because of rapidly growing global instabilities in our risk society, the more developed and institutionalized EAC, the more hybridized its identity and functions. It is no surprise that the U.S. and Russia may remain as a powerful key hybridizer, since they, claiming (at least in geographical terms) a promising and qualified member of EAC, cannot but interfere with the organization and structure of EAC, exerting further hybrid influences on EAC. In fact, the U.S. has been very active in promoting trans-Pacificism or Asian-Pacificism, giving its mind to Asia.[14] In opposition to this Asian Pacific identity, many leaders, elites, and scholars advanced a new East Asian identity. Especially the government of

Singapore and Malaysia promoted the so-called "Asian values". But the U.S. has continued to renew the status and role of APEC again in order to build the Asian Pacific identity in alliance with Japan. China is not willing to accept it.[15] This identity conflict may be reproduced since Japan has long tried to include Australia, New Zealand, and India in EAC whereas other members of EAC oppose or have reservations on this idea.

Why and How East Asianism?

The famous but now very controversial thesis of Max Weber (1930) on "the Protestant Ethic and the Spirit of Capitalism" teaches us, in contrast to the Marxian materialist interpretation of history, that a system requires a spiritual force based on some kind of ethical value orientations. Likewise, EAC as a social system needs some spiritual or ethically oriented values to justify its raison d'être and maintain its functional requirements. Since EAC is already being built on the technological infrastructure made possible by information technology revolutions, its material base is solid and stable. Given the anomic chaos all over the world, new spiritual bases or fresh ethical/value orientations are in urgent demand to effectively and legitimately construct EAC.

Furthermore, it is a normative imperative that EAC should become an alternative, though not utopian, society, achieving at least a minimum level of social improvement.[16] It is, therefore, quite natural for us to identify and reinforce certain desirable value orientations in East Asia, utilizing them to correct and balance the excessively Westernized East Asia. The coming crisis of Western modernization all over the world is distinctively illustrated in the all kinds of injustices and disasters from contemporary risk society. It is time East Asians were rediscovering the countervailing power of the East Asian way of value orientations, that is, East Asianism and Easternizing the overly Westernized East.

Five Functional Value Orientations of East Asianism

East Asianism is an invention. In order to make EAC a better or an alternative society, we must change our values and lifestyles. Drawing many relevant values from Classical East Asian Religions and also witnessing their steady growth worldwide, I invented the concept of East Asianism as a value system with which EAC can Easternize the currently Westernized East. It is no exaggeration that since the late 20th century "the currents of influence again run from the East to the West, though now at much higher overall level of interdependence and integration" (Nederveen Pieterse 2009, 137).[17]

I propose East Asianism as postmodern value orientations or lifestyles that are expected to countervail against Western modernity. Historically, East Asianism inherits and reinvents the wisdom of three great religions: Confucian moderation and communitarian moral politics, Buddhist non-materialism and post-secularism, and Taoist non-coercion and natural pacifism.

The idea of East Asianism is organized on two grounds. First, in contrast to the dominating value orientations of Westernization and modernization such as political statism, economic materialism, social competition, cultural universalism, and religious secularism, I identify five functional value orientations such as post-statist pacifism, post-materialist idealism, post-competition mutual aid, post-universalist particularism, and post-secularist mysticism that have been historical characteristics of East Asia where Confucian, Buddhist, and Taoist influences have been intermixed with each other and have maintained, if not conspicuously, these value orientations in everyday life of East Asians.

East Asianism, however, does not negate the rationalist merits and progressive power of Western modernity. The former cannot replace the latter. Rather East Asianism aims to balance the normative power of the East and the West and to create a new hybrid civilization. The crisis of Western value orientations lies just in their excessive dominations of our life. I do not contend that Western values and beliefs have been fallen into a secondary position and Western civilization is doomed to be replaced by Eastern one. Easternization of the West as well as the Westernized East is a process of hybridization between the East and the West. Similarly, the global interaction between the East and the West is a two-way hybridizing process: the East Asia is being globalized while it is globalizing the rest of the world. East Asianism is an East Asian way of shaping EAC.

Post-Statist Pacifism for a Peaceful Life

In this era of risk society, safety becomes the first priority in human desires. Political and military safety in particular is most urgent, because political violence such as war and massacre has always been inhuman and barbaric. As is well known, the state is born from war and lives on war. Taoist and Buddhist pacifism may cure the warring state in the contemporary world as well as East Asia. The political repression and violence by the state has been the ugly symbol of imperialist and colonialist coercion in modern times.

Non-violence derived from the pacifist orientation should be also applied to the micro-level of everyday life as well as the macro-level of hierarchical domination by bureaucratic organizations such as the state and government, the enterprise, and powerful associations like big unions, interest groups, and religious establishments. The state system must be transformed from deciding and ordering power to mediating and supporting resource. The statist order is necessary to manage the complexity and conflict brought by the increasing interactions among diverse people. Many times, however, freedom and liberty, often expressed in chaotic forms, has been functioning as a much desired basis of human happiness and development. A creative new order for a peaceful life may result from the destruction of old orders based on the statist violence and coercion.

Many anti-war and peace movements passionately expect the anti-statist power of globalization to weaken the militancy and hierarchical domination of the state system. EAC is required to develop a federal association of the very much decentralized governments of various forms. However, the political autonomy of non-coercive society encouraged by EAC, if excessively pursued, may fall into a trap of the Hobbesian warring state. A post-state society has to find a way to balance between collective order and individual freedom through the elimination of statist coercion on the one hand and by the generation of social individualism as a communitarian orientation on the other hand. The values of non-violence and pacifism can become the best means to prevent wars. Then, a peaceful society within post-statist EAC will emerge from the ashes of violence burnt by our passionate and strong wills for non-coercion.

Post-Materialist Idealism for a Simple Life

The great East Asian religious wisdoms have consistently stressed the joy of a simple life. After capitalist modernization of East Asia, East Asians became rapidly preoccupied with material possession and success. Thus, a reified fetishism or the power of greedy materialism like "money is everything" prevails at every corner of the capitalist world. Unlimited desires for material satisfaction produce and reproduce the polarization of society between the rich and the poor. Only a few win the battle of material competition, and hence the many losers enter the world of scarcity where severe poverty and frustration often destroys their human dignities. Given the narrowing limit of social and natural resources, there are simply no ways to satisfy fully the material desires of everybody. Unlimited economic growth or limitless capacity of production power in a Marxian sense is no longer feasible since environmental disasters will come first and destroy all of us.

What is, then, to be done? Without radically changing our lifestyle of mass consumption, we would be unable to sustain the sustainable development. The value of self-regulation must be internalized to encourage a simple life or minimalist lifestyle. Here, the East Asian philosophy of "being content amid poverty" (or to put it differently, material insufficiency) and enjoying the Taoist Way (安貧樂道) may suggest a way to go beyond the materialist life style. EAC must provide its member citizens economically the satisfaction of basic needs as minimum human rights. The minimum, not the maximum use of material resources is our principle for survival to overcome the ecological crisis. In post-materialist EAC, material insufficiency can be compensated with idealistic and spiritual pleasures such as meditation and imagination, reading, writing and listening, praying and believing, breathing, walking and exercising, and so on. A simple life based on the balance between maximum desires and basic needs can constitute the core of non-materialist society where many material necessities can be properly replaced by ideal satisfaction.

Post-Competition Mutual Aid for a Caring and Sharing Life

We are living now in the world of war of all against all. The competition is ever more increasing and intensifying by the meritocratic system based on the principle of the survival of the fittest. In the end, only a very few may survive while the vast rest becomes the loser. This is certainly a misguided consequence of human competition which has been an indispensible part of capitalist development. Unfortunately, we, brainwashed too much by the Darwinian theory of evolution, or the law of the Jungle, have forgotten the necessity of mutual aid as the other indispensible principle of human society, long argued by the great anarchist Peter Kropotkin (1954). The excessive competition in social relations must be mitigated and balanced by cooperation. Otherwise, everybody even including the winner will become sooner or later the victim of the inhuman system.

Recently, however, there has been a bright sign of growing cooperation among various social relationships such as communitarian interests and solidarities. EAC must be designed to balance the competitive orientations with the cooperative practices. A caring and sharing society may be greatly helpful in increasing efficiency as well as equality in EAC. We have to devise a dualist means to keep, on the one hand, the competitive power which does not neglect, on the other hand, the cooperative values. A mutually aiding society discriminates against neither the winner nor the loser. It cares for both of them by reducing the monopoly of resources by the winner on the basis of the principle of reciprocity. Any competition without clear awareness of caring and sharing social resources will result in a pyramid of sacrifices and defeats.

Post-Universalist Particularism[18] *for a Hybrid Life*

Cultural universalism based on the absolute infallibility and inviolability of Christianity has been a hallmark of Euro-centrism and an essential core of Westernization or Modernization. The West, with its monotheist conviction, was never skeptical about their mission to Westernize the other part of the world. Orientalism was thus invented to glorify the universal and superior status of the West and stigmatize Asian cultural practices as an underdeveloped and inferior form of particularism. But post-modern deconstructionism and relativism uncovers the myth of

Western universalism and tells us that it is nothing but another particularism. The universal, like the absolute or the pure, is no longer self-evident but a very unstable social construction devised by the powerful to maintain the status quo. It has often been used to dominate, repress, and exploit the particular and the weak.

Hybridization has always been a strong challenge to the purist essentialism and the universal way of thinking, since it infiltrates and destroys the universal boundaries established to distinguish the powerless particular or the heretical hybrid from the dominant universal and the glorified pure and to discriminate against the former. Within the framework of EAC, the universal, if such a thing exists, is impelled to be hybridized with the particular and to make itself another particularity. Any kind of nationalist, ethnocentrist, dogmatist behavior is not to be welcome to EAC. If the particular is called a small universe, then, the universal is a particularity of many particulars. A hybrid society is composed of many particularities, not of a single universal.

Post-Secularist Mysticism[19] *for an Imaginative Life*

Rationalization of social life has coincided with secularization of religions. Thus man could declare that god was dead and man became master. But the excessive secularization of churches and priests has made religions big business. Religion is becoming more and more a commodity which can be bought and sold in the market. Human spirituality has little to do with religious sincerity or faithfulness. The sacred is indistinguishable from the secular. As a result, people are increasingly disenchanted with the overly rationalist voices of many secularized religions.

Given the enormous social disorganization and serious anomic disruptions, we need some spiritual renovations with which we can endure growing uncertainties and anxieties generated by many and rapid social changes of all sorts. Thus people are becoming more and more interested in mysticism (not as magnification of world) which, they believe, may illuminate some way to get out of the tedious and often threatening realities. In fact many East Asian religious practices (Japanese Shintoism in particular) have been developed in close relationships with mystical orientations.[20] Very ironically, we, humans living in the era of highly advanced scientific knowledge are inclined to rely on some mystical ways of stabilizing and comforting ourselves.

The sacred can be sacred not because it represents some holy power of the almighty god, but because it satisfies believer's sense of meaninglessness with an imaginative world of fantastic creations. Rationality and mystical thinking are not necessarily in contradiction with each other, but the two as hybrid composition of religiosity can be reciprocal. EAC in which a vast variety of religious sects and beliefs will flourish, has to tolerate the religious mysticism and hybridize this mystical orientation with the secularized religions of today. The balance between the sacred and the secular may be achieved through the mediation of the mystic. To repeat, the mystic is neither non-scientific nor superstitious but very much reasonable as well as probable. There is nothing absolutely certain in our world. If we could recognize the useful power of mysticism and make it play the role of mediating and hybridizing between the sacred and the secular, EAC would become an imaginative world of all heterogeneous beliefs. Furthermore, this tolerating force of religious imagination can facilitate the coming of a cosmopolitan society all over the world as well as in EAC, for religious conflicts become most explosive and dangerous when any attempts to unify religious differences are made.

The main points of my discussion in this section are summarized in Table 5.1.

Table 5.1 Hybridization and East Asianism

Regional Category and Power/ Function	*The Past West*		*The Coming EAC*	*The Future East*	
	Balanced	*Excessive*	*Hybridization*	*Balanced*	*Excessive*
Political	Order and power	Coercion and violence	Post-statist, pacifism for a peaceful life	Autonomy or anarchy?	Egoism and chaos
Economic	Satisfaction of desires	Materialism, fetishism, Inequality	Post-materialist idealism for a simple life	Basic needs	Poverty
Social	Competition and meritocracy	War of all against all	Post-competition mutual aid for a caring and sharing life	Cooperation	Free rider and inefficiency
Cultural	Universalism	Euro-centrism	Post-universalism for a hybrid life	Particularism and relativism	Exclusion and isolation
Religious	Rationalism	Secularism and snobbism	Post-secularist mysticism for an imaginative life	Transcendentalism and spiritualism	Retreatism
Social typology	Modern capitalist, state system		Communitarian/ libertarian de/re-territorialization	Post-modern, cosmopolitan, federal association, and global civil society	

CONCLUSION: TOWARD A COSMOPOLITAN WAY

This study has started with the grand but practical assumption that hybridization becomes normal and usual all over the world and hence EAC as a hybrid must play the role of hybridizing the West with the East, seeking for a balance of power between the two and then a cosmopolitan society where all divisive boundaries and discriminating distinctions become weaker and weaker.

In fact, EAC is certainly being hybridized with the internal and external influences from ASEAN+3, ASEM, APEC, NAFTA, and EU. Its historical mission is not to purify or essentialize East Asia and refute or marginalize the West but to hybridize the East with the West. Since the East has been excessively Westernized or modernized under the prevalence of Eurocentrism, EAC has to correct the imbalance by the medium of East Asianism as hybridizing force.

Reflecting on the imperialist distortion of historical change in East Asia by Japan, Yoshimi (1960)[21] suggested a method to do this task of balancing. First, the East recognizes its limitations as well as the merits of the West and then reinterprets the Western merits from the Eastern point of view. Finally, we should try a reciprocal development of both the East and the West in order to recreate a hybrid but "highly universal and matured."[22] Despite the reciprocal and subjective dimension of his approach, he seems to anticipate a highly upgraded future of some universal values. In my post-modern view, the principle of the Yin/Yang and Five Ways can offer a more realistic approach to the construction of EAC. Like the cyclical movements between Yin and Yang, the decline of the West is being followed by the rise of the East. It is then quite spontaneous to go beyond the Western excess through the Eastern moderation, that is, East Asianism as new value orientations and to achieve a balance between the East and the West. But any balance in any time is just a new beginning for another balance, since all balances are destined to be broken and hence just temporary. With this recognition of cyclical shifts of all power relations, we do not mystify the promises of EAC, though it is surely an improvement from the present condition of East Asia. Furthermore, EAC as hybridization may contribute to the expansion of cosmopolitanism which might become substantial and realistic only if our world is fully hybridized.[23]

To borrow the terminology of Castells (1998a), EAC is historically a postmodern project identity while EU has been a modern project. One of the hidden aims of EU EU seems to be the recovery of its old glorious hegemony, that is, Eurocentrism over the other world. The decline of the West is becoming a reality in which the rise of East Asia becomes a new reality. The global hybridization itself may reflect the power shift from the West to the East. The postmodern turn in the 21st century will be strengthened by the postmodern quest for EAC with which East Asia can develop new project identities of radically transforming existing social structure and building alternative societies.

In this light, EAC is not simply a regional blockade against other blockades but a critical regionalization of establishing communitarian solidarity as well as libertarian value orientations in East Asia. Since its historical missions are not to be confined to East Asia, EAC can become a cosmopolitan movement, de-territorializing itself and re-territorializing a global federal association or a global civil society.[24]

The politico-economic and socio-cultural diversities or differences, often regarded a major hindrance to forming a regional identity, can play a very positive role in building a transnational regional identity. Especially, East Asian hybrid cultural forms may provide favorable milieu for the development of cosmopolitanism that has been encouraged by the civilizational heritage of East Asia and its ancient religions. EAC is expected to encourage and strengthen the basic preconditions for creating hybrid society in which cosmopolitanism has become more of a popular phenomenon than an elite mission (Delanty and He 2008, 333–334).

NOTES

1. In this study, the boundary of East Asia, though very controversial, runs east-west from India to Japan and south-north from Indonesia to Mongolia. After EAC is solidly constructed, it may include Russia, the U.S., and Australia and New Zealand if they wish. Regions are neither fixed nor neutral but socially constructed and politically contested and open to transformation. In this light, EAC may be an imagined or invented community.
2. A self-fulfilling prophecy, a term coined by Robert K. Merton, is a prediction that, once in being made, actually causes itself to become true. It is seen as a manifestation of positive feedback in human society, since a given prophecy may affect people's actions. The power of visionary ideas like East Asian Community can overcome many barriers and impediments built in realities.
3. One key point of all pessimisms and criticisms on the possibility of EAC comes from the historical and empirical comparison of East Asia/EAC with Western Europe/EU (Cummings 2002). In my view, EU is neither the best model nor the only goal for EAC. I agree with Tsunekawa's (2002) proposal that despite the lack of a common identity and a well-institutionalized framework, East Asia approaches to EAC quite successfully by paying greater attention to human security or safety problems such as nuclear issues, poverty, environmental pollutions, and crimes.
4. These days the lack of EU-like institutionalization is considered a serious impediment to regional cooperation in East Asia. The positive evaluation on "EU as a catalyst of cosmopolitanism" (Delanty and He 2008, 830) is supported by realistic judgment that European countries will never again go to war. But, according to Castells (1998b, 855), EU has not realized a historical project of building a European society, since it is "essentially a defensive construction on behalf of European civilization to avoid becoming an economic colony of Asians and Americans."
5. Realistically, a political image of EAC will resemble what Schmitter (2002, 154) called "a multi-level and polycentric governance" network.

6. Easternization, historically begun again from the 1960s, is the counter-construct of Westernization (Campbell 2007). The 1960s countercultural movements in the West as self-criticism of the capitalist materialistic dominance have provided fertile ground for a non-Western alternative, encouraging an enthusiasm for the wisdom or religious spirituality of the East.
7. Jung's conception of Easternizing the East is directed to refute the essentializing the East. Therefore my use of Easternization (of the Westernized East) as balancing or hybridizing the power of the East and the West is not in contradictory with Jung's. Hybridization is an antithesis to essentialism.
8. Jung's conception of transversal middle path seems to be linked to Confucian moderation or middle way (中庸) which tries to achieve, without adopting any dogmatism, a dynamic equilibrium in conflicting situations by benevolence.
9. In this study, five ways such as ways of wood (木), fire (火), soil (土), metal (金), and water (水) are respectively matched to the five hybrid functions of East Asianism.
10. The principle of Yin/Yang does not approve any essential superiority of either the West (Yang) or the East (Yin). It suggests only a balance between the two opposing but reciprocal forces.
11. Imperialist hegemonic conception was expressed in Great East Asia Co-Prosperity Zone based on Great Asianism.
12. In 1907 Anarchists of Japan, Korea, China, India, Vietnam, and Malaysia founded Asian Solidarity and Friendship to fight against imperialism. They organized Eastern Anarchist Association in 1928.
13. Li Dazhao (1919), a founder of Chinese Marxism, proposed new New Asianism to ultimately build a global federation of three regional federations (Europe, America, and Asia) based on the free and equal association of each nation and each people.
14. For example, in July 1993, President Clinton proposed the idea of a "New Pacific Community" at the Group of Seven meeting in Tokyo and emphasized the significance of APEC.
15. APEC did not play any significant role in responding to the Asian Financial Crisis in 1997/1998. In fact, APEC supported "the IMF's crisis-management" and did little to mitigate the crisis. Many countries were disappointed by this act, and the reputation of APEC was injured seriously. Despite the indispensible role of the U.S. as one of the principal markets for most East Asian countries, the position of the U.S. is, as Evans (2002, 143) describes, "like the ghost at the party called 'toward an EAC'. The U.S. presence is ubiquitous but not acknowledged, denounced or applauded."
16. As mentioned earlier, a minimum but highest goal of EAC is to build a state of no more wars in East Asia.
17. Frank (1998) shows very convincingly the rise of East Asia.
18. In my usage, particularism does not mean either exclusiveness or isolation. It is employed to represent the relative uniqueness or specificity of everything.
19. Mysticism is closely connected to transcendentalism which allows us to approach to another world without necessarily relying on the almightiness of religious god.
20. The four pillars of the Cyclic Eight Characters for the year, month, day, and time of one's birth, the theory of geomancy (used in choosing auspicious sites for grave and housing), physiognomy, and palmistry in Korea are, though neither religion nor superstition, becoming more and more popular even in young generations.
21. He is famous for proposing an idea of East Asia as a method.

22. As a post-universalist, I would like to understand Yoshimi's "universal" as contingent or temporary universal.
23. Hybridization is conceptually linked to cosmopolitanism which might be plausible only when the power of hybridization can shatter away the state/national boundaries (Nederveen Pieterse 2001, 225).
24. EAC may learn some lessons from EU, but it should go its own way, for EU is going to remain for a while within the statist iron cage of modern project. EAC may borrow its future images from Proudhonian Libertarian Associationism (Chomski 2005; Kojin 2006).

REFERENCES

Alexander, Jeffrey C. 2006. *The Civil Sphere*. New York: Oxford University Press.

Attali, Jacques. 2005. Homo Nomad, translated by Hyo-Sook Lee. Seoul: Woongjin.

Bhabha, Homi K. 1994. *The Location of Culture*. New York: Routledge.

Campbell, Colin. 2007. *The Easternization of the West: A Thematic Account of Cultural Change in the Modern Era*. Boulder: Paradigm Publishers.

Castells, Manuel. 1998a. *The Power of Identity*. Oxford: Blackwell.

Castells, Manuel. 1998b. *The Rise of the Network Society*. Oxford: Blackwell.

Chomski, Noam. 2005. *Government in the Future*. New York: Seven Stories Press.

Cummings, Bruce. 2002. "Historical, Economic and Security Realms in East Asian Community Building: Regional Regimes in Search for a Future." In *Building an East Asian Community: Visions and Strategies*, 161–182. Annual International Conference, Asia Research Center, Korea University, December 12.

Delanty, Gerard, and Baogang He. 2008. "Cosmopolitan Perspectives on European and Asian Trans-Nationalism." *International Sociology* 23(3): 323–344.

Evans, Paul. 2002. "East Asian Regionalism: Supplement or Alternative to an American-Centered Pacific Order." In *Building an East Asian Community: Visions and Strategies*, 130–150. Annual International Conference, Asia Research Center, Korea University, December 12.

Hardt, Michael, and Antonio Negri. 2000. *Empire*. Cambridge: Harvard University Press.

Frank, Andre Gunder. 1998. *Reorient: Global Economy in the Asian Age*. Berkeley: University of California Press.

Jung, Hwa Yol. 2010. "Transversality: What 'Global Asia' Means in an Age of Hyphens and Hybrids." *Global Asia* 5(4): 88–97.

Kim, Seung Kuk. 2005. "Self-Fulfilling Prophecy for East Asian Community: Toward a Postmodern View." Paper presented at the East Asian Sociologists Conference in Hitotsbash University, Tokyo, October 18–21.

Kim, Seung Kuk. 2006. "Modernity in East Asia and Post-Modern Alternative: A Reflection on Theories of East Asian Community." *Society and Theory* 9: 7–52.

Kojin, Karatani. 2006. *Toward the World Republic*. Tokyo: Iwanami Shoten.

Kropotkin, Peter. 1954. *Mutual Aid: A Factor of Evolution*. Montreal: Black Rose Books.

Li, Dazhao. 1919. "Great Asianism and New Asianism." *Guomin* 2(1).

Nederveen Pieterse, Jan. 2001. "Hybridity, So What? The Anti-hybridity Backlash and the Riddles of Recognition." *Theory, Culture & Society* 18(2–3): 219–245.

Nederveen Pieterse, Jan. 2009. *Globalization & Culture: Global Melange*. New York: Rowman & Littlefield.
Negri, Antonio. 2006. Guihwan[The Return], translated by Soo-Jong Yoon. Seoul: Ehak.
Schmitter, Philippe. 2002. "Vices & Virtues of Competing Theories of European Integration and Their Implications for Building an East Asian Community." In *Building an East Asian Community: Visions and Strategies*, 151–160. Annual International Conference, Asia Research Center, Korea University, December 12.
Tsunekawa, Keiichi. 2002. "Cooperation Without a Community: Human Security Issues and a Pragmatic Approach to Regional Integration in Asia." In *Building an East Asian Community: Visions and Strategies*, 203–222. Annual International Conference, Asia Research Center, Korea University, December 12.
Weber, Max. 1930. *The Protestant Ethic and the Spirit of Capitalism*, translated by Talcott Parsons. London: George Allen & Unwin.
Yoshimi, Takeuchi. 1960. *Asia as Method*. Tokyo: Iwanami.

6 Japan, Globalization, and East Asian Dynamism

Hidetaka Yoshimatsu

INTRODUCTION

Globalization has had significant impacts on various dimensions of political and economic affairs in the current world. It has transformed economic conditions of the states and the world economy as a whole through the diffusion of goods, services, capital, technologies, and even development ideas. Such transformations in the economic domain have changed political power constellation, which is illustrated by the growing presence of the Group of Twenty in world politics.

East Asia is a region where globalization has notable influences on inter-state relations, as well as social and economic conditions of states. The region as a whole has developed as "the manufacturing factory," providing a wide range of electronics and other machinery products for the world market. Moreover, steady economic growth has raised the region's political presence, sending four countries as a member to the Group of Twenty. In particular, China has emerged as an economic power center in the world, becoming the hub of trade and investment in East Asia.

For more than 40 years from the late 1960s, Japan has been the leading economic power in East Asia. It has formed tight linkages of trade, investment, and financial transactions with East Asian countries, serving as the main source of capital, technologies, and foreign aid. Indeed, globalization encouraged Japan to intensify economic linkages with various parts of the world. However, it influenced the Japanese political economy through evolving linkages with the East Asian economies. This is because Japan's political economic interests were deeply integrated into East Asia.

The main objective of this chapter is to examine how Japan has reacted to globalization, which adopts the form of East Asian dynamism and the Chinese ascendancy. The arguments that this chapter advances are threehold. First, the Japanese government has intensified initiatives to draw benefits from globalization in pursuit of enhanced economic integration with dynamic East Asia. Second, such initiatives have been faced with opposition from domestic actors who sought to avoid negative influences of globalization on the Japanese society. Third, the Japanese government has adopted dyadic policies to the Chinese economic ascendancy—competitive and cooperative—and the alleviation of political tensions is the key to develop bilateral relationships in the economic domain.

GLOBALIZATION AS A STIMULANT TO CHANGE ENVIRONMENTS SURROUNDING JAPAN

In the new millennium, there are two significant evolutions in the global political economy, which has crucial impacts on Japan. The first is continuous dynamism of the East Asian economies and the gradual shift in the gravity of economic power from the west to Asia. In 1990, the total gross domestic product (GDP) of the broad East Asia was $5.0 trillion compared with $6.6 trillion of the North American Free Trade Agreement (NAFTA) and $7.1 trillion of the European Union (EU).[1] The GDP of the broad East Asia increased to $15.2 trillion in 2009, and is projected to reach $24.4 trillion in 2015 when the region will overcome the NAFTA (21.6 trillion) and the EU (19.5 trillion) (Ministry of Economy, Trade and Industry [METI] 2010, 157). East Asia as a whole has achieved steady economic growth to become the world's manufacturing factory. The region has developed as the provider of major manufacturing products from steels to home appliance equipments and to automobiles. The global financial crisis caused by the Lehman shock in autumn 2008 had serious negative influences on the East Asian economies largely through a drop in exports to the U.S. and European markets. However, the economies recovered rather quickly from the crisis through massive fiscal expenditure for stimulus programs. The success of East Asia in riding out the global financial crisis impressed the strength of the East Asian economies and contributed to the recognition of the solid economic center in the world.

The economic dynamism of East Asia on the rise of globalization has significant implications for Japan. While Japan's economic growth has been sustained by global-scale trade and investment linkages, East Asia has maintained a special position in such linkages. In 2009, East Asia accounted for 53.0 percent of Japan's exports and 43.9 percent of its imports. Indeed, the presence of East Asia in terms of foreign direct investment (FDI) has been low: 22.5 percent of Japan's accumulated FDI at the end of 2009. However, Japanese firms have gained higher profits from East Asia compared with Europe and North America. In the 1990s, the Japanese government and business established productive and administrative networks in East Asia to the extent that Japan and East Asia were deeply integrated into an Asian-wide division of labor (Hatch 2010). Accordingly, continuous dynamism in East Asia provides significant opportunities for Japan to support its industrial upgrading and economic prosperity.

The second global evolution surrounding Japan is China's economic ascendancy. The Chinese economy has continuously shown high performance. China achieved the GDP growth of 8.0 percent or more in 2000–2010, raising its share in the world GDP to 9.5 percent in 2010. China's economic growth has been accompanied by increased economic linkages with East Asian countries. This is typically shown in changes of trade values for parts/components in East Asia (Table 6.1). While China's exports to the newly industrialized economies (NIES) and Association of Southeast Asian Nations (Thailand, Malaysia, Indonesia, and the Philippines ASEAN-4) increased by 5.5 times and 11.1 times between 1998 and 2008, its imports from the NIES and ASEAN-4 grew by 7.1 times and 9.5 times in the same period. The strength of China-centered trade linkages becomes apparent compared with corresponding figures for Japan. While Japan's exports to the NIES and ASEAN-4 increased by 2.2 times and 2.3 times between 1998 and 2008, its imports grew by 2.7 times and 3.3 times in the same period. The global financial crisis after the Lehman shock strengthened China's economic position in the world. The Chinese government adopted decisive fiscal expending measures, using $585 billion, 13.3 percent of GDP to stimulate domestic consumption and sustain industrial sectors that suffered from the economic slump (METI 2010, 159). As a consequence, it could achieve a quick recovery from the crisis, recording a 10.3 percent growth in 2010. China's economic performance became outstanding *vis-à-vis* the U.S. Indeed, the U.S. economy gradually entered into a recovery trend in 2010. But, it still lacked dynamism in consumption due to low-level income growth and slow improvement in unemployment.

Table 6.1 Trade Values for Parts/Components in East Asia (U.S. $ billion)

		Importer			
Exporter	*Year*	*China*	*Japan*	*NIES*	*ASEAN-4*
China	1998		9.2	28.5	3.2
	2008		50.4	157.5	35.5
Japan	1998	20.8		54.6	24.1
	2008	100.5		117.4	54.3
NIES	1998	22.4	14.8	51.4	27.8
	2008	159.3	39.4	121.6	84.6
ASEAN-4	1998	6.2	14.8	34.2	8.8
	2008	58.6	48.3	96.3	33.4

Note: NIES = newly industrialized economies (specifically South Korea, Taiwan, Hong Kong, and Singapore); ASEAN-4 = Association of Southeast Asian Nations, including Thailand, Malaysia, Indonesia, and the Philippines (Ministry of Economy, Trade and Industry 2010, 171).

China's expanding power is easily interpreted as a potential threat to Japan. Not only do Japan and China have crucial sources of conflict including the historical problems and territorial disputes but they have also competed over leadership in East Asia. Japan has serious concerns that China's economic might change into military build-up that will be directed toward it. At the same time, Japan has deepened economic interdependence with China through trade, investment, and financial transactions, which expanded an opportunity that China's economic strengths bring about plus-sum effects on Japan. Moreover, Japan and China are the two great powers that propel the development of regional multilateral institutions represented by the ASEAN+3 to tackle common challenges and create stable inter-state relations in East Asia. The complicated relations with China are likely to urge Japanese policymakers to formulate multiple strategies to manage the rise of China by taking into account positive and negative sides of the rise.

In brief, there are two global transformations that have significant impacts on Japan: a gradual economic power shift from the west to East Asia and the ascendancy of the Chinese economy. The former encourages Japan to adopt policies that are conducive to embedding its economy into East Asian dynamism. The latter has more complicated implications for Japan. The rise of China would undermine Japan's relative political and economic position in East Asia, on the one hand, and provide possible opportunities for augmenting political and economic interests for its neighboring countries including Japan, on the other hand. Accordingly, Japan is forced to adopt the dyadic strategy of "competition and cooperation."

JAPAN'S RESPONSES TO EAST ASIAN DYNAMISM AS A GLOBAL TREND

For a long time, the Japanese economy achieved its growth by depending on trade and investment linkages with the global market. In the new millennium, the growing presence of the East Asian economies in globalization trends has encouraged the Japanese government and business to search for renewed linkages with East Asia in order to maintain industrial vigor. Initiatives for this objective are divided into outward-looking and inward-looking policies.

The Outward-Looking Policies to Integrate Japan into East Asian Dynamism

The Japanese government has adopted policies to promote the advance of Japanese firms into dynamic East Asia. The first important attempt is deployment of integrated infrastructure systems. In East Asia, continuous economic growth has produced growing demand for development of infrastructure. According to the Asian Development Bank (ADB), infrastructure investment in energy, telecommunications, transport, and water/sanitation in Asia is estimated to be $8 trillion in 2010–2020 (ADB 2009, 167). Infrastructure development is conducive to producing substantial economic benefits by upgrading industrial clusters and the networking of industrial corridors. In the new millennium, the bidding for infrastructure projects tends to adopt an integrated style of combining a master plan, designing, procurement, construction, finance, and operational management (Maeda 2011, 44).

The Japanese government developed institutional frameworks to formulate strategies to support Japanese firms' involvement in infrastructure development in Asian countries. In September 2010, the government set up the Ministerial Meeting on Deployment of Integrated Infrastructure Overseas. The members of the meeting discussed possibilities of and strategies for Japanese firms' overseas deployment by focusing on specific fields such as railways, nuclear power generations, and coal-fired power generations, or specific countries including Vietnam and Indonesia. The meeting, headed by Chief Cabinet Secretary, had strength in making decisions by going beyond ministerial sectionalism.

On the basis of discussions at the ministerial meetings, the Japanese government adopted several measures to promote deployment of integrated infrastructure systems. The Japan Bank for International Cooperation was separated from the Japan Finance Corporation in order to strengthen functions of export finance to developed nations and the provision of funds for Japanese firms' merger and acquisition of foreign enterprises. The Nippon Export and Investment Insurance was also allowed to make the total amount of important overseas loans by private financial institutions the target of trade insurance. Furthermore, the Japan International Cooperation Agency's overseas investment loans were resumed for specific cases through verification and improvement of a new implementation system, as well as a pilot approach that works out the rules for selection. These new measures adopted in the government-affiliated organizations aimed to strengthen financial environments to assist Japanese firms' advancement in overseas projects.[2]

A relevant policy regarding Japan's outward-looking initiatives was a strategy for international standardization. Japanese firms have developed high-level technologies in several crucial industrial fields such as next-generation automobiles and energy conservation. However, they have not necessarily been successful in developing the technologies into innovative business models and diffusing them to firms in other countries as common platforms. This fact was recognized as a crucial problem given that management of technologies and business models is increasingly linked to international competitiveness.

The government regarded global standard-setting as an indispensable issue to sustain Japanese firms' international competitiveness and deepened debates on standardization. In April 2010, the government decided to set up a taskforce on the strategy for international standardization, and the outcomes of discussions at the taskforce were delivered to the Strategic Headquarters of Intellectual Property. In October 2010, an Action Plan for International Standardization was formulated, and seven industrial fields were designated as the target of global standard-setting: advanced medical care, water, next-generation vehicles, railways, energy management, contents media, and robots.

The Japanese government's commitments to deployment of integrated infrastructure systems were partially responses to requests from the business community. The business community hoped to strengthen public-private partnership in promoting Japanese firms' international operations. *Nippon Keidanren* (Japan Business Federation), in its policy proposals in April 2008 and April 2009, advocated international cooperation from a strategic standpoint through enhanced public-private linkages.[3] *Nippon Keidanren* also issued a policy proposal in December 2010 in which it required the strength of financial functions to support the deployment of integrated infrastructure systems.[4] The government formulated concrete polices by paying attention to appeals from the business community.

The government itself had a serious concern about the future of Japan's industrial competitiveness in the global market. Given the prospect of a long-term decline in domestic demand due to aging population combined with the dwindling birth ratio, external demand is a key to maintain the continuous growth of the Japanese industry. Indeed, Japan's economic power has been sustained by industrial and technological strengths. However, such strengths have been heavily dependent on four manufacturing sectors—automobiles, electronics, machineries, and steels. Not only were sources of industrial competitiveness concentrated and unbalanced but these competitive sectors have been also confronted with rising competition in the global market. In order to maintain a position of an economic power, Japan was required to broaden the scope of industrial sectors that are capable of undertaking global operations beyond the narrow manufacturing sectors and integrate these sectors into growth potential in the newly emerging Asian markets. The fostering of new global companies was an answer to free from a dilemma between the maintenance of competitive edge of the Japanese industry and the prevention of the "hollowing-out" effects that invite high unemployment.

Importantly, deployment of integrated infrastructure systems encouraged the Japanese government and business to reconsider government-business relations. Since businesses in infrastructure are normally managed under the strong involvement of the government, commitments by the private sector alone have limitations to win the bidding for infrastructure projects. Additionally, since businesses in infrastructure require huge capital, the private sector often finds difficulty in meeting such capital and risk accompanying it. Accordingly, the Japanese government and business searched for a new form of public-private partnerships such as the top-level diplomacy, the formation of consortiums, and the adoption of package assistances.

The concrete approaches to deployment of integrated infrastructure systems reflect renewed ideas about government-business relations. One of the major features of the Japan-initiated "developmental state" is close government-business relationships. The government works closely with sectors and trade associations to promote rapid industrialization. The intimate relationship facilitates information sharing for economic management and sectoral development and guides capital channeling into favored industries. The government and business also set up institutional arrangements represented by advisory councils in order to dampen the likelihood of government failure (World Bank 1993). In the 1990s and early 2000s, the Japanese government departed from the developmental state model, promoting neo-liberal reforms of deregulation, privatization, and public finance reform. These reforms contained the reduction of the scope of state intervention in the market and creating a transparent and open relationship between the government and business. However, intensive competition in the global market encourages the Japanese state to revisit the government-business partnership as the base for successful expansion of business operations overseas.

The Inward-Looking Policies to Promote Inward Foreign Investment and Free Trade Agreements

In addition to outward-looking policies, Japan sought to transform domestic systems and regulations in order to take East Asian dynamism in the domestic economy. An important inward-looking policy is a set of reform initiatives designed to invite globally operating companies and skilled human resources to Japan. Such initiatives had much to do with the prolonged recession after the Lehman shock. The government hoped to revive Japan as an industrial center in Asia by boosting inward FDI, which has been small compared with outward FDI (Figure 6.1).

The Japanese government developed institutional frameworks to implement projects for domestic reforms to invite globally operating companies and skilled human resources to Japan. In September 2010, the government set up the Meeting of the Roundtable on the Promotion of Inward Investment, which comprised ministers of relevant ministries, private representatives from major industrial associations and labor unions, as well as the American and European business associations. The meeting set forth the Inward Investment Promotion Program two months later. The program proposed that the government build an open, global-standard investment environment through the reduction of the effective corporate tax rate and the review of regulations and systems hindering inward investment. The program also encouraged the enhancement of Japan's capability as a pivotal industrial base for Asia. For this objective, it proposed the development of incentives and subsidies for locating in Japan and special immigration treatment. The acceptance of high-level foreign human resources was particularly important, and the government adopted new systems that include preferential treatments such as an approval framework with a point system, simplification and prioritization of entry/stay procedures, and easier conditions for permanent residency.

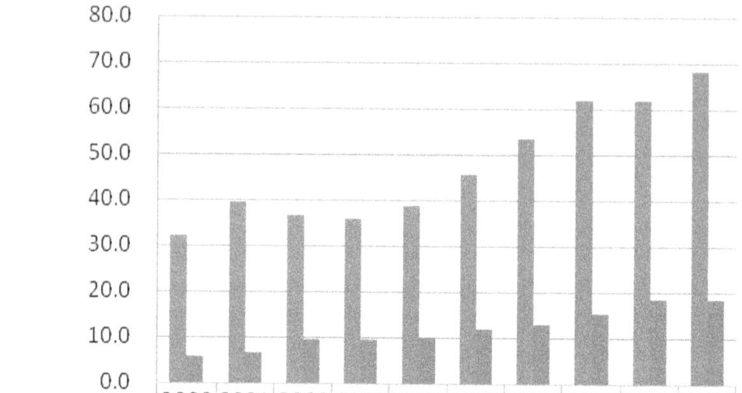

	2000	2001	2002	2003	2004	2005	2006	2007	2008	2009
Outward FDI	32.0	39.6	36.5	35.9	38.6	45.6	53.5	61.9	61.7	68.2
Inward FDI	5.8	6.6	9.4	9.6	10.1	11.9	12.8	15.1	18.5	18.4

Figure 6.1 Trends of Japanese foreign direct investment (FDI) amounts, 2000–2009 (trillion yen). Data compiled from Ministry of Finance (various years).

Several policies were implemented to materialize these policy prescriptions. The government contained measures to lower the effective corporate tax rate for combined national and local taxes by 5 percent in the 2011 Tax Reform. The tax reform also contained a new tax measure regarding a 20 percent deduction from income for approved companies, which aimed at encouraging global companies to establish Asian headquarters and research and development bases in Japan. Furthermore, the government planned to enact the Law on the Promotion of Japan as an Asian Industrial Centre, which would provide further measures to support the advancement of global companies into Japan.

For a long time, low-level inward investment was recognized as a serious constraint on dynamic development of the Japanese industry, and the previous cabinets adopted measures to promote inward investment. For instance, in 2003 the Japan Investment Council Expert Committee compiled the Program for the Promotion of Foreign Direct Investment in Japan. The program suggested the dissemination of information, improvement in business environments, and the revision of administrative procedures (METI 2003, 119–120). Distinctive in the 2010 program compared with the previous ones was its deep commitments. The measures adopted in the 2010 program contained the lowering of the effective corporate tax rate, which was raised as one of the most serious hurdles for foreign companies to advance into Japan.[5] It also contained concrete provisions of incentives to attract foreign firms and human resources.

A major feature in commitments to growing inflow of foreign investment and human resources is that Japan began to locate domestic structural reforms as a means to bring in globalization. The Japanese government and business avoided substantial structural reforms of their political economy in response to overwhelming force of globalization by extending Japanese production and administrative networks to developing Asia (Hatch 2010). However, such closed, patchwork responses gradually robbed the Japanese economy of innovative ideas and industrial dynamism. The 2010 program could be regarded as Japan's attempts to face the wave of globalization directly and to draw benefits from globalization that facilitates freer moves of global companies and skilled human resources.

An additional important inward-looking policy is the promotion of free trade agreements (FTAs)/economic partnership agreements (EPAs). In the late 1990s, the Japanese government began to shift its stance on trade policy from multilateralism to bilateralism and regionalism. In line with this shift, Tokyo signed an FTA with Singapore in January 2002. The government then entered into formal negotiations on FTAs with Mexico in November 2002, South Korea in December 2003, and Malaysia in January 2004. Major progress in FTA policy was seen in 2006–2007. In July 2006, the Koizumi cabinet adopted the cabinet decision, the Basic Policies for Economic and Fiscal Management and Structural Reform 2006. The decision contained the phrase that "the value of trade with countries having concluded EPAs with Japan is expected to account for 25 percent or more of Japan's total trade value by the year 2010."[6] This decision adopted the numerical target for FTA policy for the first time. The formulation of the new FTA policy contributed to the expansion of FTA partners. The government entered into formal FTA negotiations with Vietnam, Australia, India, and Switzerland in the first half of 2007.

Although it had passed more than 10 years since the Japanese government converted its trade policy, outcomes in the FTA policy were not substantial. By the end of 2010, Japan ratified FTAs with 11 partners including 7 ASEAN members. Its FTA partners did not include major trading partners such as China, the U.S., and the EU. Consequently, the ratio of trade with FTA partners in total trade was just 17 percent. In order to change the situation, the government adopted further measures. In November 2010, the Kan cabinet adopted a cabinet decision, the Basic Policy on Comprehensive Economic Partnership. The decision stipulates that "the government would promote high-level economic partnerships with major trading powers," and "press ahead with fundamental domestic reform."[7] After adopting this decision, the government resumed negotiations on an FTA with Australia and searched for the opening of those with Mongolia and the EU. Furthermore, Prime Minister Kan announced that the Japanese government would make decisions about its stance on participation in the Trans-Pacific Strategic Economic Partnership Agreement (TPP) by June

2011 at the Asia-Pacific Economic Cooperation summit held in Yokohama in November 2010.

The FTA is an important policy to link the Japanese economy and industry to the global market. The promotion of FTAs is indispensable for keeping up with a global trend that regionalism and bilateralism are main vehicles to achieve market liberalization. Such a trend caused the "domino effect" on the global scale.[8] More specifically, the steady development of FTA networks is required in terms of corporate competition, in relation to South Korea in particular. Japan and South Korea hold international competitiveness in similar industrial sectors represented by electronics and automobiles. The Korean government has responded positively to globalization trends, concluding FTA negotiations with its major trading partners, the U.S. and the EU. Since the U.S. and the EU provide important markets for the Japanese manufacturing sectors, differences in tariff imposition would lead to significant disadvantages for Japanese firms in competition against their Korean rivals.

In Japan's past FTA negotiations, two issues have constituted serious impediments to smooth development of negotiations: agricultural protection and labor migration. The agricultural groups have maintained internal cohesion that constitutes the base for strong voting machines and retained close linkages with supportive politicians. The interests and pressure of such groups have had significant influences on the progress of FTA negotiations (Yoshimatsu 2006; Mulgan 2008). The Japanese Nursing Association opposed the introduction of foreign healthcare workers on the ground that foreign workers would compete with them and depress their wage level (Er 2010, 151). Accordingly, the Japanese government accepted only small numbers of foreign nurses under its FTAs with the Philippines and Indonesia. The government searched for clues to resolve problems in these two fields by deepening discussions at newly established institutions. In November 2010, the government established the Headquarters to Promote the Revitalization of the Food Industries, Agriculture, Forestry and Fishery in order to promote high-level FTAs and improvement of Japan's food self-efficiency. The government also set up a study group under the Minister of State for National Policy to discuss the issue of nurses and healthcare workers from overseas. The identification of major stumbling blocks and concrete actions to remove such blocks indicate the government's decisiveness in that the promotion of FTAs is an inevitable way to keep up with a global trend of the FTA diffusion and avoid losses resulting from the lack of FTAs.

Reform Initiatives and Domestic Politics

The previous two sections explained how Japan has responded positively to globalization trends by seeking to integrate the Japanese economy into dynamism in East Asia. However, there are uncertain elements regarding to what extent the Japanese government's attempts will produce expected outcomes.

As a consequence of a landslide victory in the lower house general election, the Democratic Party of Japan (DPJ) government was formed in September 2009. The DPJ gained power by criticizing public policies implemented by the former Liberal Democratic Party (LDP) cabinets. Yukio Hatoyama, the first Prime Minister of the DPJ government, pushed forward the concept of *yu-ai* (fraternity). Hatoyama was critical of neoliberal reforms undertaken under the LDP cabinets, which led to growing income gaps among the people.[9] Hatoyama (2009, 136) pointed out that:

> In Japan, opinion was divided on how far the trend toward globalization should be taken on board. Some people advocated the active embrace of globalism and supported leaving everything up to the dictates of the market. Others favored a more reticent approach, believing that effort should be made instead to expand the social safety net and protect our traditional economic activities. Since the administration of Prime Minister Koizumi, the LDP has stressed the former while we in the DPJ have tended toward the latter position.

This view indicates Hatoyama's preferences for anti-globalism and anti-market fundamentalism. Hatoyama's preferences were incorporated into the DPJ's election promises. The DPJ government in its 2009 election platform (*manifesto*) promised to extend employment insurance coverage to all workers in order to strengthen safety net for the people, to implement a fundamental review of postal reforms, and to ban, in principle, the dispatch of temporary workers to manufacturing jobs (DPJ 2009, 20–21). These policies aimed to remedy problems caused by deregulation measures under globalization trends.

In June 2010, Hatoyama was forced to step down from the office in less than 10 months largely due to awkward handlings of the U.S. Marine Corps Futenma Air Station problem in Okinawa. Even after the resignation of prime minister, Hatoyama remained as a leader of an influential faction within the DPJ, and considerable numbers of DPJ members still had preferences for maintaining the party's left-center stance, which are incompatible with the neo-liberal policy stance. These politicians were critical of the Kan cabinet's tendency to depart from the left-center policy stance.

Domestic opposition was particularly fierce over the promotion of FTAs. Several influential societal groups such as the Japanese Agricultural Cooperatives, the Japan Medical Association, and the All Japan Dockworkers' Union have expressed a strong anxiety about Japan's participation in the TPP. Moreover, politicians including ruling party members were involved in activities opposing the FTA promotion. In February 2011, the National Conference Regarding the TPP was formed as a main group to oppose the TPP. The conference, one of whose initiators was Masahiko Yamada, former Agricultural Minister, contained DPJ politicians who were critical of the government's reform programs.

Around 2010, Japan was in a critical point in that it could ride the tide of globalization or not. To open up the Japanese economy and integrate it into East Asian dynamism was necessary to regain vitality of the Japanese industry in the long run. However, some societal groups that would be forced to assume serious burdens in the short run and their supporters in the executive and legislative branches strongly oppose market-opening measures. Given these situations, policymakers are required to confirm the appropriate route that Japan should pursue in globalization trends. In this regard, strong leadership by the Prime Minister and the cabinet are required. As far as a relationship with the society is concerned, the government needs to overcome "collection action problem" that small groups that have negative influences from globalization exert strong political influence to avoid such influences. The government is required to explain courteously compensation measures that will be provided for the groups that suffer from globalization. At the same time, the government needs to maintain political legitimacy for domestic reforms in response to globalization by persuading the general public about the necessity of such reforms. Given that Japan cannot avoid the tide of globalization, a crucial issue is not the blocking of globalization itself but the way to respond to it.

THE RISE OF CHINA AND JAPAN'S COMPETITIVE AND COOPERATIVE STRATEGIES

The rise of China has significant impacts on Japan. Indeed, the Chinese economic ascendancy implies a challenge for Japan that has been the dominant economic power in East Asia. At the same time, the rise of China provides significant opportunities for Japan as a source of its economic growth, and China's growth raises its potential as Japan's partner for achieving regional stability in East Asia. The bifacial impacts of the Chinese ascendancy encourage Japan to adopt a range of approaches that include both competition and cooperation.

Competition against China

Competitive, strategic orientation in response to the rise of China has been exhibited in Japan's trade policy in the new millennium. Japan originally took the lead in the FTA formation in East Asia by agreeing on a bilateral FTA with Singapore. China showed quick moves in FTA policy after it finalized negotiations on the World Trade Organization accession, and signed the Framework Agreement on Comprehensive Economic Cooperation between ASEAN and China in November 2002. This move was perceived by Japanese officials and politicians with great surprise.

Japan chased China by advancing negotiations on the ASEAN-Japan Comprehensive Economic Partnership (AJCEP). When Prime Minister

Koizumi made a formal visit to Southeast Asia in January 2002, he proposed an initiative for the AJCEP. The leaders of ASEAN and Japan signed the Framework for the AJCEP during the Bali Summit in October 2003. Japan and ASEAN commenced formal negotiations on the AJCEP in April 2005, and all ASEAN members and Japan completed the signing of the agreement by April 2008.

Although Japan was forced to follow the route that China and ASEAN had already traced, it sought to take the lead in the FTA formation in East Asia through three methods. The first was the formation of "comprehensive" FTAs with Southeast Asian countries. Japan aimed to formulate an EPA, not a conventional FTA. Japan's EPA strategy was derived from a strong belief that EPAs are superior to conventional FTAs as they would serve to promote the overall reform of economic structures by targeting broad areas from investment and intellectual property rules, competition policy, and economic cooperation (Oike 2006). At the same time, Japan's EPAs were intentionally aimed to differentiate them from China's FTAs. The Ministry of Foreign Affairs (2009, 11) provided a contrast between Japan's and China's approach to ASEAN. The ministry characterized Japan's EPAs in the ASEAN region as comprehensively working on not only border measures such as tariffs and investment regulations but also measures to create an environment that is conducive to fostering cooperative elements in both Japan and ASEAN and undertaking negotiations on each item for trade in goods in pursuit of a high-level agreement.

The second was the establishment of bilateral networks with each ASEAN member. Even before beginning negotiations with ASEAN as a whole, Japan made strong commitments to a bilateral FTA with Southeast Asian counties. Tokyo accelerated negotiations with Southeast Asian countries after early 2004 by beginning formal negotiations with Malaysia, the Philippines, and Thailand. By October 2009, Japan's EPA with Singapore, Malaysia, the Philippines, Thailand, Indonesia, Brunei, and Vietnam came into effect. Japan signed an Investment Agreement with Cambodia in June 2007 and later with Laos in January 2008. Thus, Japan committed to bilateral trade pacts with all ASEAN members except for Cambodia, Laos, and Myanmar, with the aim to formulate substantial EPA networks with ASEAN members.

The third was the advocacy of the Comprehensive Economic Partnership Agreement in East Asia (CEPEA). This initiative, proposed formally in the METI report *Global Economic Strategy* in April 2006, aimed to create an EPA among the ASEAN+6 including India, Australia, and New Zealand. The report proposed starting negotiations on this EPA in 2008 after all FTA negotiations centered on ASEAN would likely be concluded in 2007 (METI 2006, 52–53). At the second East Asia Summit (EAS) meeting in January 2007, the leaders endorsed an agreement to begin private-level works to explore the CEPEA idea. The CEPEA aimed to reduce the relative importance of China-initiated ASEAN+3 FTA. A senior METI official explained the objective of the concept, stating that "China will take the lead in +3 negotiations. We should promote +6 negations ahead of the curve."[10] Japan's CEPEA proposal was an attempt to balance China's growing influence and show leadership in East Asia.[11]

As already explained, Japan had serious domestic constraints on the FTA promotion. Despite such constraints, Japan sought to counter China's FTA initiatives in East Asia. It appealed comprehensiveness in its FTA approach and pursued a "sandwich" strategy to forge virtual FTA networks in East Asia through a bilateral FTA with each ASEAN member and a broader ASEAN+6 FTA. Indeed, Japan was behind in moves to conclude an FTA with ASEAN, but it sought to maintain its presence in the formation of overall FTA networks in East Asia.

Mekong development is another field where Japan launched strategic policies to counter the rise of China. Support for the Mekong development has been a diplomatic concern for Japan since the 1990s, and the government set up specific institutions for this objective such as the Forum for Comprehensive Development of Indochina and the ASEAN Economic Ministers (AEM)-METI Economic and Industrial Cooperation Committee. In the new millennium, the Chinese government has gradually intensified cooperation with the Mekong countries through the ADB-initiated Greater Mekong sub-region (GMS) economic cooperation program. The Chinese government began to show clearer leadership at the GMS ministerial and summit meetings, making the Guangxi Zhuang Autonomous Region one area covered by the GMS Program in 2005.

Japan's Mekong policy in the new millennium has a clear strategic orientation to balance China's growing influence in the region. Geopolitical nature was obvious in the holding of the summitry and ministerial meetings with the Mekong countries. In January 2008, the first Mekong-Japan foreign ministers' meeting was convened in Tokyo. At the meeting, Japan pledged $20 million from the Japan-ASEAN Integration Fund for improving "efficiency of logistics and distribution of the East-West Economic Corridor and Second East-West Economic Corridor in the region" and the holding of a senior officials' meeting to coordinate the projects. In November 2009, the first Japan-Mekong summit was held in Tokyo. At the meeting, the leaders issued the Tokyo Declaration, in which Japan expressed its commitments of more than 500 billion yen of official development assistance (ODA) in the next three years for further development of both hard and soft infrastructure and environment conservation to achieve a "Green Mekong."

The holding of the summitry and ministerial meetings was a prominent departure from Japan's conventional diplomacy toward Southeast Asia because the meetings constituted linkages between Japan and the Mekong countries alone, excluding the old ASEAN members. The specific membership raised Japan's position in the relationship, enabling it to reflect its policy preferences in a straight manner. More importantly, these meetings provided Japan with the same status as China that has held summitry and ministerial meetings with the Mekong countries under the GMS Program.

Geopolitical nature was shown in a main project that the Japanese government committed to the Mekong development. At the second Mekong-Japan summit in October 2010, leaders referred to the Mekong-Japan Economic and Industrial Cooperation Initiative (MJ-CI). The main pillar of the MJ-CI was the development of the East-West Economic Corridor and the Second East-West Economic Corridor.[12] The government sought to differentiate its approach by developing "soft infrastructure" such as a program for supporting human resources with the logistics manager registration system and the establishment of the ASEAN single window system, in addition to the construction of hard infrastructure. China has committed to the development of the North-South Economic Corridors linking Kunming and Bangkok as well as Kunming and Hai Phong in Vietnam. Japan hoped to retain influence in the development of transport infrastructure by pushing forward the horizontal economic corridors against China-initiated vertical economic corridors. Furthermore, the Japanese government, through the newly established Economic Research Institute for ASEAN and East Asia (ERIA), supported the construction of a new highway called the "East Asia Industrial Corridor," which extended the Second East-West Economic Corridor from Bangkok to the East Coast of India.[13] The development of the logistics infrastructure aimed at integrating the Mekong countries into the broader regional and international economies. Such an attempt was expected to support industrial growth of these countries and to reduce their dependence on China.

The trade and Mekong development are the policy fields where Japan had shown prominent presence in East Asia. The Japanese manufacturing industry set up intensive production networks in East Asia, making Japan a major trading partner for most East Asian countries. Japan has, since the early 1990s, provided intensive support for industrial development and human resources development in the Mekong region. China's gradual increases of presence in these fields implied the shrinkage of the status and assets that Japan accumulated for a long time. Accordingly, the Japanese government had strong incentives to arrest the eclipse of its presence and influence.

Cooperation with China

While Japan adopted strategic countermeasures against the rise of China in order to maintain its presence and influence in East Asia, government officials recognized that their government had to pursue close collaboration with China given its political and economic importance for Japan and other regional countries. Such recognition led to the initiatives to promote cooperation with China in bilateral and regional dimensions.

In the current Sino-Japanese relations, one of the most promising areas for bilateral cooperation is energy conservation, which is linked to energy security. As the Chinese economy has achieved rapid growth, demand for energy has risen sharply, making China a net oil importer in 1993. The adoption of new technologies for building a resource-efficient, environmentally friendly society was a vital and urgent issue for the Chinese government. The Chinese government hoped to introduce advanced Japanese technologies and experiences in energy saving that Japanese industries have accumulated since its high economic growth period. The Japanese government and business hoped to take advantage of its advanced technologies and expertise in order to increase business contracts in the rapidly growing Chinese market. China was expected to be a lucrative market for environment- and energy-related businesses for Japanese firms.

A concrete initiative in promoting bilateral cooperation in energy conservation began in 2006. In May, the first Japan-China Energy Conservation Forum was held in Tokyo. Although this event was named just a "forum," it was an important opportunity for both governments illustrated by the attendance of high-ranking government officials—the Ministers of Economy, Trade and Industry and of the Environment from Japan, and the Minister of Commerce and vice-chief of the National Development and Reform Commission (NDRC) from China. The three-day forum, involving some 500 participants from Japan and 300 from China, provided high-level speeches and theme-specific discussions. Moreover, a section meeting was organized in six fields: energy conservation laws and regulations, ESCO (energy service company) programs, iron and steel, construction materials, energy, and automobiles. Afterwards, both governments have held the conservation forum annually in rotation in Tokyo and Beijing.

The energy conservation forum has served to launch cooperative projects in a wide range of areas. The number of cooperative business projects increased from 5 in the first forum to 19 in the third forum in 2008 and to 44 in the fifth forum in 2010. Not only did the target of cooperation expand to water treatment and resource recycling, but geographical area for cooperation in China also extended from coastal to inner areas. Moreover, collaboration between Japanese and Chinese industrial associations produced concrete projects at the fourth forum. This move could be regarded as a significant contribution to advancing comprehensive cooperation through institution-building at the industrial level.

In accordance with the development of the energy conservation forum, the Japanese and Chinese governments have launched several cooperative initiatives. The first is the establishment of model projects for energy conservation. The energy ministers reached an agreement to launch the Energy Conservation and Environmental Business Promotion Model Project. The project aimed at searching for business matching between Japanese and Chinese enterprises, which would be a model for improving energy conservation in China. METI and NDRC set up a committee for administering the joint works, and individual model projects have been announced at the conservation forums.[14] Secondly, both governments agreed to begin joint research on energy policy.

The Institute of Energy Economics, Japan, and the Energy Research Institute of the NDRC exchanged the memorandum of understanding regarding joint research. The research covered the Energy Conservation Law and relevant legal systems as well as a bench-mark analysis of high energy consumption industries in China. Thirdly, the Japanese government agreed to strengthen cooperation in human resource development for energy conservation. The government accepted 300 trainees from Chinese government agencies and organizations for a three-year period in order to enhance human capabilities to manage institutions for energy conservation.

In the regional dimension, the Japanese government searched for close collaboration with China under the framework of the ASEAN+3. The ASEAN+3 members have advanced regional institutions for financial cooperation such as swap agreements for financial liquidity—Chiang Mai Initiative (CMI)—regional surveillance mechanisms and Asian bond markets. They have developed the cooperative process in the incremental manner, reaching the signature of the CMI Multilateralization (CMIM) agreement in December 2009. The CMIM agreement decides the individual country's contribution, borrowing accessibility, and common decision-making methods. The ministers also agreed to establish the ASEAN+3 Macroeconomic Research Office (AMRO) as a surveillance unit to monitor and analyze regional economies.

In the evolution of regional financial cooperation, Japan and China played a leading role in propelling cooperative initiatives. During the Asian financial crisis in 1997–1998, the Japanese government unsuccessfully tried to establish the Asian Monetary Fund. Afterwards, the government made efforts to develop the networks of bilateral swap agreements. The Japanese Ministry of Finance undertook informal negotiations behind the scenes in order to gain explicit support for the CMI from the U.S. and other East Asian countries. The networks of the swap agreements deepened centered on Japan. The progenitor of the CMI was the New Miyazawa Initiative, which was announced by then Finance Minister Miyazawa in 1998.[15] Under the Initiative, Japan signed a bilateral agreement with South Korea and Malaysia in January and July 1999, respectively. By July 2002, Japan concluded the bilateral swap agreement with South Korea ($7 billion), Thailand ($3 billion), the Philippines ($3 billion), and Malaysia ($3.5 billion). Therefore, Japan was the main organizer of the CMI in a few years after the start of the initiative.

China took the stance of objecting to Japan's leadership role in launching the Asian Monetary Fund during the Asian financial crisis. Afterwards, China changed its stance on financial cooperation. In 1998, Chinese Vice-President Hu Jintao proposed a meeting of Deputy Finance Ministers and Central Bank Vice-Governors of the ASEAN members together with China, Japan, and South Korea. This proposal led to an ASEAN+3 Finance Ministers meeting in Hanoi in March 1999. Chinese Premier Wen Jiabao officially proposed converting the CMI's separate bilateral swap agreements into a unified multilateral currency swap agreement at the ASEAN+3 summit in October 2003 (Dent 2005, 391–392).

In the process of advancing subsequent financial cooperation, Japan and China failed to coordinate their policy stances in several important issue-areas. For instance, China did not support Japan-initiated Asian Currency Unit because of possible constraints on the domestic financial system and economic development and opposition to the light weight of its currency in the basket (Jiang 2010, 616–617). In other cases, the Japanese government was forced to make compromise with China after intensive debates. According to the CMIM agreement, Japan and China would provide $38.4 billion each—32 percent of total $120 billion—and would have an equal voting share of 28.41 percent. Japan accepted the equal share on the ground that it would nominally maintain the leading position because 2.98 percent of China's share comes from Hong Kong. Japan and China also competed over the appointment of the first director of the AMRO, and they reached the consensus that the Chinese director would serve for first year of the three-year term and the Japanese director would serve for the remaining two years. These cases indicate that severe competition over regional leadership was implemented in the development of financial cooperation.

Despite such confrontation, China and Japan could have common interests in advancing financial cooperation in East Asia. Although 13 countries have engaged in financial cooperation under the ASEAN+3, Japan and China are genuine creditor nations. The two states found the common stance on increasing autonomy of Asian countries with the maintenance of the disciplines for borrowers including the maintenance of the International Monetary Fund link (Searight 2009, 230). China and Japan also found common interests in changing International Monetary Fund policy conditionality and governance. In particular, they hoped to get larger quotas and voting rights in the Executive Board and Board of Governors (Henning 2009, 3). For instance, the message of the China-Japan-Korea finance ministers meeting in 2006 contained a phrase that "we acknowledged the importance of addressing the issue of significant under-representation of the countries whose current economic strength and the relative position in the global economy are not properly reflected in the IFIs and ensuring its legitimacy."[16]

Given the declining position due to the rise of China, Japan is forced to adopt strategies to maintain its presence and influence in East Asia. Under such conditions, the Japanese government has implemented policies to promote cooperation with China primarily to attain its national interests in augmenting economic benefits and maintaining political influence. At the same time, the Japanese government intended to advance cooperation with China for sustaining sound development of the Chinese and Asian economies.

Going beyond Political Tension

The explanation in the previous two sections reflects the two sides of a coin that China's economic growth brings about effects on the Japanese economy. While the Japanese government seeks to maintain Japan's economic presence in East Asia in confrontation with China's economic growth, it attempts to take advantage of benefits that China's economic growth produces.

In addition to economic factors, political elements have made Sino-Japanese relations more complicated. For a long time, Sino-Japanese political relations have been chilly and unstable largely because of various political issues including the Yasukuni Shrine issue, historical textbook issue, Taiwan issue, and territorial disputes over Senkaku/Diaoyu Islands. Such political tensions have cast a long shadow on the development of economic relations. For instance, the first Japan-China Energy Conservation Forum in May 2006 was organized as an event to change frosty bilateral relations in 2005–2006. In April 2005, a series of anti-Japanese demonstrations broke out in major Chinese cities including Beijing and Shanghai. The following month, Chinese Vice-premier Wu Yi, who had made a formal visit to Tokyo, suddenly cancelled a meeting with Japanese Prime Minister Koizumi. Koizumi's visit to Yasukuni Shrine in October led to the cancellation of a planned China-Japan-Korea summit in late 2005. In the context of such severe political relations, the forum was organized as one of the largest bilateral events of that time, being sponsored by Japanese METI and the Japan-China Economic Association, as well as China's NDRC and Ministry of Commerce.

After the DPJ gained power in September 2009, its government paid attention to establishing stable diplomatic ties with China. The government sought to develop the strategic mutual relationship with China through senior leaders' direct contacts. For one year after September 2009, summit meetings were organized six times, while foreign ministers' meetings were seven times. The DPJ's Secretary-General, Ichiro Ozawa, made a formal visit to Beijing in December 2009 with some 600 delegates including 143 Diet members, one third of the total DPJ politicians. When Xi Jinping, vice-president of China, made a visit to Tokyo soon after, the DPJ made special treatment to grant him an audience with Emperor. The DPJ cabinet paid attention to the historical issue. In 2010, every cabinet member abstained from visiting the Yasukuni Shrine on August 15th, the day marking the end of the war. No cabinet member's visit to the shrine was the first occasion in the past 25 years.

Despite the DPJ's attempts to stabilize the Sino-Japanese relations, a series of diplomatic concerns between Japan and China continued. China intensified their maritime activities around the East China Sea. In April 2010, Chinese submarines and destroyers navigated Southeast-ward on the high seas between the main island of Okinawa and Miyako Island. A Chinese helicopter flew within around 90 meters of a Japanese destroyer. The following month, a Japan Coast Guard vessel that was engaged in seafloor research was chased by a Chinese marine survey ship inside the Japanese exclusive economic zone. These incidents hinted at China's strategic intent to check Japan's reactions under conditions when Japan's diplomatic relations with Washington became loose.[17] Tension in the East China Sea rose critically in September 2010 when a Chinese fishing boat collided with Japan Coast Guard vessels near the disputed islands, and the Japanese coast guard arrested the boat crews. The Chinese government reacted to this incident decisively, announcing the suspension of ministerial-level exchanges with Tokyo and restrictions on exports of rare-earth metals. This problem settled by the end of September as the Japanese government released all crew members. Yet, shaky relations continued afterwards.

Given politically sensitive bilateral relations, it is unrealistic to expect the establishment of trustworthy relationships in a short run. The Japanese and Chinese governments are required to focus on projects that are linked to core interests that are expected to produce greater positive-sum feedbacks from cooperation. In bilateral relations, for instance, the Chinese government urged Japan's positive commitments to the Caofeidian development zone through various occasions.[18] The extension of partnership in energy conservation to the development zone will consolidate partnership for positive-sum benefits. Furthermore, it is useful to expand the base for positive-sum cooperation by urging the involvement of non-state actors who have vital stakes in stable bilateral relations. Indeed, it is difficult to expect the emergence of business linkages in a short time span. However, public and private partnership paves the way for extending the base for business chances, and the emergence of business collaboration will consolidate the ground for stable bilateral relations.[19]

In the regional dimension, it is useful to take into account commonality in leadership style by Japan and China. Some scholars have identified a specific manner in Japan's leadership, calling it "leadership from behind" (Rix 1993). Indeed, China has raised its economic and political presence in a short period, but it made efforts to be a responsible member of the regional and global community rather than an explicit leader (Tsang 2008). Dent finds "a communal approach to leadership" by Japan and China, "whereby exercises of regional leadership are formulated in a more consensual or collective way, both in terms of interests and decision-making processes" (Dent 2008, 293). Based on the communal leadership style, Japan is required to collaborate with China in establishing common principles for realizing an East Asian community. In this respect, ASEAN members have advanced their diplomatic relations and promoted regional cooperation through the ASEAN Way.[20] The ASEAN members have transformed some norms in the ASEAN Way in accordance with the launching of the ASEAN Charter (Thomas 2009, 17–18). Northeast Asia is required to develop and present specific principles that would be put in parallel to the ASEAN Way, and these principles would be the core tenets for community-building in East Asia.[21]

CONCLUSIONS

In this chapter, I have examined the ways in which Japan has responded to globalization trends, as well as characteristics and problems that were seen in such responses. The article highlighted the influence of globalization on Japan in the form of growing economic dynamism of East Asia and the ascendancy of the Chinese economy.

In order to integrate the Japanese industry into East Asian dynamism, the Japanese government has implemented both outward-looking and inward-looking policies. Assistance to deployment of integrated infrastructure systems is a representative of outward-looking policy. The assistance aimed to broaden the scope of industrial sectors that would be capable of undertaking global operations and were accompanied by evolved ideas about government-business relations. The government also adopted inward-looking policies to promote structural reforms for the invitation of global companies and excellent human resources from overseas as well as the promotion of FTAs. In particular, the FTA promotion has become an important policy as a means to avoid disadvantage in global competition as well as to promote the opening of the Japanese economy and society.

The Japanese government was forced to adopt dyadic policies in the face of the rising China. Japan, which had been the leading economic power for more than 40 years in East Asia, sought to maintain its strong economic and political presence in the region. For this objective, the government implemented strategic policies to counter China's regional influence, which were typically seen in regional trade integration and support for the Mekong development. At the same time, the Japanese government launched cooperative initiatives to sustain the sound development of the East Asian and Chinese economies. While Japan has, in collaboration with China, assisted the development of feasible architectures for regional financial stability, it has committed to energy conservation in China under joint public-private partnership.

The Japanese government, with deepened understanding about the implications of globalization, has gradually intensified positive policies to meet the globalization challenge. However, such policies were confronted with opposition from groups that were apprehensive about the negative impact of the market-opening on Japan. The government is required to explain benefits that market-opening will bring about in the long run. China's economic ascendancy raised the importance of economic partnership in Sino-Japanese relations. Nonetheless, economic partnership is heavily influenced by political tension. The identification of core interests and the expansion of the base for realizing such interests are required to make economic partnership as a linchpin to establish sound political relations. Sino-Japanese partnership is required to develop regional cooperation into the phase of community-building. The countries in East Asia need specific principles that drive the cooperative process and symbolize the objectives for community formation, and Japan's successful commitment to China for developing such principles will become a crucial drive for creating an East Asian community.

NOTES

1. The broad East Asia refers to 10 ASEAN members, three Northeast Asian countries (China, Japan, and South Korea) plus India, Australia, and New Zealand. They are the original members of the East Asia summit.
2. The government's intensive commitments produced successful outcomes. When Prime Minister Naoto Kan made a formal visit to Hanoi in October 2010, Kan and Vietnamese Premier Nguyen Tan Dung signed an agreement to select Japan as a partner for a construction of two reactors at the second new power plant site. At the meeting, the Vietnamese government also expressed a decision to select Japan as a partner to develop rare earth elements.
3. Nippon Keidanren, "Proposal on Future International Cooperation: Stress on a Strategic Stance and the Strength of Public-Private Cooperation," April 15, 2008; and Nippon Kendaren, "Pursuing Strategic, Enhanced International Cooperation Through Public-Private Cooperation," April 8, 2009.
4. Nippon Keidanren, "The Strength of Financial Functions for the Deployment of Integrated Infrastructure Systems," December 6, 2010.
5. According to questionnaire surveys on foreign companies' attitudes toward direct investment in Japan, "reduction in corporate taxes" was ranked the third (12.3 percent)—following "increase in number of talented staff available" (15.6 percent) and "introduction of special treatment more attractive than that in other countries" (14.1 percent)—as conditions needed to be satisfied to establish a regional management base in Japan (Japan External Trade Organization 2008, 18).
6. "The Basic Policies for Economic and Fiscal Management and Structural Reform 2006," July 7, 2006, Cabinet Decision. Accessed February 12, 2011 from http://www5.cao.go.jp/keizai-shimon/cabinet/2006/decision060707.pdf.
7. "Basic Policy on Comprehensive Economic Partnerships," November 9, 2010, Cabinet Decision. Accessed February 13, 2011 from http://www.npu.go.jp/pdf/20101109/20101109_en.pdf.
8. The domino effect indicates that the creation of a regional trade arrangement raises incentives for excluded states to apply for membership, in order to avoid the disadvantage resulting from non-member status. See Baldwin (1995).
9. The Koizumi government promoted neoliberal reforms through the privatisation of the postal services, as well as the reduction of subsidies to local governments and social security benefits (Uchiyama 2010).
10. *Asahi Shimbun*, August 27, 2006.
11. METI prepared for the pair proposal to the CEPEA: the establishment of the ERIA. This proposal aimed to show Japan's leadership role in guiding regional economic affairs.
12. The East-West Economic Corridor is a highway route running from Da Nang Port in Viet Nam, through Laos, Thailand, and to the Mawlamyine Port in Myanmar. The Second East-West Economic Corridor is a highway route linking Bangkok, Phnom Penh, and Ho Chi Minh City.
13. The Japanese government proposed the establishment of the ERIA, an East Asian version of the Organization for Economic Cooperation and Development, at the second East Asia summit in January 2007, and the institute was formally set up in June 2008.
14. The number of the model projects increased from 5 in the second forum in 2007 to 22 in the fourth forum in 2009.
15. The initiative aimed to provide packages of support measures totalling $30 billion, of which $15 billion would be made available for the mid- and long-term

development while another $15 billion would be used for the short-term capital need during the process of implementing economic reform.

16. "Joint Message, the 6th Trilateral (China, Japan and Korea) Finance Ministers' Meeting," May 4, 2006, Hyderabad, India. Accessed March 2, 2011 from http://www.mof.go.jp/english/international_policy/convention/triateral_meetings_among_jp_ch_kr/060504joint_message.htm.
17. The DPJ government began to re-examine the relocation of U.S. Marine Corps Futenma Air Station, which led to unstable relations with Washington.
18. The Caofeidian development zone has special importance in this respect. This new development zone spans 50 km in Tangshan city, Hebei Province. The area was listed as a model area for the development of a recyclable/circular economy in October 2005. Beijing Capital Iron and Steel Group constructed a steel plant in 2007, and other companies such as Huadian Power Group and PetroChina established some of their energy bases.
19. The fact that the energy conservation forum was held as planned in October 2010 when political tension was high illustrates the value of such partnership.
20. The ASEAN Way is a set of norms that include the non-interference principle, informal consultation, pragmatic expediency, consensus-building, and flexible incrementalism (Acharya 1997, 329–333).
21. Taniguchi (2006, 312) raises forgiveness to other cultures and resultant moderateness, self-reliant efforts, and co-existence with the nature as examples of principles for an East Asian community.

REFERENCES

Acharya, Amitav. 1997. "Ideas, Identity, and Institution-Building: From the 'ASEAN Way' to the 'Asia-Pacific Way'?" *Pacific Review* 10(3): 319–346.

Asian Development Bank. 2009. *Infrastructure for a Seamless Asia*. Tokyo: Asian Development Bank Institute.

Baldwin, Richard E. 1995. "A Domino Theory of Regionalism." In *Expanding Membership of the European Union*, edited by Richard E. Baldwin, Pertti Haaparanta, and Jaakko Kiander, 25–53. Cambridge: Cambridge University Press.

Democratic Party of Japan. 2009. *Minshuto Seiken Seisaku, Manifesto* [The DPJ's policy platform for government, Manifesto]. Tokyo: Minshuto Honbu. Accessed November 20, 2010 from http://www.dpj.or.jp/special/manifesto2009/.

Dent, Christopher M. 2005. "Taiwan and the New Regional Political Economy of East Asia." *China Quarterly* 182: 385–406.

Dent, Christopher M. 2008. "Regional Leadership in East Asia: Towards New Analytical Approaches." In *China, Japan, and Regional Leadership in East Asia*, edited by Christopher M. Dent, 275–304. Northampton: Edward Elgar.

Er, Lam Peng. 2010. "Challenges and Prospect for Japan's Ageing Population: No Easy Choices." In *Ageing and Politics: Consequences for Asia and Europe*, edited by Wilhelm Hofmeister, 139–156. Singapore: Konrad-Adenauer-Stiftung.

Hatch, Walter F. 2010. *Asia's Flying Geese: How Regionalization Shapes Japan*. Ithaca: Cornell University Press.

Hatoyama, Yukio. 2009. "Watashi no Seiji Tetsugaku: Sofu, Ichiro ni Mananda 'Yuai' to Iu Tatakai no Hatajirushi" [My Political Philosophy: Fraternity, A Banner of Fight Learned from My Grandfather, Ichiro]. *Voice* (September): 132–141.

Henning, C. Randall. 2009. "The Future of the Chiang Mai Initiative: An Asian Monetary Fund?" *Policy Brief* 09–5: 1–9.

Japan External Trade Organization. 2008. *Survey on Attitudes of Foreign-Affiliated Companies toward Direct Investment in Japan 2007*. Tokyo: Japan External Trade Organization.

Jiang, Yang. 2010. "Response and Responsibility: China in East Asian Financial Cooperation." *Pacific Review* 23(5): 603–623.

Maeda, Tadashi. 2011. "Ogata Purojekuto wo Meguru Kokkakan Kyoso to Nihon no Senryaku," [Inter-State Competition over Large-Scale Projects and Japan's Strategy] *Kokusai Mondai* 598: 41–50.

Ministry of Economy, Trade and Industry. 2003. *Tsusho Hakusho 2003* [White paper on International Economy and Trade 2003]. Tokyo: Keizai Sangyo Chosakai.

Ministry of Economy, Trade and Industry. 2006. *Gurobaru Keizai Senryaku: Higashi Ajia Keizai Togo to Nihon no Sentaku* [Global Economic Strategy: Economic Integration in East Asia and Japan's Choice]. Tokyo: Gyosei.

Ministry of Economy, Trade and Industry. 2010. *Tsusho Hakusho 2010* [White Paper on International Economy and Trade 2010]. Tokyo: Nikkei Insatsu.

Ministry of Finance. various years. "International Investment Position of Japan". Accessed January 20, 2011 from http://www.mof.go.jp/english/international_policy/reference/iip/index.htm.

Ministry of Foreign Affairs. 2009. "Nihon no Keizai Renkei Kyotei (EPA)" [Japan's Economic Partnership Agreement (EPA)], October. Accessed December 5, 2010 from http://www.mofa.go.jp/mofaj/gaiko/fta/pdfs/kyotei_0910.pdf.

Mulgan, Aurelia George. 2008. "Japan's FTA Politics and the Problem of Agricultural Trade Liberalisation." *Australian Journal of International Affairs* 62(2): 164–178.

Oike, Atsuyuki. 2006. "Nihon no EPA Kosho no Tenkai to Tenbo" [The Evolution and Prospect of Japan's EPA Negotiations]. *Boeki to Kanzei* (December): 24–39.

Rix, Alan. 1993. "Japan and the Region: Leading from Behind." In *Pacific Economic Relations in the 1990s: Cooperation or Conflict?* edited by Richard Higgott, Richard Leaver, and John Ravenhill, 62–82. St. Leonards: Allen & Unwin.

Searight, Amy. 2009. "Emerging Economic Architecture in Asia: Opening or Insulating the Region?" In *Asia's New Multilateralism: Cooperation, Competition, and the Search for Community*, edited by Michael J. Green and Bates Gill, 193–242. New York: Columbia University Press.

Taniguchi, Makoto. 2006. "Kikiteki Ajia Gaiko wo Ikani Tatenaosuka" [How to Reconstruct Asian Diplomacy in Crisis] *Chuo Koron* (April): 304–314.

Thomas, Nicholas. 2009. "Understanding Regional Governance in Asia," In *Governance and Regionalism in Asia*, edited by Nicholas Thomas, 1–31. Abingdon: Routledge.

Tsang, Steve. 2008. "China's Place in East Asia," In *China, Japan, and Regional Leadership in East Asia*, edited by Christopher M. Dent, 84–100. Northampton: Edward Elgar.

Uchiyama, Yu. 2010. *Koizumi and Japanese Politics: Reform Strategies and Leadership Style*. Abingdon: Routledge.

World Bank. 1993. *The East Asian Miracle: Economic Growth and Public Policy*. New York: Oxford University Press.

Yoshimatsu, Hidetaka. 2006. "The Politics of Japan's Free Trade Agreements." *Journal of Contemporary Asia* 36(4): 479–499.

7 China's New Development Stage

Peilin Li

Since China began to implement the reform and opening up policies in 1978, its development and reform have been centered on Two-T Change, namely the transition of economic institution and the transformation of social structure. Over 30 years, China has undergone rapid economic growth and enormous social transformation. But all this comes at a heavy cost, especially the cost of natural resources and ecological environment.

After the international financial crisis, China has now put forward a new concept of "changing the mode of development." The theme is closer to the meaning of "sustainable development," but it covers even broader contents than the common understanding of "sustainable development." "Changing the mode of development" at least conveys three shades of meaning. First, economic growth should no longer rely excessively on investment and export but more and more on domestic consumption. Second, the mode of economic growth should be changed from low-cost quantitative expansion into qualitative technological improvement, and from "Made in China" to "Created in China" to promote industry upgrade. Third, the mode of development at the expense of natural resources and environment should be changed into a resource-saving and environment-friendly mode; development should no longer be driven largely by industry but by modern service industry to a greater extent; and low-carbon economy should be energetically promoted.

Instead of talking about sustainable development from the angle of protecting the ecological environment, I am trying to look into issues about the sustainable development of China and the world from the angle of increasing China's domestic consumption.

It is often said that there are three main factors that drive a country's economic growth: investment, export trade, and domestic consumption. As for export trade, the international financial crisis inflicted heavy losses on China's export, which had undergone negative growth of over 20 percent in 2009 for a dozen of consecutive months and bottomed out only in 2010[1]. Impacted by the international financial crisis, international trade protectionism prevails in many countries due to the unemployment pressure, giving rise to many trade disputes between China, America, and the

European Union. Therefore, even after the crisis, China is not likely to resume its 60 percent high dependency (the ratio of the total volume of imports and exports to gross domestic product [GDP]) on foreign trade. Besides, different from export-oriented small economic entities in East Asia and Southeast Asia, China has a large population, so it is risky, unsustainable, and unstable if its economic growth relies excessively on foreign trade. For the equivalent of a Boeing airplane, China has to export about 100 million pairs of jeans. To preserve and increase the value of foreign exchange earned through exports of large quantities of cheap products, China has to buy the relatively secure U.S. treasury bonds. However, in order to stimulate its economy, the U.S. increases its investment by printing money, leading to the depreciation of the U.S. dollar and dilution of its debts.

Since the reform and opening up, China's development mode has always featured high saving and investment ratios. From 1978 until now, the investment ratio has maintained a high level of 30 percent to 45 percent, averaging around 37 percent. Especially after 1993, China's investment ratio showed a rapidly rising trend. In 2007, it reached an even higher level of 45 percent. But this kind of high-investment and high-growth development mode is not sustainable whatsoever. Long-term high investment is bound to cause excessive production capacity, reduced investment gains, redundant construction, and increase in non-performing bank loans.

Therefore, to meet the requirements for sustainable development and to keep the trade balance of the international economic order, China must increase its domestic demands and increase consumer spending, so as to shift to a development mode in which China's future economic growth will rely largely on domestic consumption. According to some scholars at home, China's economic growth should still rely largely on investment, because in the short term, it will be difficult to stimulate economic growth by increasing domestic consumption, although it is a must. Moreover, it is believed that high saving and investment ratios are a feature of China's national conditions and have been China's primary means of economic growth for quite a long time, so the transformation of the development mode should still rely more on changing the investment structure and increasing the investment efficiency.

Let's look into the hypothesis that "in the short term, it is difficult to stimulate economic growth by increasing domestic consumption." At a first look, it makes some sense. But a critical eye will discover its problems. First, the hypothesis is based on the development experience of the past. In the past, when the economic growth rate declined, we always stimulated the economy by expanding finances and enlarging investment. To stimulate the economy by increasing consumption is only a wish that has never been fulfilled. On the other hand, high investment, as an alternative, would always lead to redundant construction, excessive production capacity, increased inventory, reduced investment gains, or even inflation after the crisis. It is hard to tell if these old problems would come back following the international financial crisis.

We have to see a new possibility, a new future—that is, China's economic and social development has reached a new stage of growth, featuring significant changes from the past. We have been used to the old practices, but in the next 30 years we need to make some changes during the process of growth.

Why do people lack confidence in consumption? In the short term, consumption is restrained by income, and it's time to change the situation. In China, the proportion of resident income to the national income is constantly declining. For example, from 1992 to 2007, the proportion of disposable income of Chinese residents to the national income declined from 69 percent to 53 percent. Meanwhile, the proportion of disposable income of enterprises to the national income rose from 12 percent to 23 percent, and the proportion of disposable income of the government to the national income increased from 19 percent to 24 percent. Why is consumption at a low ebb now? According to statistics, the State lacks no money: from 1994 to 2008, China's tax revenue (in renminbi [RMB]) increased from over RMB500 billion to RMB5.4 trillion, with an average annual growth of 18 percent, which was far higher than the GDP growth; Chinese people seem to lack no money either: from 1994 to March 2009, the savings balance of urban and rural residents increased from over RMB2 trillion to RMB24.1 trillion, with an average annual growth of 18 percent. Where has the huge amount of money gone? Why are people not spending? From 1985 to 2008, Chinese residents' consumption rate, namely the proportion of consumer spending to GDP, actually declined from 52 percent to 35.4 percent, which represents a very low level in the world. Needless to say, the rate was far lower than America's 70 percent and Japan's 65 percent. The 300 million American people consume more than $10 trillion's worth of commodities every year, while 1.3 billion Chinese people consume only over $1 trillion every year. The two consumer markets differ widely.

The fundamental reason for China's sluggish consumption lies in the structure of income distribution, that is to say, the greatest challenge that China faces in terms of consumption is actually the problematic structure of income distribution. For a little over the last 30 years, China's greatest achievement has been its rapid economic growth, whereas its most challenging problem lies with income distribution. The growth curve of Gini coefficient, against which the income gap is measured, is surging all the way up, just like the GDP growth curve. In the history of modernization, there was no country but China that had increased the Gini coefficient from 0.2 to around 0.5 in over 30 years,[2] no country but China that had widened the gap of income distribution at such a great speed. According to existing research findings, nearly 60 percent of China's overall income gap can be explained with the income gap between cities and rural areas (Shi 2008). This is the primary problem in the income gap. In recent years, China has lifted the agricultural taxes and increased its investment and fiscal transfer payment for rural areas. In 2008, cities and rural areas saw nearly the same speed of growth in resident income. This had never happened before in more than a decade. In 2009, however, the international financial crisis brought great impacts to the income of farmers that migrate to cities for employment or doing business. Reducing the number of farmers and transferring rural labor are important means for China to increase the income of farmers and improve its overall consumption power, and increasing farmers' consumption power serves as the determining factor for the overall increase of the consumption capacity.

The consumption structure is also closely related to the structure of social stratification. The coming of a mass consumption era depends largely on the expansion of the middle class, that is to say, the structure of social stratification has to change from the pyramid shape into an oval shape. Theoretically, the coming of a mass consumption era relies on the growth of the middle class. Admittedly, "middle class" is an ambiguous conception: economists often define the middle class by income and property, while sociologists place emphasis on the index of occupation. In other words, it is only when the tertiary industry of a country accounts for the largest proportion of the whole industrial structure and when the white-collar class accounts for the majority of the labor force, could the country's middle class be in the majority. According to our research, if the middle class is to be defined by the three indexes including income, occupation, and education, by 2006, China's middle class will account for 12 percent of the country's total active population, and around 25 percent of the urban active population (Li and Yi 2008). As a matter of course, since China has the largest population in the world, every percentage point of growth of the middle class represents a huge consumer group, that is, an enormous consumer market.

As we know, household consumption rate, namely the proportion of household consumption to household income, decreases progressively along with the increase in household income. This rule is very obvious in China. According to our sample survey of nationwide social conditions in 2008, the household consumption rate showed an obvious declining trend along with the increase in income: the lower the income of a household, the higher its consumption rate; the higher the income of a household, the lower its consumption rate; and the consumption rates differ greatly (Peilin and Wei 2008). This means how to distribute the increased income of the whole society has much to do with consumption. To increase consumption, we have to increase the proportion of resident income to national income and increase the proportion of the income of low-income groups to resident income. In other words, on the one hand, we have to prevent saturated consumption among the rich. On the other hand, we have to prevent the situation that those who need consumption have no money.

According to the analysis of the survey data, there are three main factors that affect the day-to-day consumption of a normal household in China: educational spending, medical spending, and housing spending.

Educational spending and medical spending, in particular, contribute to far higher proportions of the total consumption of low and medium-income households than high-income households. Only housing spending is an exception: the higher the income of a household, the higher the proportion of its housing spending to its total consumption. This shows that many high-income households have transformed their housing spending from a cost of living into an investment for property income. However, this kind of housing investment, which is detached from consumption and based on the expectation of rapid appreciation, is likely to turn into asset bubbles. But the excessively high proportions of educational consumption and medical consumption of low and medium-income households have restricted their day-to-day consumption and instant consumption. A survey of the purposes of various resident savings also shows that the spending for offspring education and medical spending are often ranked the first two places among the purposes of saving. Chinese people's propensity to save is based on reasonable considerations and is intended to avoid the risk of future household consumption, so this is not only a cultural issue. If we say that American people live in a culture of credit consumption, that is, the current generation spends money of the next generation, then Chinese people live in a culture of savings accumulation, that is, the current generation saves money for the next generation.

To change people's consumption behavior, we have to establish and improve a series of relevant systems, and it will also involve a series of social policies and social reforms. First, we have to establish a mechanism for normal growth of labor wages, namely a mechanism for the annual growth of labor wages according to the growth of enterprises' profits. Meanwhile, we have to establish a mechanism for the growth of governmental salary according to the economic growth and the growth of enterprises' labor wages. Secondly, the structure of income distribution must be adjusted by such levers as finance, taxation, social security, and social benefits, so as to divert more increased income to low-income groups that need consumption, and constantly expand the medium-income groups as the backbone of mass consumption. Third, we have to provide public products and services more effectively and universally; establish and improve social security system that cover both urban and rural residents; equalize basic public services in urban and rural areas; and stabilize the public's anticipation of consumption for education, medical care, housing, old age, and so on.

To increase consumer spending is more of a social issue than just an economic issue and is closely related to many social institutions. From an economic perspective, an oversized income gap inhibits the consumption of the low and medium-income classes, bringing negative impacts to the general growth of consumption and making the economic growth rely excessively on investment and exports; from a social perspective, the oversized income gap has become the underlying cause of many social problems, leading to general discontent of the public. As early as 1993, Deng Xiaoping had given his admonition by saying "distribution poses an enormous problem. We talk about preventing polarization. In fact, it takes place naturally. We need to solve these problems by various means, methods and solutions." Otherwise, "such a way of development would eventually lead to unpredictable problems." (Party Literature Research Center of the CPC Central Committee 2004, 1364)

If the high-speed growth of China's economy in the past 30 plus years relied mainly on investment and exports, then its growth in the next 30 years should rely more on the growth of domestic consumption. That is, the primary driving force for economic growth should be diverted to domestic consumption. This is not impossible, but quite plausible. In China, a new stage of mass consumption has arrived.

The first feature of the new stage of growth is the coming of the mass consumption era. In the past, it was considered a far cry. In fact, the era has come today. If calculated in U.S. dollars, China's per capita GDP only increased from over $300 to over $800 in 20 years from 1980 to 2000. But since 2003 when it exceeded $1,000, the per capita GDP has gained speed: in 2006, it exceeded $2,000; in 2008, it reached over $3,300; and by the end of 2010, it is estimated to reach around $4,000. This kind of leap-forward development is closely related to three factors: high-speed economic growth, diminished net increase of population, and appreciation of RMB. The Engel coefficient of Chinese residents is continuously declining. The proportion of food consumption to the total household consumption has actually reduced to nearly 30 percent, because we have always underestimated the housing spending. According to the experience of various countries, when the Engel coefficient reduces to around 30 percent, it signifies the coming of a mass consumption era. In this era, large consumer goods, such as houses, automobiles, and so forth, begin to gain popularity among average households, and a new type of consumer spending on education, medical care, tourism, communications, and so forth becomes a fast-growing hot spot of consumption. In the face of the mass consumption era, however, we are not well prepared, haven't conducted enough research, and lack confidence in mass consumption.

The second feature of the new stage of growth is that industrialization and urbanization come to an intermediate stage of acceleration. This stage is also closely related to consumption growth. In industrialized and urbanized countries, consumption has been saturated, so it is difficult to be stimulated. But in China, the situation is different: China's structural transformation shows great elasticity, and its consumption has great potential of growth. According to international experience, the hallmarks of a major transformation of the economic and social structures include a lower than 5 percent proportion of agricultural added value in GDP, a lower than 30 percent proportion of agricultural labor in the employment structure, and a higher than 50 percent urbanization level. China's three major structures, including the production value structure, the employment structure, and the urban-rural structure, have all come to a stage of transformation. Of China's GDP, the proportion of agricultural added value will decline to below 10 percent in 2010 and to around 6 percent in 2015; of the employment structure, the proportion of agricultural labor will decline to below 38 percent in 2010 and to around 33 percent in 2015; and of the urban-rural structure, the urbanization level, as indicated by the resident urban population, will reach around 50 percent in 2010. These indicators show that China, in general, has reached an intermediate stage of acceleration in the process of industrialization and urbanization, and its economic and social structures will undergo a profound transformation. However, China faces such a problem that urbanization lags behind industrialization, and the transformation of its social structure lags behind the transformation of its economic structure. For example, hundreds of millions of migrant workers in China are doing non-agricultural jobs but maintaining their identity as peasants. They live in cities, but their consumption is still in the rural style.

The third feature of the new stage of growth is that the population structure is undergoing significant changes, producing two results. The first result is the aging of population. Starting from 2015 or 2016, the dependency ratio of the whole society will turn around to the augmentation as a result of the rapid increase of the elderly dependency ratio. This tendency forces us to promptly establish social security systems, particularly an old-age pension system, which cover both urban and rural residents. The second result is the gradual termination of the low-labor-cost era. That the working-age population stops growing and starts to decline will force up the market price of labor, compel China to transform its mode of development from "made in China" into "created in China" and its status from a major power of population to a world power of human resources, and make it rely more on the labor training and education to maintain its comparative advantages. To that end, China will inevitably choose to establish a mechanism for the normal growth of wages. Both results are related to the expansion of consumption. The former is conducive to stabilizing the consumption anticipation, while the latter is conducive to increasing the consumption power.

Of all the outstanding issues concerning China's expansion of consumption in the next decade, acceleration of urbanization, particularly housing consumption, as we might say, are essential issues to be properly addressed. In that regard, we can introduce a major policy, that is, to allow farmers' houses to enter the leasing and trading markets. By doing so, we will see that farmers' houses have their market prices, and farmers may obtain more property income. Meanwhile, we will see an enormous increase in the housing supply, thereby stabilizing the costs of housing and making it more affordable.

In addition, in respect of the expansion of consumption, income distribution remains an inevitable issue. The adjustment of the structure of income distribution entails not only properly adjusting the proportion of labor payment to capital gains in the primary distribution but also well balancing the proportions of the incomes of the State, enterprises, and residents to the national income: the proportion of labor payment in the primary distribution should be increased, so should be the proportion of resident income to the national income. Furthermore, the role of such levers as finance, taxation, social security, and social benefits should be brought into play in the redistribution.

To adapt to the "transformation of the development mode" and the needs of the new stage of growth, China needs to conduct a comprehensive social reform to provide momentum for future development. It has been more than 30 years since China's reform and opening up, and our primary approach is largely oriented toward the reform of the economic institution system, although concurrently we have introduced reforms to other sectors. By far, China has basically established a socialist market economic system. But the great changes of the economic and social structures require continued adaptation of the systems of all sectors. As the reform expands from the economic sector to the whole social spectrum, it is now urgent to implement social reforms involving the institutions of employment, income distribution, social security, management of migration, social governance, operation of non-profit organizations, and whole civil society. To fully promote and deepen the social reform will become a hallmark of the new stage of growth and a major task for China to accomplish in that stage.

NOTES

1. Unless otherwise specified, all figures in this article are measured according to the data published by the National Bureau of Statistics.
2. Measured according to data obtained from the comprehensive survey of China's social conductions conducted in 2006 by the Institute of Sociology, CASS, the Gini coefficient for China's per capita household income in 2005 was 0.496. Source: Li Peilin, Chen Guangjin, and Li Wei. 2006. "A Report on the Situation of Social Harmony and Stability of China in 2006." In *Analysis and Forecast on China's Social Development (2007)*, edited by Ru Xin, Lu Xueyi, and Li Peilin, 19–31. Beijing: Social Sciences Academic Press.

REFERENCES

Party Literature Research Center of the CPC Central Committee. 2004. *Chronicle of Deng Xiaoping's Life 1975–1977*, Vol. II. Beijing: CPC Central Committee Literature Press.

Li, Peilin, and Li Wei. 2008. "Investigative Report on People's Livelihood Issues, 2008." In *Society of China: Analysis and Forecast (2009)*, edited by Ru Xin, Lu Xueyi, and Li Peilin, 15–32. Beijing: Social Sciences Academic Press.

Li, Peilin, and Zhang Yi. 2008. "The Scope, Identity, and Social Attitude of Middle Class in China." *Society* 2: 1–19.

Li, Shi, ed. 2008. *Research on Income Distribution in China III*. Beijing: Beijing Normal University Publishing Group.

8 Global Specialization and the China-U.S. Economic Imbalance

Min Gong

Economic globalization is regarded as "the most powerful force to have shaped the post-war world" (Frankel 2006). Economic specialization and international competition are the main ways that globalization affects bilateral and multilateral economic relationships in regional and global economies. By integrating into a world market, an economy can realize more efficient use of factors of production through relocation of resource and supply chains geographically, leading to higher output and income.

The U.S. and China have become a critically important market for each other since China's opening-up policies in 1978. Because of global specialization, U.S. companies can produce more of what they are best at producing, such as telecommunications and computer equipment, electrical machinery, software, movies, financial services, soybeans, and wheat. At the same time, rapid economic integration into the global market in the 1990s has transformed China into a sort of trade bridge or link between the industrialized East (Japan and South Korea) and the industrialized West (the U.S. and European Union [EU]), promoting not only China's economic growth, but also regional and worldwide trade expansion (Gong and Li 2008).

China's entry into The World Trade Organization (WTO) in November 2001 marks an important point in its economic development, as it strengthened its economic role in the region as well as in the global area. The huge economic imbalance between China and the U.S. that has followed, however, has given rise to antitrade sentiment, that poses a threat to the global economy.

In this chapter, I first describe the development of the China-U.S. economic relations with China's integration into the world economy in the late 1990s. Second, I analyze the China-U.S. economic imbalance from a perspective of economic integration and global specialization among the U.S., China, and Eastern Asia. And then, I point out that given China's comparative advantage, the China-U.S. economic imbalance is an outcome of global specialization between China and its main trade partners, which cannot be solved merely by their currency adjustments.

CHINA'S INTEGRATION INTO THE WORLD ECONOMY

China has experienced phenomenal economic growth with an average annual gross domestic product (GDP) growth rate of 9.8 percent for about 30 years. There is little doubt that exports and foreign investment have played an important role in China's development.

China's emergence as a major player in the world economy follows its entry into WTO in November 2001. Prior to this date, the volume of China's trade with the rest of world was modest. However, subsequently, Chinese foreign trade has increased dramatically. For example, in 2007, the contribution of the net export to China's GDP growth was 19.2 percent of a GDP growth rate that was reported to be as high as 13 percent. So far China has become the largest surplus export country in the world. Its foreign exchange reserves have also passed Japan's to become the largest in the world.

Figure 8.1 shows shares of certain economies' exports in world total exports during 1990–2008. Compared with those countries running trade surplus such as Japan, South Korea, and Germany, the growth rate of China's exports has been impressive. In 2008, China accounted for 8.9 percent of exports of the world's total exports, up from 5.02 percent in 2002, equivalent to the share for Germany, higher than the 4.8 percent for Japan and the 2.6 percent for South Korea. So far, China has been closely tied to advanced economy markets, with the U.S., the EU, and Japan as its most important export markets. This is the case despite the fact that its share of exports to Japan has shrunk since 2002. In 2009, exports to the U.S. and EU accounted for over 42 percent in China's total exports (Figure 8.2). Recently, albeit comparatively small, the share of China's exports to developing Asian economies is rising, reflecting China's efforts of diversifying its export markets.

Whereas China's export performance has been impressive, its import performance has been even more so. In 2008, for example, China purchased 6.93 percent of total world imports (Figure 8.3), higher than 4.67 percent of Japan, 2.66 percent of South Korea, and close to 7.34 percent of Germany. China has been the main market to which Japan and South Korea's products export. The share of China's imports from Japan reached to a maximum of 23 percent in the beginning of the 1990s, followed by a continuous decline. In 2009, Japan still is the largest import supplier to China, though the share of Japanese goods fell to 12 percent (Figure 8.4). By contrast, China's imports from South Korea and developing Asian economies appear to be following an upward trend, as compared with a downward trend of shares of China's imports from the U.S. and EU.

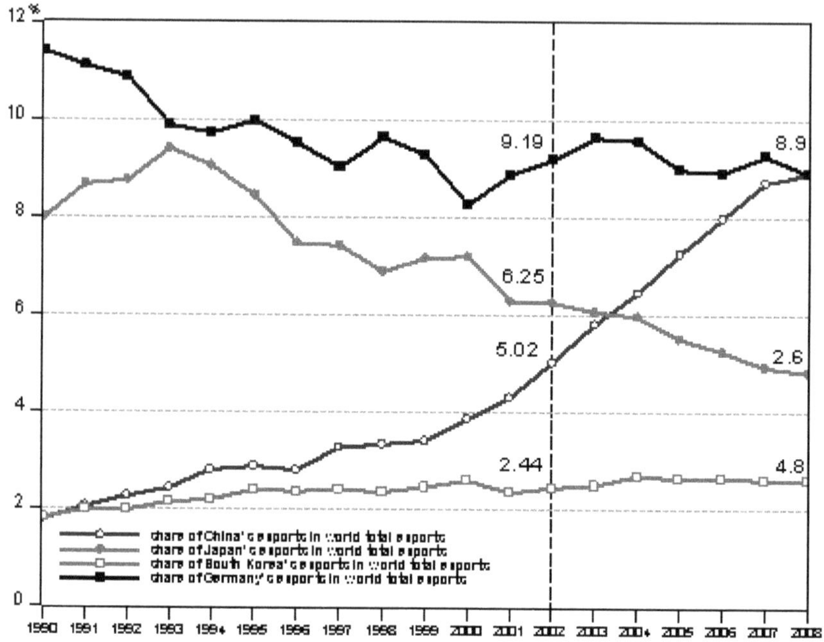

Figure 8.1 Shares of certain countries' exports in the world market (CEIC data bank and Handbook of Statistics, UNCTAD, 2009).

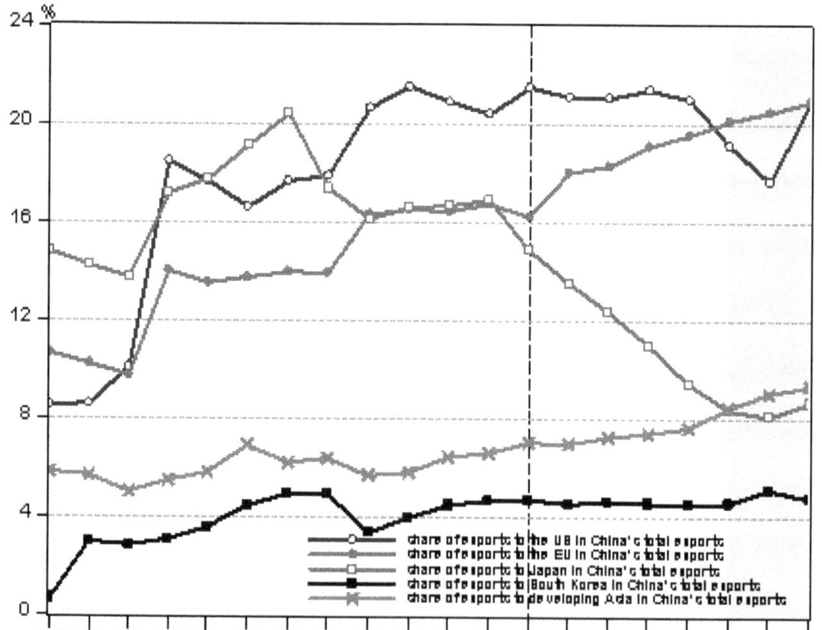

Figure 8.2 China's main export destinations (CEIC Data Bank).

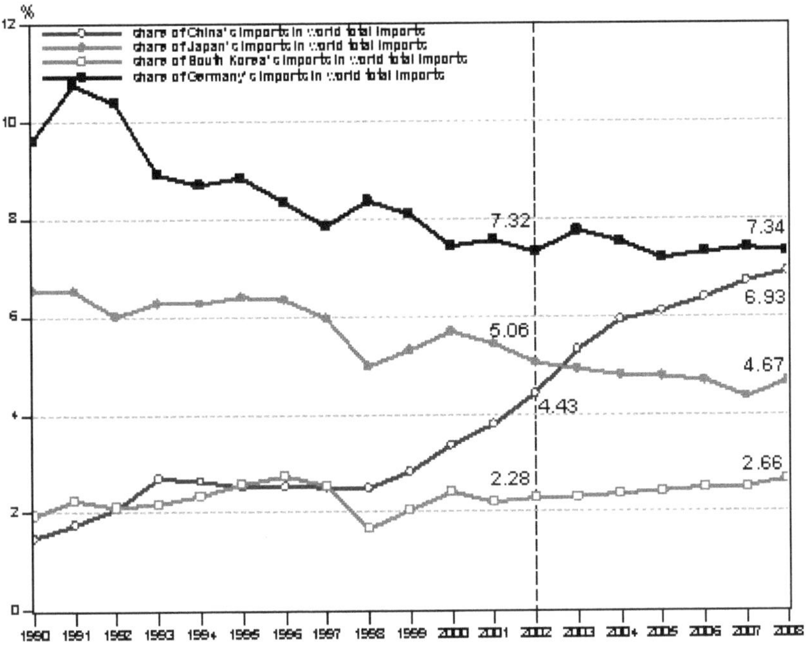

Figure 8.3 Shares of certain economies' imports in the world market (CEIC Data Bank and Handbook of Statistics, UNCTAD, 2009).

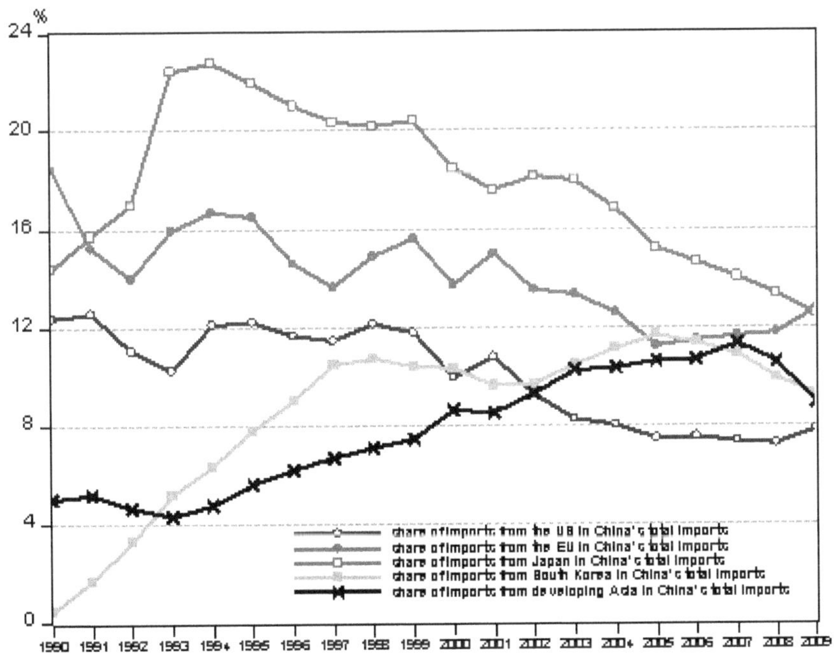

Figure 8.4 China's main import suppliers (CEIC Data Bank).

Continuous growth in exports and imports reflects the importance of inter-nation trade in China's economy. The ratio of net exports to GDP soared to 8 percent in 2008 from 2.5 percent in 2002. Over the same time, China's trade surplus with the world increased to $298.1 billion from $30.4 billion in 2008, and China's trade surplus with the U.S. increased to $171.1 billion from $42.7 billion in 2002 (Figure 8.5). Meanwhile, China's trade dependent degree, which is the ratio of the sum of merchandise exports and imports to GDP, increased dramatically from 38.5 percent in 2002 to 66.3 percent in 2006. For comparison, this ratio stood at 29.6 percent in 1990. As a result of these developments, the Chinese economy has become extremely vulnerable to adverse shocks from the rest of the world. The huge economic imbalance between China and the U.S. also has given rise to antitrade sentiment that poses a threat to the global economy.

However, if we examine the bilateral trade relationships between China and its main partners, it is clear that China has increasingly been running trade deficits with such countries as Japan, South Korea, and developing Asia economies (Figure 8.6). Although between July 2005 and July 2008 the value of the Chinese currency (RMB) rose 21 percent against the U.S. dollar to $0.1464 from $0.1208 where it had been pegged since 1997, the large trade surplus with the U.S. and the EU led to China having an overall trade surplus with the rest of the world.

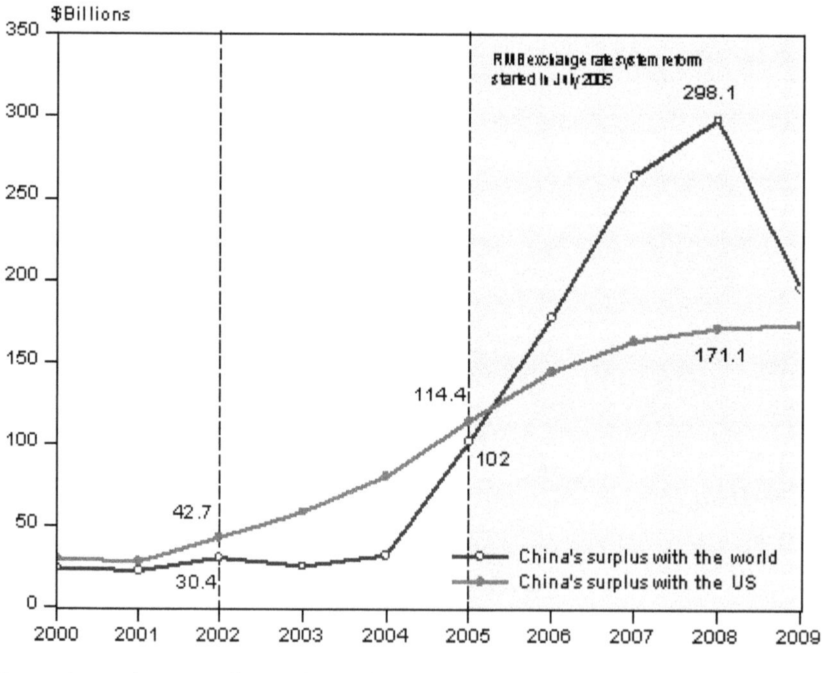

Figure 8.5 China's trade surplus with the U.S. and the world (CEIC Data Bank).

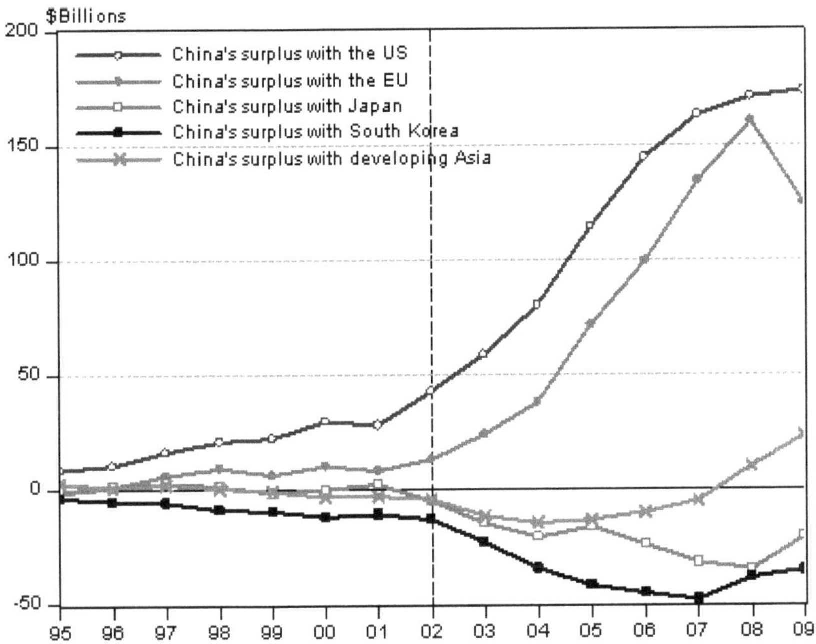

Figure 8.6 China's trade balance with certain economies (CEIC Data Bank).

Considering FDI (foreign direct investment) flow from Japan and South Korea to China, it would make sense that there exists connection between China's trade deficits with the industrialized East (Japan and South Korea) and China's trade surplus with the industrialized West (the U.S. and EU), which I will discuss in detail in the next part.

Finally, it is instructive to take a longer view of relationships between the U.S. trade deficit and U.S. dollar's exchange rate. The U.S. trade deficit with the world has been increasing since 1980 regardless of the value of the dollar. Japan contributed about 40 percent of the U.S. trade deficit during the 1980s and accounted for 35.7 percent on average during the 1990s (Figure 8.7). The Japanese yen rose by 80 percent against the dollar in the three years after the Plaza Accord in 1985, but this had little impact on the U.S. deficit with Japan until 2000. About this time, there is a switch from Japan to China, which started to become the key contributor to the U.S. trade deficit since 2000. The roles of Japan, as well as Taiwan (China), South Korea, Hong Kong (China), and Singapore all declined sharply.

In fact, if we measure the value of the Chinese currency in terms of the nominal effective exchange rate, which is a trade-weighted index of the average value of RMB, or in terms of the real effective exchange rate, which calculates a trade-weighted exchange rate based on real exchange rates instead of on nominal rates, it can be observed that the value of RMB has been on a upward trend since July 2005 (Figure 8.8), implying

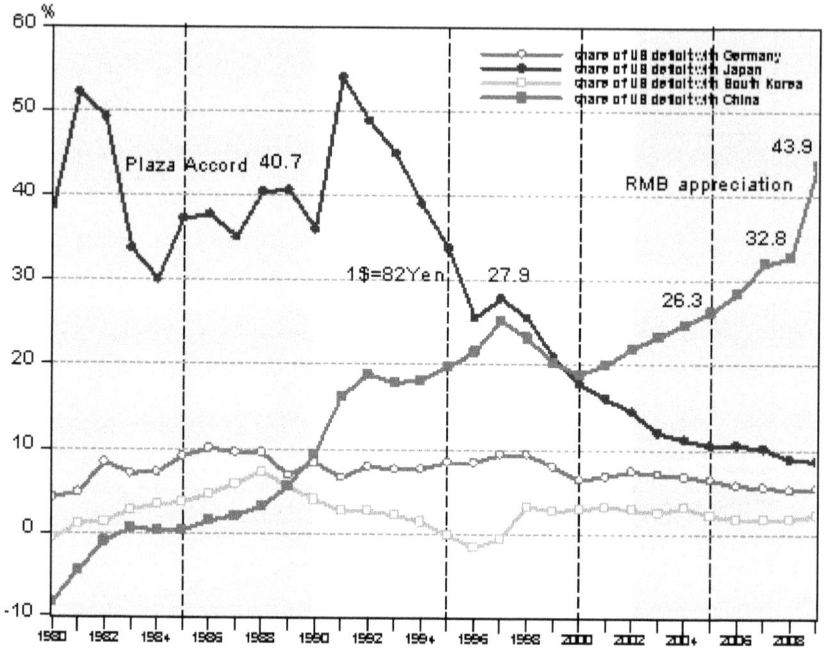

Figure 8.7 U.S. trade deficits with certain economies (CEIC Data Bank).

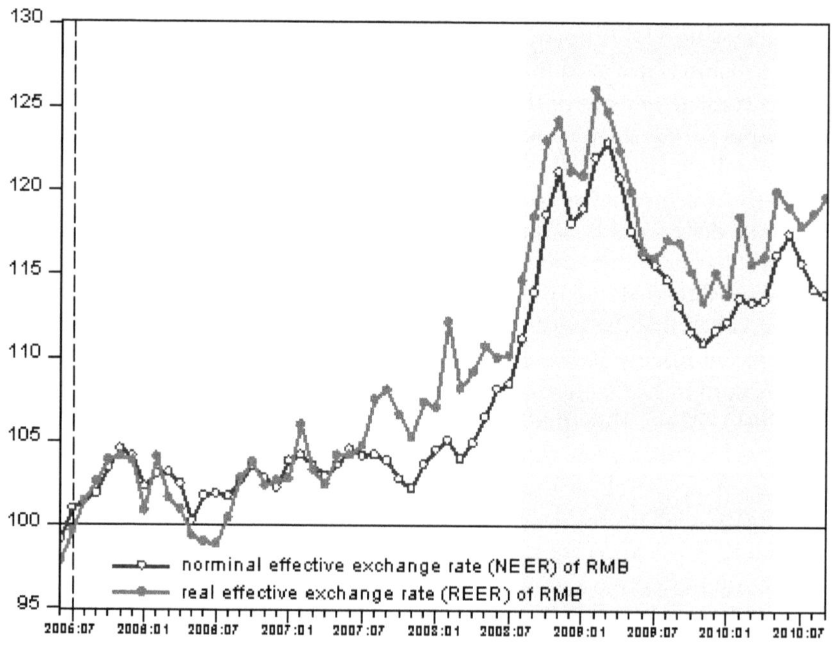

Figure 8.8 Nominal and real effective exchange rate of RMB (CEIC Data Bank).

that the value of the Chinese currency continues to rise against major currencies after the reform of RMB exchange rate system. The growth in Chinese imports into the U.S. has resulted in imbalanced trade, expanding U.S. deficits with China considerably. China's contribution to the overall U.S. trade deficits has increased significantly from 18.9 percent in 2000 to 32.8 percent in 2008. The bilateral deficit kept rising in spite of RMB appreciation in July 2005.

Expanding U.S. deficits with China regardless of the value of the dollar and a change in the roles of China and East Asian economies in the U.S. trade deficit lead us to the hypothesis, which is that China's external imbalance might be associated with relocation of production from the East Asian economies to China in response to the Asian financial crisis in 1997–1998, as well as a stagnant Japanese economy since 1990.

INVESTIGATING ECONOMIC IMBALANCE FROM A GLOBAL POINT

Understanding the External Imbalance

Cooper (2007), Caballero et al. (2008), and Mendoza et al. (2007) all argue that differences in saving-investment patterns and portfolio choices across countries reflect differences in levels of development, demographic patterns, and other underlying economic fundamentals. Thereby, deficits and surpluses on current accounts are "good" if they reflect optimal allocation of capital across time and space from a global point of view. On the other hand, some deem that imbalances are "bad" if they reflect distortions, externalities, and risks at the national and international level. Distortions include lack of a comprehensive social safety nets, as in the case of China, for example, and failures within the financial system.

Blanchard and Milesi-Ferritti (2010) hold that the imbalance between global demand and supply of goods and services is another important factor that causes global imbalances. The large U.S. current account deficits would be "ugly" if there already was more than enough effective demand in the world, which is true. The surpluses in some European countries, in oil exporting countries, and more recently in China would be "ugly" if there was a chronic lack of effective demand, which is also true. Akyüz (2010) examines contributions to global demand made by the major economies including the U.S., Germany, Japan, and China in an attempt to explain global imbalances. He finds that global imbalances are related to insufficient effective demand globally, excluding the U.S. Moreover, he mentions that currency adjustments merely alter relative growth rates rather than raising the overall global growth.

In this chapter, I try to investigate the determinants of economic imbalance between China and the U.S. from a perspective of economic integration and global specialization among the U.S., China, and Eastern Asia. In fact, global specialization via economic integration has been one of the most important factors in determining bilateral or multilateral trade relations in regional and world economies since the mid 1990s, which has fundamentally changed the pattern of regional production and trade in Asia as well as in the world economy. To some extent, economic integration of China, Japan, and the U.S. over the past two decades via vertical integration of production chains has reshaped the economic division relations of Asia and the world and contributed to the recent economic prosperity in developing Asia, incidentally, contributing to global imbalances as well.

Global Specialization and China's External Imbalance

In my view, global specialization in the process of economic integration is a key factor contributing to global imbalances. I will divide the impact of global specialization on the China-U.S. trade imbalance into three cases.

Complete Specialization and Inter-Industry Trade between China and the U.S.

Based on traditional factor endowment theory, as a country's international trade increases there is a shift of resources out of non-comparative advantage sectors into comparative advantage sectors. China has comparative advantage in labor -intensive industries in the current stage of development. Trade liberalization leads advanced economies to move their labor-intensive industries into China. At some point, advanced economies start to import labor-intensive goods from China instead of producing and exporting them by themselves. In reality, a significant amount of what the U.S. imports from China is no longer produced in the U.S., including clothing, toys, furniture, and basic household appliances, and so on.

The U.S. trade deficit with China resulting from inter-industry and completely specialized trade is irreversible because labor-intensive industries in the U.S. cannot be revived due to high labor costs there. Consequently, an increase in the prices of Chinese imports due to RMB appreciation simply makes the American consumer worse off. More importantly, if U.S. imports from China decrease because of RMB appreciation, Americans will buy more from India, Vietnam, Mexico, Indonesia, Bangladesh, and other low labor-cost economies instead. Thus, the U.S. trade deficit is not likely to decrease.

Fragmentation of Production and Intra-industry Trade among China, East Asian Economies, and the U.S.

Fragmentation of production, which sometimes is referred to as "slicing of the value chain," is viewed as a consequence of trade liberalization in developing countries (Jones and Kierzkowski 2001). The East Asian economies, led by Japan, then followed by South Korea, have succeeded in slicing their low-end value chain and in building efficient assembly plants in China since the 1990s. Over the last 25 years, U.S. firms have sliced some of the value chain to low-wage East Asia and Mexico by off-shoring or outsourcing, moving up the value chain. The change in the rearrangement of production in regional and world economies has transformed China's bilateral trade relationships with its main partners.

Theoretically, vertical intra-industry trade between developed countries and developing countries can be explained by the "Flying-Geese" model of shifting comparative advantage (Akamatsu 1962), which applied to the Chinese machinery products trade (characterized by processing trade) since the 1990s (Ljungwall and Sjoberg 2007; Kwan 2002) without exception. Practically, the choice to produce inputs abroad or purchase inputs from abroad is a part of the global strategies of multinational firms. Figure 8.9 shows how it actually works and how it affects the U.S. trade deficit with China.

For instance, in terms of the stage of economic development, Japan is an industrialized country with a large capital stock and advanced technology. Hence, Japan can serve as an exporter of capital and technology. South Korea is a newly industrialized country, which is just starting to become a main exporter of capital in the northeastern region. Compared with these two countries, China is a transitional country at a catch-up stage, thus, a natural recipient of capital, technology, and industry transfer in the region.

As a result of global division of industry, China has been the main place that accepts FDI from developed countries. In fact, China has become the first largest FDI recipient in the world since 2009 as a result of China's export-promotion growth strategy. Most FDI into China from Japan, South Korea, and the U.S. is export-oriented (Greaney and Li 2009; Zhang

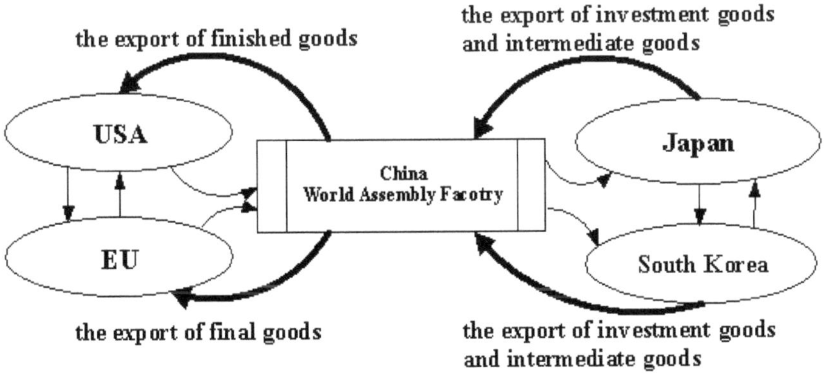

Figure 8.9 China as a trade bridge and a world assembly factory.

2005). From the late 1990s up to the present, the majority of FDI in China have been in manufacturing industries. China's low labor cost has been one of the major considerations for foreign investors or outsourcing companies. Those nations, including Japan and South Korea, as well as the U.S., supply parts and components to China and export the final goods via the assembly factories in China to the U.S. and EU. Consequently, China has been running increasing trade deficits with Japan and South Korea, while running increasing trade surplus with the U.S. and EU.

Gong and Li (2008) estimated a vector-autoregressive model to investigate the trade relations between China and its main trade partners. They found that substantial FDI-induced indirect trade from Japan and Korea to the U.S. through China and between Japan and Korea through China. These indirect trade flows lead to increases in China's trade deficit with Japan and Korea as well as China's trade surplus with the U.S.. These findings can be seen in the work by Xu and Wang (2008) and Deng et al. (2007).

We conclude that China functions as a trade bridge or trade link for many exports from industrialized Asia (Japan and South Korea) to the U.S. and EU. From the viewpoint of world trade growth, as a trade bridge, China contributes to the stable growth of the regional and world economies (Das 2008). However, China's exports depend heavily on the processing trade, which is characterized as labor-intensive and low value-added trade. Some research asserts that the value-added of China's exports in China only counts for 10–20 percent of the total price. Ikenson (2010) found that Chinese value-added accounted for about 37 percent of the total value of U.S. imports from China. Koopman et al. (2008) found the number to be closer to 50 percent. More importantly, as Japan and South Korea are expanding their exports to the U.S. via China, trade tensions that used to exist between Japan and the U.S. have shifted to tensions between China and the U.S. (or the EU).

Finally, the U.S. trade deficit, which resulted from vertical intra-industry trade in line with shifting comparative advantage, is also irreversible. The impact of RMB appreciation on the China-U.S. economic imbalance is not clear. RMB appreciation encouraged the import demand for intermediate goods, which in turn, speeded up the export of processing trade even faster because the reserve of labor pool in rural China has suppressed the wage rate, ballooning China's trade with the world between 2005 and 2008.

Intra-industry Trade Based on New Factor Endowment Theory between China and the U.S.

This is the second type of a division of labor that exists between China and the U.S., as explained by the neo-classical comparative advantage theory (Falvey 1981). Developed countries should produce and export human capital-intensive, high-quality products and import labor-intensive low-quality products from the same merchandise category, while developing countries should do the opposite. For example, the information technology is one of fast growing sectors in China, but China still lags behind the U.S., Japan, and other Asian countries in terms of export competitiveness. As a result of the division of labor, the U.S. can specialize in high-value-added products and China in low-value-added products that are associated with relatively less skilled labor inputs. Similar to the previous case, this kind of intra-industry trade is associated with complete specialization, which will cause displacement for less skilled workers in the U.S.

To sum up, trade imbalances among China and its main trade partners can be considered an outcome of inter-industry and intra-industry trade based on their dynamic comparative advantage. China is currently destined to be an ideal manufacturing base because of its different comparative advantage and different development stage from its trade partners. Although the global imbalances have to be corrected, manufacturing will not return back to the U.S., and Japan will not resume its low-end manufacturing production. An adjustment in the production and trade pattern among China, Japan, and the U.S. will not take place until China's comparative advantage has changed. Otherwise, China's trade surplus will be going away soon.

EXCHANGE RATES, WAGES, AND CHINA'S EXTERNAL IMBALANCE

China and the U.S. have been badly shaken by the financial crisis. After the financial crisis, although the U.S. trade deficit with China fell to $143.3 billion in 2009 from $171 billion in 2008, the U.S.-China economic tensions have intensified. The U.S. blames the undervalued Chinese currency for its trade deficit with China and the losses in U.S. jobs (Krugman 2010a, 2010b). Some call for RMB revaluation as a means of addressing the U.S. trade deficit with China and quickly creating U.S. jobs. Some assert that unless China raises the real value of the Chinese Yuan by at least 40 percent, the U.S. trade deficit and job losses will continue to grow rapidly.

However, the relationship between currency and current account improvement is weaker than many expect. History suggests that the impact of an increase in the value of the Chinese currency against the U.S. dollar on bilateral trade imbalance is complicated. As mentioned previously, China's currency rose 21 percent against the dollar from 2005 to 2008, but its trade surplus with the U.S. continued to increase given the feature of China's processing trade export.

According to World Economic Outlook by IMF, April 2010, there is absolutely positively no relation between adjustments of exchange rate and current account improvement. Although exchange rate appreciation often played a role, other policies also were needed to facilitate the current account rebalance, including macroeconomic policies that stimulated domestic demand and, in some cases, structural reforms. Since real appreciation seems to have slowed growth, other measures are provided to offset this adverse effect.

Based on this analysis, we hold that global specialization and economic integration of the U.S., China, and Japan (as well as South Korea and developing Asia) contributes more to economic imbalance between China and the U.S. than the relative value of their currency. In the long run, the division of labor and comparative advantage is going to rule the world economy, making the U.S. trade deficit sustainable, even if not with China, but with developing Asia economies.

From the point of China, with its current stage of economic development and abundant labor force, China has adopted opening-up policies. Intra-regional industrial division promotes rapid development of labor intensive industry. Strong outside demand consolidates China's exports-driven growth model, which depends heavily on exports and labor-intensive industry that can take advantage of low wages, and its economic growth has been driven by high investments and high exports.

Although low wages were a comparative advantage for China to promote labor-intensive industries before the global financial crisis, it became a problem in the wake of the financial crisis when the government wanted to stimulate domestic demand through consumption. Due to underdeveloped financial markets, the absence of a comprehensive social safety nets, the declining share of labor income in national income, as well as income disparity between the urban area and rural area, high precautionary savings are responsible for the low consumption-output ratio. The Chinese government has recently focused on promoting domestic consumption to rebalance the economy. On the demand side, rebalancing requires reducing the reliance on exports and fixed asset investment. On the supply side, it requires a shift to services from low-end manufacturing.

In fact, theoretically, both adjustments in real wages and currency appreciation can help reduce China's trade imbalance, help the Chinese demand shift from external to domestic sources, and help rising consumption. Moreover, they will change China's export composition toward higher value-added goods—that is, by an upward movement on the export quality ladder. More importantly, with resources shifting from the export sector to the service sector, they will facilitate the Chinese supply rebalanced.

However, compared to RMB appreciation, raising wages may be a better way to rebalance internal and external imbalance in China. Given the fact that China's per capita income is still low, a majority of Chinese people cannot take advantage of RMB revaluation. Hence, the relationship between strong RMB and higher purchase power could be weaker too. In contrast, the wage hikes will directly increase household purchasing power, thus accelerating the shift of China's final demand composition.

In order to correct for low wages suppressed by the abundant supply of labor, China's local governments have been asked to raise minimum wages at least every other year since 2004. In the depth of the financial crisis in late 2008 when the growth rates of both exports and imports plunged, the government stopped scheduled increases in minimum wages and pegged the RMB to the U.S. dollar. In the face of a relatively stable global economy, China's government has resumed increases in minimum wages and re-introduced more flexibility in the exchange rate regime.

Although wage increases may possibly lead to loss of manufacturing competitiveness in China, the overall competitiveness is also affected by factors such as infrastructures, a domestic market, supply chain, and skilled industrial workers. As long as wage increases are supported by labor productivity increase and improvement in business environment, benefits should outweigh costs. Wage increases are more effective not only in rebalancing China's current account but also in reversing the downward trend of household consumption share than RMB revaluation.

CONCLUSIONS

I have examined various factors contributing to the China-U.S. trade imbalance from the perspective of global specialization and shifts in global production. That is, China's trade surplus with the U.S. is explained by its role as a trade bridge in regional and world economies. China's 2001 accession in the WTO is an important event in becoming this trade bridge between the industrialized East (Japan and South Korea) and the industrialized West (the U.S. and EU). As a result, China has been running increasing trade deficits with Japan and South Korea, while running increasing trade surplus with the U.S. and EU.

Trade imbalances among China and its main trade partners can be considered as an outcome of inter-industry and intra-industry trade based on their dynamic comparative advantage. Global specialization and economic integration among the U.S., China, and Japan (as well as South Korea and developing Asia) contributes more to economic imbalance between China and the U.S. than the relative value of their currency. In the long run, the division of labor and comparative advantage is going to rule the world economy, making the U.S. trade deficit sustainable, even if not with China, but with developing Asia economies.

China's external imbalance will not be corrected by exchange rate adjustment, unless their comparative advantage itself has changed. As compared to currency appreciation, wage increases are more effective not only in rebalancing China's external imbalance but also in reversing the downward trend of household consumption share.

REFERENCES

Akamatsu, K. 1962. "A Historical Pattern of Economic Growth in Developing Countries." *Journal of Developing Economies* 1(1): 3–25.

Akyüz, Y. 2010. "Global Economic Prospects: The Recession May Be Over but Where Next?", Research Paper 26, South Centre Research Papers. Accessed Feb. 12, 2012 from http://www.iadb.org/intal/intalcdi/PE/2010/05046.pdf.

Blanchard, O.J., and G.M. Milesi-Ferritti. 2009. "Global Imbalances: In Midstream?"
IMF Staff Position Note, December 22, 2009. Accessed Feb. 12, 2012 from http://www.imf.org/external/pubs/ft/spn/2009/spn0929.pdf.
CEIC Data: CEIC Data Company Ltd. The website is http://www.ceicdata.com/.
Caballero, R., E. Farhi, and P. Gourinchas. 2008. "An Equilibrium Model of 'Global Imbalances' and Low Interest Rates." *American Economic Review* 98(March): 358–393.
Cooper, R.N. 2007. "Living with Global Imbalances." Brookings Papers on Economic Activity 2: 91–110. Accessed Feb. 12, 2012 from http://scholar.harvard.edu/rcooper/publications/living-global-imbalances. .
Das, D.K. 2008. "Winners of Globalization." CSGR Working Paper 49/08(August). Accessed Feb. 12, 2012 from http://www2.warwick.ac.uk/fac/soc/csgr/research/workingpapers/2008/24908.pdf. .
Deng, Z., H. Guo, and Y. Zheng. 2007. "How East Asian Industry Transfer Affects the U.S.-China Trade Imbalance: Economic Mechanisms and Policy Implications." *Issues & Studies* 43(3): 165–197. Accessed Feb. 12, 2012 from http://iir.nccu.edu.tw/attachments/journal/add/4/43–3-165–197.pdf.
Falvey, R.E. 1981. "Commercial Policy and Intra-industry Trade." *Journal of International Economics* 11: 495–511.
Frankel, J.A. 2006. "Twin deficits and twin decades." In *The Macroeconomics of Fiscal Policy*, edited by R. Kopcke, G.M.B. Tootell, and R.K. Triest, 321–336. Cambridge: MIT Press.
Gong, M., and W. Li. 2008. "China's Role as a Bridge to Expand the Regional Trade." Working Paper No. 41, the Centre for International Governance Innovation, Canada.
Greaney, T.M., and Y. Li. 2009. "Assessing Foreign Direct Investment Relationships between China, Japan, and the United States." *Journal of Asian Economics* 20(6): 611–625.
Ikenson, D.J. 2010. "China Trade and America Jobs." The Wall Street Journal, April 2. Accessed Feb. 12, 2012 from http://online.wsj.com/article/SB10001424052702304739104575153473028804234.html.
Jones, R., and H. Kierzkowski. 2001. "A Framework for Fragmentation." In *Fragmentation: New Production Patterns in the World Economy*, edited by S. Arndt and H. Kierzkowski, 17–34. New York: Oxford University Press.
Koopman, R., Z. Wang, and S. Wei. 2008. "How Much of Chinese Exports is Really Made in China? Assessing Domestic Value-Added When Processing Trade is Pervasive." NBER Working Paper 14109. Accessed Feb. 12, 2012 from www.nber.org/papers/w14109.
Krugman, P. 2010a. "Chinese New Year." *The New York Times*, January 1. Accessed Feb. 12, 2012 from www.nytimes.com/2010/01/01/opinion/01krugman.html.
Krugman, P. 2010b. "Taking on China." *The New York Times*, March 14. Accessed Feb. 12, 2012 from www.nytimes.com/2010/03/15/opinion/15krugman.html.
Kwan, C.H. 2002. "The Rise of China and Asia's Flying-Geese Pattern of Economic Development: An Empirical Analysis Based on U.S. Import Statistics." RIETI Discussion Paper Series 02-E-009. Accessed Feb. 12, 2012 from http://www.rieti.go.jp/jp/publications/dp/02e009.pdf .
Ljungwall, C., and O. Sjoberg. 2007. "The Economic Impact of Globalization in Asia-Pacific: The Case of Flying Geese." China Center for Economic Research, Peking University, Beijing, Research Paper No. E2005007.
Mendoza, E.G., V. Quadrini, and J. Rios-Rull. 2007. "Financial Integration, Financial Deepness, and Global Imbalances." NBER Working Paper 12909. Accessed Feb. 12, 2012 from http://www.nber.org/papers/w12909.

UNCTAD Handbook of Statistics: United Nations Conference on Trade and Development, 2009. Data is available from UNCTAD's website: http://unctadstat.unctad.org/ReportFolders/reportFolders.aspx

Xu, M., and S. Wang. 2008. "The Empirical Analysis of Sino-U.S. Trade Imbalance under the View of Industry Transference." Paper presented at the Asia-Pacific Economic Association Conference, Central University of Finance and Economics Beijing, China, December 13–14.

Zhang, K.H. 2005. "Why Does So Much FDI from Hong Kong and Taiwan Go to Mainland China?" *China Economic Review* 16(3): 293–307.

9 Whither Democracy?

South Korea under Globalization Revisited[1]

Hyun-Chin Lim and Jin-Ho Jang

INTRODUCTION

Are new democracies stable and viable? Freedom House finds that there have recently been signs that an erosion of new democracies is getting underway. By historical standards, the overall state of freedom in the world has clearly improved over the last two decades. However, we can see a continued erosion of freedom in terms of political rights and civil liberties worldwide, with setbacks in Latin America, Africa, the former Soviet Union, and the Middle East. In particular, 2009 marks a fourth continuous year of deterioration in the area of freedom; declines of political rights and civil liberties were registered in 40 countries, representing 20 percent of the world's polities (Freedom House 2010). This is close to what Larry Diamond (2008) has labeled "democratic recession."

South Korea's democratization has been known to be a rare success case in the postwar Third World context, since it has not been challenged by military coups or dictatorial anti-constitutionalism after the country's 1987 democratic transition. Based on the government system of a single five-year presidency, there have been five presidential elections since 1987. In 1987, Roh Tae-Woo won the presidential election in the wake of feuds among pro-democracy movement leaders, such as Kim Dae-Jung and Kim Young-Sam. In 1992, Kim Young-Sam, a candidate who allied with Roh Tae-Woo's ruling party, was elected as president after about 30 years of rule by three presidents with military backgrounds since the 1961 coup, while early two presidents in the country between the years of 1948 and 1961 had had civilian backgrounds. In 1997, the oppositional political party won the presidential election, making Kim Dae-Jung president. In 2002, Roh Moo-Hyun, who had been a labor-rights lawyer in the 1980s, was unexpectedly elected as president, and the younger generation of politicians (so-called "386 generation politicians") who were associated with Roh and experienced student activism in the 1980s entered the power elite circle collectively. In 2007, the conservative party ("Grand National Party" [GNP]) became the ruling party again in 10 years after it had lost power in 1997 and Lee Myung-Bak, a candidate of GNP, became president in February

2008. According to Huntington's (1991) standard of formally measuring democracy, this peaceful second-time ruling-party shift by free and regular elections makes sufficient case for South Korea to have entered democratic consolidation following Greece, Spain, and Portugal.

According to *World Freedom Report 2009*, South Korea still maintains the score of 1 in terms of political rights and the score of 2 in terms of civil liberties. It was during the Kim Young-Sam government that South Korea first received the score of 2 both in political rights and civil liberties; during the Roh Moo-Hyun government, its political rights improved from 2 to 1 while civil liberties remained at 2.[2]

It is tempting to ask how the incumbent Lee Myung-Bak government's democratic performance will be assessed in the near future. People in the country have expected that South Korea is on its way of reaching its freedom score of 1 not only in political rights but also in civil liberties. Contrary to such expectations, however, there are worries that democracy is in decline under the Lee Myung-Bak government. It can be argued that South Korea has achieved democratic consolidation after the transition in 1987 from authoritarianism of the past decades. It can be questioned whether what South Korea enjoys at present is "electoral democracy" rather than "liberal democracy." Even though the country has open, transparent, inclusive, and competitive elections, it fails to uphold political rights and civil liberties on a full scale (Schedler 2001). The president often alienates the parliament in that party politics halts to function as the central organ of representing diverse public interests. The rule of law is sometimes evaded in the name of social stability. There are still the outbreaks of political scandal and corruption, the decline of trust in political institutions, and restrictions on the freedom of expression and association and so on.

In addition to the formal aspects of democracy in South Korea, concerned scholars of the topic have paid close attention to its mode of transition in terms of dynamics between internal and external factors: above all, democratization has been driven and achieved mainly by people's struggles against authoritarian regimes (Abelmann 1996). While Huntington (1991) emphasized the significance of globally diffusive forces toward democratization during the postwar period by using such a generalizing term as the "Third Wave," it has been noted that the explanation is not applicable to the South Korean case with no reservation (S. Kim 2001). South Korea's democratization has not been generated decisively from the outside in ready-made form. Rather, the political transition can be considered to have been achieved by people's struggles and movements resisting and overcoming such obstacles as (both civilian and military) authoritarian rule and repression which sometimes demanded people's lives (Koo 2001).

By the way, the current situation of democracy in the country has been facing another challenge. The challenge comes in large part from globalization. The term "globalization" implies many things (Nederveen Pieterse 2003, 2004). Here, the concept is used mostly to mean "economic" globalization.[3] The global economic integration has placed increasing pressures on domestic political processes. Above all, the increase of business influence and market power in a national government's policymaking and implementation has been closely linked to the globalization effects. In South Korea, the growth of *chaebols* and their power in domestic affairs in the recent decades represents such globalization effects.[4] Their growth has capitalized on the global market, and their resources now can be utilized to significantly influence domestic political processes and policy outcomes as they prefer. On the other hand, not only domestic big business groups such as *chaebols* but also global market forces such as transnational investors give a serious challenge to the stability and deepening of democracy by influencing policymaking and restructuring people's social and economic conditions (Robinson 2004; Soederberg 2005; Teivainen 2002). For example, the 1997 financial crisis and economic reforms have restructured society as well as the economy in the country. Since 1997, civilian governments which were democratically elected and supported even by politically progressive citizens have had to meet global standards as the norms and rules of governance. Such "globalization-generated" domestic reforms have largely liberalized domestic markets and radically reduced government regulations in the economy, resulting in the increase of socio-economic insecurity and the continuing gap between the "haves" and the "have-nots." The effects of economic globalization on democracy in Korea thus need to be examined and explained across the boundaries between politics and the economy.

One of the co-authors of this chapter has already examined the impacts of globalization on democracy in South Korea (Lim 2008). The main argument was that South Korea has a long way to go before the country can enjoy a high quality and empowered democracy. Keeping the main argument in mind, several issues will be addressed in this chapter. First, the nature of the historical transition to democracy in 1987 is discussed. If the Korean case is not that of the "Third Wave" transition, what was a decisive force in the transition process? Then, what were the achievements and limitations of the democratic transition? Second, the dilemma between the rapid growth of business influence and democracy is discussed. Third, the dilemma between the globalized economy and democratic politics will be examined regarding the topic of the financial crisis and the subsequent economic reforms. Finally, the implications of ongoing neoliberal reforms on the future prospect of democracy will be discussed in terms of socio-economic disparities.

EARLY HISTORICAL PHASES AND DEMOCRATIC TRANSITION IN 1987

Regarding the aspect of democratic struggles in South Korea, the pre-1987 period can be divided into three phases. The first phase is between 1948 and 1960. This period can be characterized by contradictions between "liberal political values" formalized by new political actors, which emerged immediately after Korea's 1945 liberation on the one hand and the "authoritarian legacies of real politics" inherited from pre-modern and colonial times on the other. When the presidential election in March 1960 turned out to be manipulated by the government, then-president Syngman Rhee had to resign under the pressure of students' and citizens' demonstrations, the decisive one of which occurred on April 19, 1960 ("April 19 Revolution").

The second phase is between 1961 and 1979. When the military junta led by Park Chung-Hee made a coup on May 16, 1961, they took power from the then-civilian government which had been democratically established after Syngman Rhee's fall in 1960. Park's military government lasted until his death in October 1979. During this period, anti-communist authoritarianism ruled widely in society, reaching its peak in the "Yushin (restoration) Regime" from 1972 through 1979. On the other hand, the political authoritarianism was combined by strong economic developmentalism, which established not only modern heavy industries and business, but also capitalist class structuration in South Korea (Amsden 1989; Chang 2003; E. M. Kim 1997). During the entire period of this phase, Park Chung-Hee's rule had been challenged by students, church, and workers. These three actors together pursued the liberalization of the political order, such as restoring the civilian rule of government and free and direct presidential election, which had been eliminated under the "Yushin Regime" (S. Kim 2001). From the early 1970s, workers had been organized into labor unions with support from church activists and students (Koo 2001). Key oppositional politicians, such as Kim Dae-Jung and Kim Young-Sam, whose political activities were oppressed by Park's military government in the late 1970s, worked together to open the liberal political space against such government oppressions during this period.

The third phase is between 1980 and 1987, when the "new" military junta took power by making a mini-coup in December 1979 after the assassination of Park Chung-Hee in October of the same year. Chun Doo-Hwan who led the mini-coup in late 1979 became president in March 1981 after a constitutional revision. A short moment of political liberalization in early 1980, which was called the "Spring in Seoul," was soon closed by the new military. Against this new military junta's attempt to take power and impose political oppression in society, there was an uprising by students and citizens in the city of Kwangju[5] in May 1980 ("Kwangju Uprising"), which is located in the southwestern area of the Korean peninsula and was also Kim Dae-Jung's political home. The military suppressed the uprising by violently killing people, and the blood-shedding incident in Kwangju of 1980 became a critical turning moment for radicalizing college students as well as political activists in South Korea, resulting in the strong democratization movement of the 1980s.

Under the shadow of the "Kwangju Uprising" which was harshly suppressed by the new military junta, students' political activism became massive and radicalized in the 1980s compared with that of the 1970s. In June 1987, there were massive demonstrations by students and citizens demanding a constitutional revision for the open presidential election ("June Uprising"), while then-president Chun Doo-Hwan wanted to extend his rule by maintaining the status quo. Millions of people gathered on the streets in Seoul shouting "Dictatorship Out!" In the 1980s, many college students voluntarily dropped out of school and became labor activists by entering factories while concealing their identities as former college students (Oh 2010). "Solidarity between workers and students" became their motto, and this movement contributed to the eruptions of massive labor strikes by organized workers in July and August 1987 ("July and August Great Struggles") leading to a rapid increase in the number of labor unions.

Chun's new military government surrendered to people's massive demonstrations in June 1987 and finally accepted the constitutional revision that would restore the free and regular presidential election in December 1987, the previous one of which was held in 1971. Thus, the year 1987 became the year of Korea's democratic transition. This transition was, however, made possible not only by the students' and citizens' demonstrations on the streets but also by the compromise among key political figures who were mostly conservative or liberal and would later become the candidates of their own political parties in the 1987 presidential election. There were discussions in Korean academic circles on the "1987 Regime" indicating the fact that the establishment of formal democracy in 1987 has had both positive and negative sides (J.-Y. Kim 2009). The former impact comes from more open possibilities for democratic development as seen in the "June Uprising" and the rise of political activism during the 1980s, while the latter side comes from the nature of the transition as a conservative compromise among top-level politicians, excluding or postponing the institutionalization of class-based party politics.[6]

In spite of the limitations of the "1987 Regime," workers' power grew in large part until the late 1980s. This political development reflected the fact that big business in Korea, which had hired an increasing number of male workers in heavy industry sectors for producing exports since the 1970s, was unable to prevent those workers from unionizing and demanding higher wages and better working conditions as the number of democratic labor unions exploded in the late 1980s. Over the previous decades, the export-oriented industrialization of domestic big businesses in heavy industries produced an increasing number of male workers. The working-class formation combined with their unionization and labor activism during the 1980s contributed to higher wages and better working conditions for a wider range of workers in Korea.

CHAEBOL GROWTH, GLOBALIZATION, AND THE "1997 REGIME"

Even though the free and regular presidential election was restored in 1987, Roh Tae-Woo, another former military man and key player in the 1979 mini-coup, was elected as president in the 1987 election, and the new military junta's conservative political party became again the ruling party in 1988. Even in 1990, the conservative ruling party incorporated two other conservative parties ("Three Party Merger"), one of which was the party led by Kim Young-Sam, a long time oppositional leader. This is called the Korean case of "Trasformismo (Transformism)" by some political scientists (Choi 2002, 110). This political merger of three parties (the grand conservative alliance) again showed the limitations of the "1987 Regime" as a conservative compromise. After becoming the ruling party's candidate, Kim Young-Sam won the 1992 presidential election, while Kim Dae-Jung lost it again as an oppositional leader with his own political party.

By the way, in the 1992 presidential election, another significant presidential candidate, namely, Chung Ju-Young, then chairman of the Hyundai *chaebol*, unexpectedly appeared by creating his own nationwide political party. This phenomenon symbolized the growth of *chaebol* power in the country, because for the first time a well-known businessman and *chaebol*-owner, who had had little political career in the past, became a presidential candidate challenging long-time political leaders both in ruling and oppositional parties. The growth of *chaebols* with their business being globalized and expanded might have encouraged the Hyundai owner to pursue another career in politics. Military regimes had been able to discipline *chaebols* until the 1980s, but from the 1990s, the *chaebols* began even to challenge political leaders as seen in the case of Chung Ju-Young's failed attempt to become president. After Kim Young-Sam's victory in the 1992 presidential election, Chung who was afraid of receiving political and financial backlash from the new government dissociated his short-lived political party.

During Kim Young-Sam's presidency from February 1993 through February 1998, the notion of "globalization" was popularized in Korea in the form of its domestically translated term "*segyehwa*." Globalization was then considered mainly as a national development strategy by the Kim Young-Sam government which was the first civilian government in the country since the early 1960s military coup. After coming into power, Kim Young-Sam suggested the idea of building a "New Korea" to eliminate the supposed legacies of the past authoritarian rule. No wonder his globalization (i.e., *segyehwa*) drive was the product of this "New Korea" policy. For him, *segyehwa* signified a new vision for the country's bright future.

The globalization drive during his presidency developed through a two-stage conceptualization: first, *kukjehwa* (internationalization) in May 1994, and later, *segyehwa* in November 1994. Internationalization was defined by the then foreign minister as "an inevitable process which every nation must undergo to ensure sustained stability and prosperity" by "trying to induce foreign investment, liberalizing its financial market and preparing to join the OECD" (Gills and Gills 2000, 36–37). Yet, *segyehwa* as a national development policy "entails rationalizing all aspects of life" and "reforms in every area." The concept meant "a sweeping transformation of society" requiring "productivity and flexibility" (Gills and Gills 2000, 38). *Segyehwa* was publicized as a necessity for the country to prosper.

In his *segyehwa* drive, Kim Young-Sam launched a series of reforms in almost every area, including the fields of military, politics, economy, finance, labor, education, law, and welfare. He might have thought that *segyehwa* was a panacea to cure irregularities inherited from the past. Without clearly recognizing potential risks inherent in globalization, Kim Young-Sam approached and accepted it mainly as a national development strategy. In fact, his *segyehwa* drive reflected both hasty financial liberalization and the globalization of production by Korean *chaebols* in the early and mid-1990s (E.M. Kim 2000; Shin and Chang 2003). Such financial liberalization was the outcome of the Kim Young-Sam government's attempt to seek South Korea's OECD membership, which went together with the bilateral U.S.-Korea Financial Policy Discussion Talks in the early and mid-1990s, making the blueprint for the schedule of financial liberalization and market opening in the country (Sakong 1993, 182, 200; Kwon 2004, 82–84). In addition, regarding the background of Korea's globalization drive in the 1990s, some studies draw attention to the creation of the World Trade Organization in 1995 after closing the 10-year long Uruguay Round talks (Moon 2000, 127). Due to the result of the talks, the Kim Young-Sam government had to accept a large-scale market opening for agricultural products, reversing its previous promise to South Korean farmers, which was made during the 1992 presidential campaigns. *Segyehwa* was used as a justification for this reversal of the promise.

The Kim Young-Sam government pushed financial liberalization and capital-market opening along with a series of deregulation for international capital flows. Without emplacing sufficient safeguards for the economy, however, the *segyehwa* drive paved the way for the financial crisis in the region-wide contagion of 1997. At the end of his presidency, thus, the Kim Young-Sam government had to ask for an emergency bail-out from the International Monetary Fund (IMF) against national default in the wake of plummeting currency value and the rapid exhaustion of dollar reserves, in part, exacerbated by the exit of invested global capital. The financial bail-out was accompanied by conditionality programs which included the shut-down of insolvent financial institutions; the termination of bank loans to financially distressed firms; the furthering of trade and capital-account liberalization; the establishment of the flexible labor-market, privatization, and improvement in transparency; and debt-to-equity ratios in the corporate sector. The IMF also demanded government budget-cuts, higher interest rates, and a reduced growth pattern. Such conditionalities and structural-reform programs had strong "neoliberal" characteristics, which have been criticized to have negative socio-economic outcomes due to their market fundamentalism (Bello 1994; Chossudovsky 1996).

When Kim Dae-Jung, a long-time oppositional party leader, was elected as president in December 1997, the country was on the brink of default with the shortage of foreign exchange reserves. The Kim Dae-Jung government from its inception had an urgent task of coping with the crisis situation. The root characteristics of the so-called "1997 Regime" have been defined in Korean academic circles, and according to political sociologist Hee-Yean Cho (2009, 80), the "1997 Regime" was conditioned by two events. One was the ruling-party change from the conservative party to the democratic one that had been previously oppositional. The other factor was the financial crisis. As a sub-regime of the "1987 Regime," therefore, the "1997 Regime" was open to two possibilities. One was to expand democratic potentials, and the other was to be overwhelmed by neoliberal reforms and negative socio-economic outcomes. It is often said that the "1997 Regime" lasted until 2007 by the winning in the 2002 presidential election of Roh Moo-Hyun, who had started his political career as a labor-rights lawyer and had become the candidate of Kim Dae-Jung's ruling-party. Roh Moo-Hyun was expected by supporters to realize increasingly democratic ideals, while his policy options were as seriously limited by conditions of globalized market forces in the domestic economy as those of his recent predecessors had been.

Kim Dae-Jung's solution to the crisis was to follow with little reservation neoliberal reforms demanded by the IMF as the rescue conditionalities, retreating from his earlier stance of being critical of them. The free-market reforms proceeded under the slogan of the "Parallel Development of Democracy and Market Economy."[7] It is not clear, however, how the post-crisis administration conceived it could deal with inherent conflicts and tensions between "democratic ideals" like participation or equality on the one hand and "market rationales" like competition or efficiency on the other. There is an analysis indicating that Kim Dae-Jung's early vision of the "mass participatory economy" with a social-democratic tone was transformed into the neoliberal version of "DJ-nomics" in 1998, and that many of the problems in the post-1997 restructuring can be found in such a change (Lee 2001). The Kim Dae-Jung administration-related scholars would note that "DJ-nomics" was German social market-styled "order liberalism" or a Third Way vision rather than neoliberalism because of its welfarist elements. Retrospectively, it cannot be denied that the real outcomes of "DJ-nomics" were not so much different from those of neoliberalism. The Kim Dae-Jung government began as a democratic and crisis-management government, and the administration attempted to complete structural adjustments in a short period, even with the goal of achieving "growth" and "distribution" simultaneously. Regardless of the goal of the government, however, the IMF's conditionalities attached to its financial rescue in large part determined the ways of implementing structural adjustments in the domestic economy. Not only such conditionalities, but also the preferences of globally mobile capital which entered the South Korean market soon after the crisis, significantly limited the Kim Dae-Jung government's autonomy regarding the making and implementation of socio-economic policies. In the end, the democratic government was unable to meet the expectations of its progressive and grass-root supporters, due to both the conditional limitations and its own neoliberal policies.

LIBERAL DEMOCRACY ON TRIAL

When Roh Moo-Hyun was elected as president in December 2002, his supporters hoped and expected the further development of democracy for people, who had suffered from negative socio-economic outcomes resulting from the neoliberal reforms in Korean society since the 1997 financial crisis. Supporters' expectations of candidate Roh Moo-Hyun in the 2002 presidential election were based on an array of complex factors regarding him: his political career as a non-conformist, as well as his commoner background and his populist posture during the election campaign. He unexpectedly won the election against the candidate from the then conservative and influential opposition party ("Grand National Party"), and the conservative candidate had been prime minister during the Kim Young-Sam presidency. Roh Moo-Hyun's centrist liberal political position was contrasted with the conservative position of the candidate from the GNP which had its roots in the "Three Party Merger" of 1990 and was considered to be responsible for the 1997 crisis. Above all, the young voters largely supported Roh, and the 2002 election was also interestingly and decisively influenced by information and telecommunication technologies, the development of which the previous Kim Dae-Jung government had strongly emphasized and promoted; near the election day, many young voters sent e-mails, messenger and mobile-phone messages to one another to encourage their voting in support of Roh.

The Roh Moo-Hyun government (February 2003–February 2008) was characterized by its liberal ruling style, which was quite apart from the ruling styles of the authoritarian predecessors. The massive participation by the younger generation of politicians (so-called "386 generation") in the power-elite circle of the government and the ruling party also contributed to such a marked political style. Many of these "386 generation" politicians were former student activists who had participated in the pro-democracy movements against military rule, and some of them had been imprisoned for that reason during the 1980s when the new military junta was in a ruling position. The democratic expectations held by supporters of the Roh government came not only from Roh Moo-Hyun's down to earth and commoner characteristics as discussed earlier but also from the rise of such a younger/ new political power group. Now the Roh government had to develop and deepen democratic goals and realize them, the key element of which was to lessen negative socio-economic outcomes resulting from both neoliberal reforms and deeper global integration of the domestic market. Labor insecurity, class polarization, increasing poverty, and the high unemployment rate of young people were among those negative outcomes. Improvement in social welfare and re-orientation in economic policies (and thus lessening the poverty level and reducing socio-economic gaps in terms of incomes, assets, and opportunities) could be a critical way to meet the democratic expectation and goal. However, the government also had to satisfy the goal of economic growth expected by the people who had considered that a high growth would produce more jobs, higher incomes, and better lives. The two expectations had to be satisfied harmoniously, but the desired goal might have been a mission impossible due to the complicated formation of power relations and dynamics during the Roh Moo-Hyun presidency, which did not prefer the first option.

Above all, a small number of domestic big businesses increased their market and profit shares and thus developed monopoly in the economic area on the one hand, and they also increased their influence on politics and policymaking on the other. Above all, the Samsung group overwhelmed even other big businesses in terms of the increase of market share and political influence in Korean society (Hyun-Yean Cho 2009). The term "Samsung Republic" was used by many commentators of the country's economy to criticize such a situation (Table 9.1). In addition, the global integration of the domestic capital market went on to deepen itself. In 2004, the market share of foreign investors in the Korean stock exchange reached about 40 percent in terms of market capitalization, and global investors' signals to the domestic economy became more important than ever (Table 9.2). It was not only the case that the policy autonomy of domestic policymakers was constrained by them but also the case that by publically making convenient excuses for the emergency and inevitability of meeting the demands of the global investors, high-ranking public officials in economic ministries and bureaucracies became more powerful than those in welfare and other offices, in essence ruling over the overall socio-economic policymaking and implementation in the neoliberal direction.[8]

Table 9.1 Share of the Samsung Chaebol among the Top Five Chaebols (%)

	1987	*1990*	*1995*	*1996*	*1997*	*1998*	*1999*	*2000*	*2001*	*2002*
Assets	19.5	21.5	24.6	24.3	23.7	19.9	23.6	25.7	28.8	30.4
Sales	26.0	28.3	26.0	23.9	23.6	23.0	28.7	30.9	33.8	35.4
Value added	23.0	27.8	30.1	23.6	23.2	27.2	27.1	43.9	35.0	38.0

Note: From Hyun-Yeon Cho (2009, 129).

Table 9.2 Share of Foreign Investors in Korean Stock Markets (%)

	1998	*1999*	*2000*	*2001*	*2002*	*2003*	*2004*	*2005*	*2006*	*2007*	*2008*
Market capitalization	18.6	18.5	27.0	32.2	32.8	37.7	40.1	37.2	35.2	30.9	27.3

Note: From Korea Exchange, accessed from http://www.krx.co.kr.

Some of the new political power group including the "386 generation" politicians were also lobbied and strongly influenced by big businesses, global investors, and local economic technocrats. And their past career of pro-democracy activism and the expectation of democratic development from supporters were severely compromised, reaching the peak in the Roh Moo-Hyun government's promotion of the U.S.-Korea Free Trade Treaty in 2006, which was opposed even by many key supporters of Roh Moo-Hyun. The treaty meant the deeper global integration of the domestic economy, and more uncertainties and potential risks among already fragile and unprivileged socio-economic groups were included in the realization of the free trade agreement (FTA) treaty, while even the process of the treaty talks was neither democratic nor transparent. Many of Roh Moo Hyun's key supporters gave up further expectations of democratic development in front of the government's stubborn and illiberal posture regarding the FTA issues. Thus, between the two possibilities in the "1997 Regime" as discussed earlier, the negative and neoliberal possibility was more realized than the positive and democratic possibility until the 2007 election, and the socio-economic gaps and insecurities among people increased during the Roh Moo-Hyun period. It can be said that while the different or even opposing possibilities in the "1997 Regime" were open to domestic actors' choices and decisions for realization, the formation of the "neoliberal power bloc or alliance" including big business, global investors, economic technocrats, and key politicians led to the asymmetrical realization of the negative possibility in terms of socio-economic outcomes (Hyun-Yeon Cho 2009; Lim and Jang 2006).

Former supporters of the centrist liberal Roh government were angry because of the betrayal they felt when the U.S.-Korea FTA talks were being made in an undemocratic way, while many people were disappointed by such negative socio-economic outcomes as the increase of employment insecurities, wealth gaps, and relative poverty among people during the period. The sentiment of socio-economic deprivation among the low- and middle-income people without housing-ownership also increased due to the sky-rocketing real-estate prices during the Roh Moo-Hyun period. The conservative opposition party criticized Roh for the economic distresses, while ironically its own policy orientation was rather and even more neoliberal. Anti-neoliberal and progressive socio-political forces had been much weakened not only by the crises in labor and other social movements since the 1997 financial crisis and ongoing structural adjustments, but also by the internal conflicts and ideological division of the Democratic Labor Party (DLP). The DLP was labor- and mass-based political party with a socialist/ social democratic orientation and had first-time elected Members of Parliament since 2004. All of these factors together contributed to the victory in the 2007 presidential election of Lee Myung-Bak, the candidate of the then oppositional conservative party (GNP).

CONCLUSION: TOWARD A NEW DEMOCRATIC ALLIANCE

The 2007 presidential election symbolized the perfection of the formal aspect of "electoral democracy" in South Korea by the winning of the then oppositional party which had lost the election in 1997 as the then ruling party. At the same time, however, it also meant the delay of "liberal democracy," without a "strong" democratic alliance accompanied by fully pledged political rights of civil liberties, since people chose rather a more neoliberal and conservative alternative as the ruling party and the president with a former CEO career in big business than a centrist liberal political party or other political alternatives in the context of increasing negative socio-economic outcomes resulting from neoliberal globalization of the domestic economy and society.

The new Lee Myung-Bak government faced a serious legitimacy crisis in 2008 when President Lee promised the lessening of the import standard in Korea of U.S. beef to then U.S. president G.W. Bush, without referring to domestic democratic procedures. This act led to a series of massive candle-light protest rallies on the streets of Seoul almost daily from early May through August 2008. This response was interpreted by participants in the demonstrations and progressive scholars as the "crisis of representative democracy," characterized by "Trasformismo" which lacked among others strong popular participation in party politics. Accordingly, this political payoff clearly demanded the necessity for direct action democracy and the re-activation of movement politics. After the crisis of 2008, the Lee Myung-Bak government seems to depend increasingly on coercive state measures to manage the country's affairs, which is seemingly reversing the democratic achievements made in the past two decades. It would be interesting to point out that the ruling Grand National Party's crushing defeat at the local election in June 2010 reveals popular dissatisfaction with the government's key policy initiatives, such as refurbishing the nation's four major rivers and transforming the city of Sejong into a non-administrative capital.[9]

There are four politico-economic paths based on the past Latin American experience of neoliberal reform: the first is "organic crisis" which is characterized by unleashing a tug of war among social classes and groups amid increasing sociopolitical tensions as a result of failed restructuring; the second is "fragmented and exclusionary democracy" that manifests the fragmentation of social classes and groups, and the exclusionary design of social and economic policies in order to achieve neoliberal reform; the third is "inclusionary democracy" that discloses the incorporation of social classes and groups in the process of policy design based on sociopolitical pacts; and the last is "double democracy" which is promoted by a dual logic of state power (respect for the allied minority and disarticulation of the rest) and the unequal distribution of resources (benefits are extended only to the allied sectors of business and organized labor; Acuna and Smith 1994, 41–49). From this observation, the Lee Myung-Bak government might have so far trod an exclusionary rather than an inclusionary democratic path. It is against this backdrop that some commentators speak of the reemergence of authoritarianism embedded in the past statist capitalist development.

In South Korea, globalization has worked as a force to form a neoliberal alliance to drive democratic governments to pursue neoliberal economic reforms resulting in negative socio-economic outcomes. This process has led to the crisis of liberal democracy when people chose the conservative party as an alternative in a situation where there is no workable party politics and institutionalized democratic alliance. "Direct action democracy" represented by the candlelight protest rallies in Seoul of 2008 also led to the blowbacks of authoritarianism by the conservative government. Democracy is not automatically determined to deepen itself after its initial transition and consolidation. South Korea's experience shows the complicated possibilities and difficulties of democratic progress in the process of globalization.

NOTES

1. This work was supported by the Dasan project through a grant provided by the Gwangju Institute of Science and Technology in 2010.
2. Political rights refer to the formation of party politics that represents a significant range of voter choice and political leaders being able to compete for and be elected to positions of power in government. Civil liberties point out the protection of religious, ethnic, economic, linguistic, and other rights, including gender and family rights, personal freedoms, and freedoms of the press, belief, and association. The rating is based on a 7-point scale for both political rights and civil liberties (1 representing the most free and 7 the least free) and then divides the world into three broad categories: free (countries whose ratings average 1.0 to 2.5), partly free (countries whose ratings average 3.0 to 5.0), and not free (countries whose ratings average 5.5 to 7.0; Freedom House 2010).
3. Current economic globalization has neoliberal characteristics, such as deregulation, marketization, financialization, the ideology of lean government, and so on. In this chapter, globalization means mainly such aspects of "neoliberal globalization" (Nederveen Pieterse 2004).
4. The "*chaebol*" is well known to be a family-owned and diversified big business group which originated in Korea and are currently doing business in global markets. They have prevailed in most of manufacturing sectors in South Korea since the beginning of the country's postwar industrialization. For example, Samsung, Hyundai, SK, LG, and Daewoo are well-known

chaebol groups, while some of them have been broken into several individual firms by corporate reforms since 1998 and even one of them, that is., Daewoo, as a group, went bankrupt in 1999.

5. The city name is currently re-romanized into "Gwangju."
6. Political scientist Jang-Jip Choi (2002) used Gramsci's term "passive revolution" in describing the fruits of such a democratic transition to be taken by conservative politicians.
7. "Productive welfare" was later added to it, which may be related to 'active labor market' in Scandinavian countries (Y. Kim 2003, 317). The program aimed at improving living standards by incorporating the unemployed into the labor market through re-education and re-skilling. Apart from the statement of intention, however, its real outcomes seem to have been rather limited.
8. Finnish social scientist Teivainen (2002) characterized politics of neoliberalism as "transnational politics of economism." Based on this insight, we can note that the rising significance of both the global and the economic in the domestic arena of politics and policy discourse in Korea since the mid-1990s has conditioned the domestic structure of political economy increasingly in the neoliberal direction. Whereas military authoritarianism had been the obviously visible enemy in the eyes of pro-democracy activists between the 1960s and the 1980s, current neoliberalism often maintains formal aspects of democracy while transforming democracy into just "polyarchy" or "low-intensive democracy," which makes the new enemy of democracy more or less invisible.
9. The ruling Grand National Party secured just 7 of the 16 mayoral and gubernatorial posts. The main opposition Democratic Party was close behind with 6. The independents got 3. There are possibilities of conflicts between the central government and the local governments, since the parliament is dominated by the ruling party and the local governments are occupied by opposition parties.

REFERENCES

Abelmann, Nancy. 1996. *Echoes of the Past, Epics of Dissent: A South Korean Social Movement*. Berkeley: University of California Press.

Acuna, Carlos H., and William C. Smith. 1994. "The Political Economy of Structural Adjustment: The Logic of Support and Opposition to Neoliberal Reform." In *Latin American Political Economy in the Age of Neoliberal Reform: Theoretical and Comparative Perspectives for the 1990s*, edited by William C. Smith, Carlos H. Acuna, and Eduardo A. Gamarra, 17–66. New Brunswick: Transaction Publishers.

Amsden, Alice. 1989. *Asia's Next Giant: South Korea and Late Industrialization*. London: Oxford University Press.

Bello, Walden. 1994. *Dark Victory: The United States, Structural Adjustment and Global Poverty*. London: Pluto Press.

Chang, Sea-Jin. 2003. *Financial Crisis and Transformation of Korean Business Groups: The Rise and Fall of Chaebols*. Cambridge: Cambridge University Press.

Cho, Hee-Yean. 2009. "87nyuncheje, 97nyuncheje-wa minjugaehyukundong-ui chonwhanjeok wigi [The '1987 Regime,' the '1997 Regime,' and the Transitional Crisis of Democratic Reform Movement]." In *87nyunchejeron* [Theories of the 1987 Regime], edited by Jong-Yeop Kim, 75–120. Seoul: Changbi.

Cho, Hyun-Yean. 2009. "Minjuwha segewha 'ihu' kyongjejeok dokjeom-gwa chaebol-ui sajeok ihae-ui jeongchijeok gwancheolgwajeong yeongu [A Study on

Economic Monopoly and Chaebols' Private Interests and Political Decision-Influencing Process 'after' Democratization and Globalization in Korea]." In *Hanguk minjuwha-wa sahoegyongjejeok bulpyongdeung-ui donghak* [The Dynamic Transformation of Socio-Economic Inequality in Korea's Democratization], edited by Hee-Yeon Cho, Dong-Choon Kim, and Yoo-Seok Oh, 119–162. Seoul: Hanul.

Choi, Jang-Jip. 2002. *Minjuhwa ihu-ui minjujuui: hanguk minjujuui-ui bosujeok kiwon-gwa wuigi* [Democracy after Democratization: The Conservative Origin and Crisis of Democracy in South Korea]. Seoul: Humanitas.

Chossudovsky, Michel. 1996. *The Globalization of Poverty: Impacts of IMF and World Bank Reforms*. London: Zed Books.

Diamond, Larry. 2008. *The Spirit of Democracy: The Struggle to Build Free Societies Throughout the World*. New York: Times Books.

Freedom House. 2010. *Freedom in the World 2010: Erosion of Freedom Intensifies*. New York: Freedom House.

Gills, Barry K., and Dongsook S. Gills. 2000. "Globalization and Strategic Choice in South Korea: Economic Reform and Labor." In *Korea's Globalization*, edited by Samuel S. Kim, 29–53. Cambridge: Cambridge University Press.

Huntington, Samuel P. 1991. *The Third Wave: Democratization in the Late Twentieth Century*. Norman: University of Oklahoma Press.

Kim, Eun Mee. 1997. *Big Business, Strong State: Collusion and Conflict in South Korean Development, 1960–1990*. Albany: State University of New York Press.

Kim, Eun Mee. 2000. "Globalization of the South Korean *Chaebol*" In *Korea's Globalization*, edited by Samuel S. Kim, 102–125. Cambridge: Cambridge University Press.

Kim, Jong-Yeop. 2009. "Bundan cheje-wa 1987nyun cheje [The Division Regime and the 1987 Regime]." In *87nyunchejeron* [Theories of the 1987 Regime], edited by Jong-Yeop Kim, 29–55. Seoul: Changbi.

Kim, Sunhyuk. 2001. *Politics of Democratization in Korea: the Role of Civil Society*. Pittsburgh: University of Pittsburgh Press.

Kim, Yun-tae. 2003. "Baljeonkukka-ui jeonhwan: 1980nyundae ihu hanguk kukka-ui byunhwa [The Transformation of the Developmental State: Changes in the Korean State since the 1980s]." In *Dongasia kyongjebyunhwan-gwa kukka-ui yeokhal jeonhwan* [The Changing Role of the State in Economic Development of East Asian NICs], edited by Dae-Hwan Kim and Hee-Yeon Cho, 303–326. Seoul: Hanul.

Koo, Hagen. 2001. *Korean Workers: The Culture and Politics of Class Formation*. Ithaca: Cornell University Press.

Korea Exchange. website. <http://www.krx.co.kr>.

Kwon, Eundak. 2004. "Financial Liberalization in South Korea." *Journal of Contemporary Asia* 34(1): 70–101.

Lee, Byung-Chun. 2001. "Jeonhwangi-ui hanguk kyongje-wa kim dae jung jeongbu-ui silheom [The Korean Economy in a Transition Period and Restructuring under the Kim Dae Jung Government]." In *Hanguk kyongje jaesaeng-ui kil-un itmunga* [Search for the Revitalizing Path of the Korean Economy], edited by Byung-Chun Lee and Won-Hee Cho, 11–68. Seoul: Dangdae.

Lim, Hyun-Chin. 2008. "Stumbling Democracy in South Korea: The Impacts of Globalization and Restructuring." In *Korea Confronts Globalization*, edited by Yunshik Chang, Hyun-ho Seok, and Donald Baker, 139–166 . Oxford: Routledge.

Lim, Hyun-Chin, and Jin-Ho Jang. 2006. "Neoliberalism in Post-Crisis South Korea: Its Conditions and Outcomes." *Journal of Contemporary Asia* 36(4): 442–463.

Moon, Seungsook. 2000. "Overcome by Globalization: The Rise of a Women Policy in South Korea." In *Korea's Globalization*, edited by Samuel S. Kim, 126–146. Cambridge: Cambridge University Press.

Nederveen Pieterse, Jan. 2003. *Globalization and Culture: Global Mélange*. Lanham: Rowman and Littlefield.
Nederveen Pieterse, Jan. 2004. *Globalization or Empire*. New York: Routledge.
Oh, Ha-Na, 2010. *Hakchul: 80nyundae, kongjanguro gan daehaksaengdul* [From College Backgrounds: Students Who Went to Factories in the 1980s]. Seoul: Imagine.
Robinson, William I. 2004. *A Theory of Global Capitalism: Production, Class, and State in a Transnational World*. Baltimore: The Johns Hopkins University Press.
Sakong, Il. 1993. *Korea in the World Economy*. Washington, DC: Institute for International Economics.
Schedler, Andra. 2001. "What Is Democratic Consolidation?" In *The Global Divergence of Democracies*, edited by Larry Diamond and Marc F. Plattner, 149–164. Baltimore: Johns Hopkins University Press.
Shin, Jang-Sup and Ha-Joon Chang. 2003. *Restructuring Korea Inc.* London: RoutledgeCurzon.
Soederberg, Suzanne. 2005. *The Politics of the New International Financial Architecture: Reimposing Neoliberal Domination in the Global South*. London: Zed.
Teivainen, Teivo. 2002. *Enter Economism, Exit Politics: Experts, Economic Policy and the Damage to Democracy*. London: Zed.

10 Democratic Deepening in South Korea and South Africa in an Age of Global Rebalancing

The Potential Role of Civil Society in the Era of Internet

Wiebe Nauta

INTRODUCTION

Our world is fundamentally changing as we are witnessing "a major tipping point in history. North-South relations have been dominant for some 200 years and current trends see the onset of an East-South turn" (Nederveen Pieterse 2011, 26). Globally, regionally, nationally, and even locally the impact of emerging countries is felt in economic, political, social, and also cultural terms. This current reconfiguration of the world order is leading to major shifts in power—a global "rebalancing," although the term is contested—and gives rise to huge challenges and opportunities—"emancipatory potential" (ibid., 22)—for all actors concerned in the North, the South, and the East. In this chapter the focus is on South Korea and South Africa, two emerging nations that share some striking similarities in their relatively recent transition from autocracy to democracy in a period of intensified globalization. Thereby, I am particularly interested in their recent trajectories of democratic deepening and the role of civil society therein. This comparison is particularly valuable since striking similarities in the mid- and late 1990s have given way to clear differences impacted by levels of and accessibility to information technology. Therefore, the question at hand is whether in this context an East-South turn, chiefly in an inspirational sense—another type of Korean Wave[1]—could benefit processes of democratic deepening in South Africa.

Democratic Deepening

When broadly examining the existence of basic democratic institutions—executive branch, legislative branch, independent judiciary, and the necessary institutions like free and fair elections—in South Korea and South Africa, one can only conclude that democracy is firmly entrenched in both countries. However, as Heller contends: "a high degree of consolidated representative democracy . . . should as such not be confused with a high degree of effective citizenship" (Heller 2009, 125) because "democratic deepening requires striking a balance between the aggregative logic of political society and the deliberative logic of civil society" (124). In order to understand Heller's argument we should particularly avoid the more "neoliberal" understanding of civil society, actively promoted by the International Financial Institutions (IFIs) and mainstream development policy circles, whereby civil society is equated with non-governmental organizations (NGOs). According to Chandhoke "the post-Washington consensus . . . views protest and struggle, which happen to be an integral part of civil society, as problems that have to be resolved through managerial techniques" (2006, 45). Kaldor's definition is more valuable: "civil society . . . is the process through which individuals negotiate, argue, struggle against or agree with each other and with the centres of political and economic authority. Through voluntary associations, movements, parties, unions, the individual is able to act publicly" (2003, 585). It is precisely this more political Habermasian interpretation of civil society—civil society's role in the public sphere—that is usually ignored by mainstream development actors.

When using the term democratic deepening I follow the definition by Heller (2009, 124) who argues that there should be "evidence of an increased capacity of subordinate groups to have an effective role in shaping public policy. More specifically, both the depth of social actors who enjoy effective political power and the scope of issues over which democratic power extends have . . . expanded." Hereby Heller points to the need of closing this gap between formal legal rights in the civil and political arena and the actual capability (see Sen 1999) of the population to meaningfully participate.

Yet, if we take into account a definition of civil society that includes the public sphere, we have to be aware of the contested nature of such terms in developing country and/or post-colonial settings as for example Mamdani (1996) has shown. Kaarsholm (2009, 412) warns us that "the idea of a commonly shared 'public sphere'" may cover up "an unevenness of access to representation, the monopolisation of the realm of the 'public' by elites, or its subsumption under the rule of consumerism and commercialization." Therefore we need to examine the origin, development, and role "actually existing civil society" (Heller 2009, 125) in South Africa and South Korea to assess recent processes of democratic deepening.

Broadly Comparing South Korea and South Africa

In general one could argue that South Korea and South Africa, although on different continents and with very different historical trajectories, also share striking similarities, particularly when focusing on the democratic transition of the last three decades in a period of intensified globalization. Yet, before comparing the periodization of this transition, let us first examine some of the basic social and economic indicators, where some interesting similarities and differences are also encountered.

First, both countries have a population of around 48 million, although of course South Africa is more than 10 times larger than South Korea. However, the South African population is growing much more rapidly over the last decades, which will have serious repercussions in terms of distributing the fruits of economic performance. The two countries had roughly similar gross domestic products in the 1980s while South Korea's population was then still almost one and a half times larger. By 2007, with roughly equal populations, the "South Korean miracle" had resulted in a gross domestic product of almost four times that of South Africa (see Table 10.1).

Since welfare gains are distributed much more equally in South Korea than in post-Apartheid South Africa—still socially and economically divided along ethnic lines—the average Korean is much better off, which is also reflected in the Human Development Index (HDI) trends. While the HDI of South Korea was only marginally higher than that of South Africa[2] in the 1980s, the 2009 figures show a sharp divergence in terms of human development. Nowadays South Korea is ranked 26th in the world, in the category of very high human development, while South Africa is ranked 129th and seems to be slipping[3] United Nations Development Programme (UNDP 2010). In the latter part of the chapter it will be examined how this impacts on the role of civil society in processes of democratic deepening.

When exploring the democratic transition in both countries, it is remarkable that South Korea witnessed the election of Kim Dae-Jung in 1997, a former human rights activist, political prisoner, and the first opposition

Table 10.1 Basic Indicator Trends of South Korea and South Africa

Indicator	*Country*	*1980*	*1990*	*2000*	*2007*
Surface Area (1000 sq. km)	South Korea	99.3	99.3	99.3	99.7
	South Africa	1219.1	1219.1	1219.1	1219.1
Population (million)	South Korea	38.1	42.9	47.0	48.5
	South Africa	27.6	35.2	44.0	48.7
GDP (current U.S.$; billion)	South Korea	63.8	263.8	533.4	1049.2
	South Africa	80.7	112.0	132.9	283.7
GDP per capita (current U.S.$)	South Korea	1,674	6,153	11,347	21,653
	South Africa	2,927	3,182	3,020	5,930
Human Development Index	South Korea (HDI rank 2009: 26)	0.722	0.802	0.802	0.927
	South Africa (HDI rank 2009: 129)	0.658	0.698	0.688	0.683

Note: From World Development Report Data Base, accessed from http://databank.worldbank.org/ddp/home.do?Step=3&id=4; Human Development Report Data Base, accessed from http://hdrstats.undp.org/en/buildtables/.

candidate to come to power while Nelson Mandela came to power in 1994. Interestingly, Kim Dae-Jung, who is sometimes referred to as the Nelson Mandela of South Korea,[4] was awarded the Nobel Peace Prize in 2000 (The Nobel Foundation 2000) while Mandela was awarded the same prize in 1993. The democratic transition in South Africa can be described in terms of three eras: *the struggle era* of the 1980s; *the freedom and consultation era* between 1993 and 1996; and *the new realism era* from 1998 onwards when the neoliberal realities of the global economy could no longer be ignored (Nauta 2004). Interestingly a similar periodization is used in the South Korean context: *the period of authoritarian industrialization* (1960s–1987); *the period of democratic transition* (1987–1996); and *the era of globalization and economic crisis* (1997 onward; Koo 2007, 74).

This chapter therefore discusses the struggle for freedom in the late 1970s and 1980s when civil society organizations in both countries were engaged in a struggle against an authoritarian regime. Secondly, the chapter compares the period of the democratic transition in both countries and the harsh impact of the world market in the mid- and late 1990s. Lastly, it examines whether the era of the internet (2001–present)[5] saw processes of democratic deepening in both countries, and the role of civil society organizations therein, with a focus information technology. What lessons, in terms of an East-South turn could South Korea provide for South Africa?

THE STRUGGLE FOR FREEDOM IN SOUTH KOREA AND SOUTH AFRICA

Although this chapter focuses on the last three decades it is crucial to recognize the origin of centralized state power in both contexts. In terms of its early history, the South Korean state was exceptionally centralized (Walraven 2003, 38–40). This was reinforced by prolonged periods of colonial occupation, as is illustrated by the physical and institutional infrastructure left by the Japanese occupation between 1910 and 1945[6]. "If state power is based ultimately on the ability to extract resources and control a people's behaviour, the Japanese colonists clearly did their job very well" (Ryoo 2009, 26). This centralized state power also impacted strongly on the development and role of civil society because civil society organizations, and their related social movements, struggled against the South Korean state to effect fundamental transformations that "began in Korea on the day that Japan surrendered in August 1945" (Cumings 2007, 23). In contrast, particularly after the democratic transition in the mid-1990s, the Korean state became actively involved in the funding, stimulation, and organization of civil society.

In South Africa, after the end of the notorious "Boer War" the Union of South Africa in 1910 had serious repercussions for black[7] South Africans in terms of access to land. The 1913 Natives Land Act and the 1936

Native Trust and Land Act forced millions of black people to leave their ancestral lands and settle in reserves that eventually covered 13.7% of South Africa's area and obliged them to utilize land administered by tribal authorities, appointed by the central government. According to Mamdani (1996) this should be recognized as another example of the colonial state in Africa, ruled by means of *decentralized despotism.* After the National Party came to power in 1948, apartheid became an official policy that permeated every sphere of life, from education to marriage to economic life, ultimately resulting in the creation of ethnically defined Bantustans—or homelands.[8] Effectively South Africa became a centrally governed police state and a foreign country for millions of blacks (Beinart and Bundy 1987; Bundy 1988; Bernstein 1996; Department of Land Affairs 1997). In the next section we focus on the period of heightened struggle against the authoritarian regimes in South Korea and South Africa in the late 1970s and 1980s.[9]

THE KWANGJU UPRISING OF 1980 AND THE 1976 SOWETO STUDENT UPRISING

Every year, on the 18th of May, Korea commemorates the Kwangju Uprising of 1980, when the people of Kwangju revolted against the imposition of martial law in South Korea by Chun Doo Hwan. The uprising was violently quelled, and more than 600 people were killed (Cumings 2007, 23; Lewis 2007, 145–166). Yet, it "interjected a revolutionary fervor in the social movement at large in seeking to build a 'scientific'[10] and '*minjung*-oriented society'" (N. Lee 2007, 95). As a result the 1980s saw the emergence of a much more radical social movement led by student activists siding with the *minjung* (common people) that "pursued liberation of the oppressed and the deprived, workers, the urban poor, and peasants" (D.-Y. Cho 2006, 69). These democratic struggles were closely related to grassroots labor struggles—the industrial workers in the 1960s and 1970s were mainly women—which were initially supported by both church groups and student groups (Koo 2007, 76). But in the early 1980s the students became more dominant (N. 2007; D.-Y. Cho 2006), as many saw the church leaders as being too mild (Koo 2007, 76). They claimed to be the "true representative[s] of the *minjung*" and "defined the grounds and conditions of the social and political discourse of the 1980s." In this period another term, namely *undongkwŏn*, became paradigmatic for the *minjung* movement, literally meaning "the movement sphere," referring both to the individual activist and the *minjung* movement as a whole (N. Lee 2007, 95–96). In this view, *undongkwŏn,* which "should be conceived as a 'counterpublic sphere'" (ibid., 97), closely seems to correspond to what is termed *the struggle* in the South African context. Around the same time South Africa experienced a popular uprising that was destined to become as symbolic as Kwangju, for the brutality of its own authoritarian regime: the Soweto uprising of 1976.

Every year South Africa celebrates Youth Day—formerly called Soweto Day—on June 16 to commemorate the Soweto uprising of 1976 when thousands took to the streets to protest against instruction in Afrikaans in secondary schools and the general poor state of education for Africans.[11] In the clashes with the police that followed 700 people were killed and thousands were injured. According to Mafeje (1978, 17) "the student revolt that flared up in Soweto in June 1976 was a clear indication of the extent of mass resistance to oppression and exploitation under apartheid." Indeed, the Soweto uprising marked another phase and an added intensity of the struggle against Apartheid, which could no longer be managed by the divide and rule tactics of the regime (Charney 1991). Amongst others, it eventually led to the establishment of United Democratic Front (UDF) in 1981, an umbrella body that represented a large diversity of civic organizations (Van Kessel 2000, 288). It followed the call by the African National Congress (ANC) to make the townships ungovernable, as is reflected in the UDF's "struggle rhetoric": "the strength and sacrifice of our people, their will to be free, cannot be crushed."[12] The Apartheid regime answered by instituting consecutive states of emergency and subsequently banned the UDF in 1988.

THE LABOR UNREST OF 1987 AND THE ESTABLISHMENT OF THE MASS DEMOCRATIC MOVEMENT

Following the Kwangju uprising and the subsequent severe state repression, including purges in all sectors of society, late 1983 saw the regime somewhat liberalizing the polity, with the expectation to fragment the opposition. However, instead, new organizations, like the National Student Coalition for Democracy Struggle and the Korean Council for Labor Welfare, were established that united under the People's Movement Coalition for Democracy and Reunification in 1985. Moreover, reinstated opposition leaders set up the New Korea Democratic Party which then aligned itself with civil society groups. This signified a substantial step forward in the democratic transition (S. Kim 2007, 55–58) and eventually resulted in the establishment of the National Coalition for Democracy Movement in 1986 and the spring uprising—or labor unrest—of 1987.

As the popular protests of June 1987 grew, Chun Doo-hwan was compelled to announce the first free presidential elections in 30 years (Armstrong 2007, 3) but, at the same time, proceeded to name his successor Roh Tae-woo. This spurred huge waves of protests, in which both the middle class (Ryoo 2009, 27) and industrial workers played a major role, as many of the protests focused on the unfair, harsh, and exploitative labor conditions, particularly in the export industry (Koo 2007, 78–79). From July to September 1987 South Korea witnessed 3,311 labor incidents with the participation of 1.2 million workers (Koo 2007, 78), opening "a new political era in South Korea (Ryoo 2009, 27).

By the early 1980s activist workers had become instrumental in organizing dissent, particularly as many of the sacked and blacklisted workers became "professional labor activists." Moreover, students began to "view labour mobilization as an important strategy for the anti-authoritarian, democratic movement," whereby students-turned-workers, who were labeled "disguised workers" by the state, became instrumental in the movement for democracy (Koo 2007, 76–77). According to N. Lee (2007, 96) the student "*minjung* discourse involved and presumed the counter-image of others: the military dictatorship, conglomerates and foreign powers." It was particularly the "'386 generation'—people in their 30s who attended college in the 1980s and were born in the 1960s"—which "effectively became the main pillar of the citizens' movement in the 1990s" (D.-Y. Cho 2006, 84). Between 1987 and 1988, 4,000 new unions were established and 700,000 new members joined during the new political dispensation (Koo 2007, 79). Until that time the Korean Federation of Trade Unions had been the only legal union, controlled by the state in interest of the *chaebols*, the South Korean highly diversified business conglomerates, owned by powerful families (Cumings 2007, 27; Yanagimachi 2004, 3). It was this radical increase in unionization that provided the muscle in the 1990s to achieve yet another step in the deepening of democracy in South Korea.

When we compare the situation in South Africa in this period, it is interesting that while in South Korea the National Coalition for Democracy Movement was established in 1986, South Africa, after the banning of the UDF, witnessed the establishment of the Mass Democratic Movement (MDM) in 1988 by UDF supporters, ANC members, and leaning heavily on the structures of the Congress of South African Trade Unions (COSATU), which was established in 1985 (Nauta 2004, 17). Since the majority of black South Africans—roughly 75% of the population—did not have access to formal political institutions, the MDM, which "had no constitution, no policy guidelines, no elected leadership, no members, and no address" (Van Kessel 2000, 43), to avoid political and institutional oppression by the state, became the alternative for the opposition and gained huge momentum in 1989. It resulted in a highly polarized period in which the country became paralyzed by strikes, comparable to South Korea. In addition South Africa witnessed rent and consumer boycotts and ongoing township violence, with a highly oppressive state apparatus that issued consecutive states of emergency.

Although the exact cause will never be clear, 1989 saw the beginning of the drastic and fundamental political changes. Several factors were at play. First, the international sanctions against South Africa caused economic pain for an already shaky economy, leading the South African business sector to plead with the apartheid regime for political reforms. Furthermore, with fall of the iron curtain the "communist threat," used to justify harsh oppression, disappeared. Additionally, the internal pressure sustained by the MDM could no longer be contained. As a result, the more moderate

F.W. de Klerk came to power, who released most political prisoners in 1990 and unbanned most political parties, heralding a period of rapid change in South Africa. The next section compares the developments in South Korea and South Africa in the mid-1990s.

THE DEMOCRATIC TRANSITION IN SOUTH KOREA AND SOUTH AFRICA

The 1990s saw the establishment of firmly entrenched democracies in South Korea and South Africa. However, as this section shows, in terms of democratic deepening one can also witness a divergence between the two countries.

General Strike of 1997 and the Election of Kim Dae-Jung

Since the labor unrest of 1987, and the formation of thousands of new unions, the 1990s witnessed a dramatic increase in collective, and often violent, labor actions, particularly as the forces of globalization increasingly impacted on the Korean economy. Thus, according to Koo "workers confront[ed] not just their own employers and the state, but also the forces of global capital" (2007, 75).Yet, until 1998 labor unions were legally prevented to be politically active" (Cumings 2007, 27) while the Korean Confederation of Trade Unions (KCTU), established in 1987, was still considered illegal.

While the election of the first civilian president (S. Kim 2007, 59) Kim Young-Sam, who had defeated Kim Dae-Jung in the 1992 elections, had been a great step forward for democracy, his administration ended in controversy in 1996. His administration prepared legislation to reform the labor code—introducing labor flexibility, facilitating lay-offs and abolishing lifelong job security—and legalize the KCTU in order to join the Organization for Economic Co-operation and Development (OECD). Yet, by failing to withstand the pressures of the *chaebols* and failing to enlist the support of the KCTU, Kim Young-Sam forced the new legislation through parliament in a pre-dawn session. Not only did he circumvent the opposition, but he also delayed the legalization of the KCTU for three years (Alemán 2004, 25–26). It led severe protests, including sit-ins and street demonstrations, because in Korean society "laying off workers because of a company's temporary financial difficulty is widely considered . . . morally unjust [and] . . . losing one's job mean[s] losing the only source of one's livelihood as well as a major basis of one's social identification" (Koo 2007, 84).

The unrest, reminiscent of 1987, resulted in the first general strike since World War II and signaled a new political era under Kim Dae-Jung. Significantly, even the state- and *chaebol*-controlled Federation of Korean Trade Unions joined the strike, while internationally it was supported by the International Labour Organization (ILO), the International Confederation of Free Trade Unions, and the OECD (Cumings 2007; S. Kim 2007;

Koo 2007; Alemán 2004). Since South Korea also faced the outbreak of the Asian financial crisis and the collapse of major *chaebols*,[13] the International Monetary Fund offered a $57 billion bailout package to prevent total collapse (S. Kim 2007, 62). It was in this volatile context that Kim Dae-Jung, who embodied "the courageous and resilient resistance to decades of dictatorship" won the elections in 1997 and took office in February 1998 (Cumings 2007, 26). His administration faced extraordinary challenges but used the crisis also to effect more fundamental changes.

Impact on Civil Society Organizations

As Kim Dae-Jung aimed to deepen democracy and permanently strengthen the progressive forces and countervailing powers in South Korean society,[14] opposing the conservative "traditional" political forces and the *chaebols*, his administration enacted "the law on promotion of Nonprofit Civil Society Organizations in 2000" (E. Kim 2009, 891)[15] so that the official subsidies, hitherto only distributed to government-related organizations,[16] would also be available to others" (Isozaki 2002, 299). As a result progressive civil society strengthened significantly in the early 21st century in terms of membership and budget (Table 10.2), but concern grew that they came too close for comfort.

Before describing the changing relationship between the state and civil society, it is useful to broadly sketch the origin and development of two major civil society organizations. I will focus on the Citizens' Coalition for Economic Justice (CCEJ), established in 1989 and the People's Solidarity for Participatory Democracy (PSPD) founded in 1994 (D.-Y. Cho 2006; E. Kim 2009). The CCEJ strives for a democratic welfare society, a competent government, and economic and social justice (D.-Y. Cho 2006, 69), while the PSPD is more directly geared toward "a participatory democracy in which liberty, justice, human rights, and welfare can be realized through practical citizens' actions" (PSPD, cited in D.-Y. Cho 2006, 70). Ideologically the PSPD aligns itself with the *minjung* and democratization movements and opposes neoliberalism,

Table 10.2 Funding and Membership of the Major Civil Society Organizations in South Korea (Unit: person and won)

Classification	*CCEJ*		*PSPD*		*KFEM*	
Year	1999	2003	1999	2003	1999	2003
Membership	20,000	35,000	10,000	12,700	53,000	85,000
Full-time staff members	56	40	48	54	50	73
Budget (billion won)	1	1.4	0.8	1.68 (2001)	3.5	2.2

Note: From D.-Y. Cho 2006
Sources: *Hanguk Min-gan danche chongnam* (2000, 2003)

while the CCEJ differentiates itself from the *minjung* movement by adhering to liberalism and neoliberalism (Choi 2000, 39).

While both organizations aimed to promote transparency and participation of citizens, according to D.-Y. Cho (2006, 76) "the CCEJ proposed the introduction of a public concept of land, tax reform, and other policy issues" in the field of housing, whereby it "succeeded in bringing about a real-name system in real estate and financial transactions in the economic sector." The PSPD, on the other hand "conducted . . . a judicial reform campaign in 1995, a transparent society campaign centered around the enactment of an anti-corruption act in 1996, a minority shareholders campaign in 1998, a budget monitoring and information disclosure campaign in 1999, [and] a blacklisting campaign to block the political party nomination of unqualified candidates in the 2000 General Election" (D.-Y. Cho 2006, 77).

For the CCEJ, the PSPD and other organizations the election of Kim Young-Sam in 1992, counter-intuitively, meant a huge challenge in terms of identity, independence and capacity. It left these organizations "which had been so good at criticizing unpopular governments and so used to repression by authoritarian regimes, bewildered, demobilized and demoralized" (S. Kim 2007, 59). Furthermore, it led to a bifurcation of civil society organizations, originally united under the banner of *minjung*, whereby middle class organizations move into new fields like the environment, foreign relations, and anti-nuclear power, while leaving the labor unions to focus on "traditional" labor issues (Koo 2007, 83). Secondly, during the Kim Young-Sam and Kim Dae-Jung administrations a marked shift in relative degree of "autonomy"[17] took place. Particularly the latter actively aimed "to turn NGOs into partners" in support of continuing democratic reform (Isozaki 2002, 303). Hereby, civil society organizations risked losing their relative autonomy and critical ability and were in danger of becoming "pseudo-political parties." If, as a result, the ruling party together with sympathetic "civil society keeps on circumventing and ultimately *replaces* party politics, this may pose a threat to the consolidation of South Korean democracy" (S. Kim 2007, 67–68). Lastly, civil society capacity was compromised as civil society leaders accepted work for government and also joined "various independent commissions as well as advisory committees for major government agencies." Although the quality of government may improve, civil society can be depleted and its independence constrained. Such "vertical cooptation could weaken civil society . . . by taking away the most capable people" (E. Kim 2009, 890–891). The next section focuses on the impact of Kim Dae-Jung's administration on the role of organized labor.

Organized Labor

The International Monetary Fund economic rescue package, to assist South Korea during the Asian crisis in 1997, demanded economic and political reforms, in line with its neoliberal agenda. This restructuring "assisted proponents of reform in the battle for ideas of the Korean state" (Hundt 2005, 245), particularly incoming President Kim Dae-Jung, who endeavored to change and reduce the role of the *chaebols*. Thus, the birth of the Korea Tripartite Commission—"Social Dialogue Based on Partnership"[18]—in which business, labor, and government were all represented, signified a clear break with the past. Furthermore, it helped Kim Dae-Jung to garner support for the harsh measures to reform the economy, since "the three parties agreed on the basic principle of fairly sharing the pain and burden of economic restructuring" (Koo 2007, 86). Ultimately, however, the Tripartite Commission was not "successfully implemented or experimented with in Korea" (D.-C. Kim 2006, 114–115), particularly because the KCTU, that was fully legalized in late 1999[19] pulled out of the Tripartite Commission in 1998, rejoined a few months later and permanently pulled out in 1999, while denouncing the neoliberal character of the Tripartite Commission (Y.-s. Kim 2010, 178; Alemán 2004, 29). For the progressive labor union, this move eventually proved rather successful as it was able to expand its political influence, particularly in the General Election of 2004. In that year "the Democratic Labor Party, founded upon the KCTU, occupied ten seats in the National Assembly and acquired 13.1 percent of the votes" (Y. Lee et al. 2008, 124). Although, on a symbolic level, it was a significant step in South Korea to give the unions a voice in economic decision making, traditionally dominated by the state and business conglomerates, the commission did not live up to its promises.

Whether or not the power of *chaebols* significantly decreased in South Korean society is up for debate, although it is clear that Kim Dae-Jung instituted major changes in terms of accountability, transparency, and financial health through, for example, the obligation to appoint outside directors in *chaebols* (Yanagimachi 2004, 3). S. Kim (2007, 63), however, argues that progressive South Korean civil society complains that "in contrast with the significant progress in political democratization" there has been a lack of progress in economic democratization. In fact, D.-C. Kim (2006) contends that organizations like the PSPD have remained fiercely critical of the role played by *chaebols*, whereby some "grew more powerful" under the next president Roh Moo-hyun (113). According to Ryoo (2009, 29) organizations like the PSPD "have even asserted that Samsung's dominance is a 'dictatorship'." Next we continue by examining the role of civil society in South Africa.

Civil Society in South Africa in the Mid-1990s

With the release of Mandela from prison in 1990, and the unbanning of opposition parties, a long period of difficult political negotiations commenced in a racially, politically, socially, and economically highly polarized society. While the apartheid security forces[20] still instigated violence between black groups, the issue of federalism proved highly divisive—white groups demanding their own territory and "independent" Bantustans refusing to reintegrate into South Africa. However, after difficult negotiations[21] it was finally agreed to establish a Transitional Executive Council, adopt an interim constitution, form a Government of National Unity (GNU) after the elections. Therefore, the adoption of the interim constitution on December 18, 1993, providing the constitutional framework to achieve a multi-party democracy and reintegrate the Bantustans, should be regarded as a point of no return on the road to democracy. It was bolstered by Mandela's call for *"a rainbow nation at peace with itself and the world,"* in which the rainbow came to symbolize peace, reconciliation, consultation, and co-operation (Mandela, May 10, 1994). The GNU comprised de Klerk's National Party, Buthelezi's Inkatha Freedom Party,[22] and the tripartite alliance—a coalition between the ANC, the South African Communist Party (SACP), and COSATU.[23] This alliance was—and still is—a unique feature in South African politics, because, in contrast to South Korea, organized labor became directly involved in politics, since COSATU, like the SACP, participated in the elections on the ANC ticket. Although it meant direct access to the chambers of power, it also involved huge risks of co-optation and failure to critically monitor the government.

As reconciliation involved (re-)creating trust the ANC offered the National Party crucial positions in the transitional cabinet in order to alleviate white fears over economic instability. However, after making sure existing property rights became enshrined in the new constitution—through the so-called Property Clause—the National Party left the GNU after two years as it did not want to become associated with black empowerment and restoring black rights. This property clause protected the property rights of citizens, while allowing expropriation only under very limited conditions—*for a public purpose*—to prevent widespread expropriation, in a country where whites still held most of the country's assets. Ultimately the property clause leant toward the former, and, thus, the Mandela administration and the subsequent Mbeki administrations battled to effect fundamental socio-economic redistribution. In addition, the harsh impact of the world market and the major challenges caused by the HIV/AIDS epidemic sustained the huge disparities between the wealthy and the poor, reflected in the high Gini coefficient for the period 1992–2007 of 57.8 (UNDP 2009).

When coming to grips with the weakening of civil society in South Africa during the mid- and late 1990s it is important to first recognize that the population could now potentially access "regular" democratic institutions. Second, like in South Korea, the government incorporated, encapsulated and co-opted civil society. Lastly, it is useful to examine the establishment of the National Economic Development and Labor Council (NEDLAC) and compare it to the South Korean tripartite commission.

In the period of the UDF and MDM, self-organization in so-called *residents associations*—or *civics*—became the answer to the lack of access to formal politics by black South Africans, which, subsequently led to the establishment of the South African National Civic Organization (SANCO) in early 1992. At the same time, many NGOs were established during the struggle against apartheid by community leaders and progressive academics[24], who had been involved in various research projects, like the Surplus People Project in 1980, focusing on the forced removals of 3.5 million people to the Bantustans from 1960 to 1980 (Surplus People Project 1983). Although the prize was sometimes high,[25] civil society was vibrant.

This changed drastically after Mandela came to power in 1994, because civics and NGOs were no longer the only available route to political processes, when new local, provincial, and national government structures were gradually established. Initially the Reconstruction and Development Program (RDP)—a "coherent socio-economic policy framework" (ANC 1994, 1)—which was the result of a long consultation process between the alliance partners and other civil society organizations like SANCO, became the leading document for the GNU between 1993 and 1996. It aimed to fundamentally transform the country through consultation,[26] before new formal institutions became firmly established, by mirroring the experience of Transitional Executive Council of 1993–1994 that led the country to democracy. "Stakeholders"—representatives from communities, NGOs, government, and the private sector—participated in shaping policies, legal frameworks, and institutions like Transitional Local Councils.[27] Such structures also facilitated the cooperation between various government structures, whereby NGOs and their institutional memory, for a while, became "beacons of continuity" for a government that faced a huge shortage of progressive staff. In fact, NGOs, in this period, even trained new government staff in government legislation (Nauta 2004, 204–225).

In the end, however, most NGO experts proceeded to join government departments leaving civil society by late 1996 "largely crippled" (Nauta 2004, 225). To make matters worse, many NGOs lost their funding base, as donors turned to fund the now legitimate. This resulted in a high dependency on government contracts and, in the process, turned highly politicized NGOs, that had played a strong role in the public sphere—producing critical news articles, newsletters, and pamphlets—into mere service providers (ibid., 151). As a result civil society lost most of its countervailing power, also because those who remained behind in civil society were reluctant to criticize former comrades that had joined the government.

When comparing South Korea and South Africa on a political level in the mid-1990s, it becomes clear that the political transformation in South Africa was initially more immediate and profound, since the tripartite alliance was able to take over the country politically and fundamentally transform politics on every level. Testimony to this is the very progressive Constitution of South Africa which took effect in 1997. The alliance became the dominant political force in parliament, hovering, just below the two-thirds majority mark.[28] This meant that compared to South Korea, the conservative forces became rather marginalized in the political realm. In an economic sense, however, even though South Africa implemented Black Economic Empowerment policies, the wealth stayed largely concentrated in elite—white—hands. In other words, massive poverty and deprivation largely stayed concentrated in "black" society, keeping South Africa one of the most unequal societies on the planet.

The fact that organized labor joined the alliance and, to this day, is essentially part of the fabric of government, has had huge consequences for processes of democratic deepening, or the lack thereof. Formally South Africa is still a democratic example in Africa, as shown by the resignation of Mandela after his first term and the recall of Mbeki in 2008. However, if one examines the role of the opposition and civil society in terms of democratic deepening, the conclusion can only be negative. The relative impotence of civil society was illustrated when the macro-economic Growth, Employment and Redistribution (GEAR) program, a "strategy for rebuilding and restructuring the economy"(Department of Finance 1998, 1), was announced in 1996. It attempted to marry the ideals of the RDP with the harsh realities of a neoliberal world order. Although COSATU became one of the fiercest opponents of the GEAR strategy: "the logic of transformation, as contained in the RDP, has been overpowered by that of the forces attempting to halt transformation" and it called for "the RDP should remain the programme of the Alliance" (COSATU 1996, 6, 14), it did not manage to fundamentally influence its partners. Even though, by 1999, its message remained unchanged "we must continue to oppose the GEAR strategy" (COSATU 1999, 18) organized labor did not retreat back to its position in civil society (Nauta 2004, 36) because its leaders claimed "that to leave would usher COSATU into 'the political wilderness'" (Bassett and Clarke 2008, 795).[29] Although COSATU managed to get some of its concerns addressed in 2003, no fundamental changes were effected, as illustrated by the new economic framework, Accelerated and Shared Growth South Africa, which was launched in 2006 (ibid., 2–4).

Compared to the failed experiment of the tripartite commission in South Korea, the NEDLAC became a powerful institution in South Africa. This council, where representatives of government, organized labor, business, and what the government calls "community representatives" negotiate economic development issues through consultation and consensus-building, has managed to realize constructive solutions for challenges in the South African economy. Even NGOs were invited to take part in the fourth chamber, named "Development." Although mainstream economists applaud this approach, others, like Friedman and Reitzes (1996), recognize similar problems as encountered in the tripartite alliance, where the government effectively seems to have neutralized and co-opted COSATU and NGOs in a corporatist fashion. In their view this is a negative trend, since civil society constitutes more than a limited group of progressive organizations and a certain distance to government is needed to remain critical.

In conclusion one can indeed argue that COSATU, by being a member of NEDLAC and a faithful partner of the tripartite alliance, seems to have weakened its progressive agenda, as it has effectively become part of the establishment. As a result problems of unemployment and poverty have largely remained unsolved. COSATU should have remained outside formal politics in South Africa, like the KCTU in South Korea. A well-functioning and deepened democracy needs several strong players inside and outside the government, representing opposing views.

Only in one field did COSATU actively distance itself from the government, as it aligned itself with the South African Council of Churches and Treatment Action Campaign (TAC): "The HIV epidemic has been permitted to go too far. [This] is a disaster that is killing people in terrible numbers, and, as frightening, an epidemic where the numbers of people newly infected with HIV continues to grow. This can and must be changed" (COSATU 2005). In the next section it will be shown that this fight saw the emergence of new civic energy in South Africa.

SOUTH KOREA AND SOUTH AFRICA IN THE NEW MILLENNIUM

The Blacklist Campaign and the Anti-Impeachment Campaign in South Korea

One of the greatest triumphs of civil society in South Korea has been the so-called "blacklist campaign" of 2000. More than 400 civil society organizations established the "Citizens' Alliance for the 2000 General Elections (CAGE) to prevent the political parties from nominating 'unfit' candidates (rejection campaign), and then to defeat those who were nonetheless nominated . . . (defeat campaign)" (Choi 2000, 26). Eventually 86 politicians were blacklisted due to past involvement in bribery scandals, violation of election laws, poor performance in legislature (absenteeism), past association with authoritarian regimes or military coups, negative attitudes to anti-corruption legislation, and so on. The campaign succeeded by striking a major blow to conservative politics so that in the Seoul conglomeration alone none of the blacklisted candidates were elected. According to Choi (2000, 26), "this movement engendered powerful shock waves. Some called it a 'civic political revolution', a 'voters revolution'." Although in 2000 Choi (2000, 41) still doubted whether the campaign generated "enough momentum to create a structural change in Korean politics," the subsequent anti-impeachment campaign, the 2004 elections campaign, and the entry in the National Assembly of the Democratic Labor Party in 2004, have proven that further democratic deepening was indeed on the cards (W. Cho 2005; A.E. Kim 2006; Y. Lee 2005).

In 2002 the election of President Roh Moo-hyun represented the rise of "a new, younger, post-liberation generation," whereby the "progressives . . . entered the political establishment *en masse*." They took over from an older conservative generation and managed to implement significant democratic reforms (S. Kim 2007, 65). Unfortunately, Roh's own party, the Millennium

Democratic Party, also became embroiled in generational conflict, as a result of which the party split in two factions whereby the pro-Roh forces formed the new Uri Party in late 2003 (Y. Lee 2005, 8). Subsequently, "when Roh committed a minor breach of the election law—saying he hoped people would support the UP [Uri Party] in the general election" the president was impeached (W. Cho 2005, 525), because the remaining Millennium Democratic Party faction aligned itself with the conservative opposition (Y. Lee 2005, 8).

The progressive movement and the general public became so outraged that "tens of thousands of citizens participated in a candlelight rally in Seoul and elsewhere, protesting against Roh's impeachment" (W. Cho 2005, 526). Subsequently, "a civic coalition comprising 551 civic and labor groups . . . protested against the National Assembly's decision to oust the president, staging and/or joining . . . candlelight vigils and waging campaigns on the Internet to gather 10 million signatures" (A.E. Kim 2006, 528). Ultimately civil society proved victorious when the Constitutional Court reinstated Roh Moo-hyun in May 2004. According to D.-Y. Cho (2006), the impeachment of Roh by the conservative forces to maintain the old order backfired and actually "offered citizens' movement organizations and citizens, interconnected through the internet, an opportunity to conclude the 1987 democratization movement" (92). Consequently, the progressive forces, staged yet another blacklist campaign in 2004, partly targeted against those who had impeached Roh. Although some scholars (e.g., W. Cho 2005) believe that this blacklist campaign did not sway the elections to the same extent as in 2000, it was still significant, according to S. Kim (2007, 65) that South Korea witnessed, for the first time, "the successful entry of the Korean Democratic Labour Party into the National Assembly." It "mark[ed] the culmination of the recent ascendance of the progressives in South Korea" (ibid., 65).

Although more recently civil society has come under attack of the more conservative Lee Myung-bak administration,[30] the events that unfolded in the last decade, surrounding the elections in 2000, 2004, and the anti-impeachment campaign, have shown, in my view, how immensely important modern communication technology has become in linking like-minded groups and creating alternative public spheres which help to consolidate and deepen the democratization process in South Korea.

The TAC in South Africa: A Revival of Civil Society?

As the HIV/AIDS epidemic exploded in South Africa and the Nelson Mandela government failed to tackle the disease head-on, the TAC was born[31] on International Human Rights Day in December 1998, in order to fight for universal access to treatment. Although the TAC initially aligned itself with the South African government when it campaigned against major global pharmaceutical companies in 1999, from its inception, it was also very critical of the government, in particular the consecutive Mbeki cabinets from 1999 to 2008.

A prominent example is the march organized by TAC and its local and international allies ahead of the 13th International AIDS Conference in

Durban, in which 5,000 local and international activists participated. According to Grebe (2008, 26) "the TAC drew heavily on its civil society networks, particularly . . . South African trade unions, NGOs and CSOs to mobilise support for the march. . . . While the principal focus of mobilisation was local . . ., [i]t was endorsed by at least 258 organisations from across the world." It symbolized its strength as an activist organization, rooted in local communities while, simultaneously, being globally connected. In August 2001 TAC proceeded to take the South African government to court—after pressuring it for three years—for failing to establish a Mother to Child Transmission Prevention Programme. In December 2001 the Court, agreeing with TAC's argument that people have a constitutional "right to life," ordered the state to provide the drugs and implement a Mother to Child Transmission Prevention Programme in public health facilities.

In the following years the TAC became a large respected and vocal civil society organization in South Africa, battling a government that was under the influence of President Mbeki's denialism—"Personally, I don't know anybody who has died of AIDS" (Washington Post 2003)—and Health Minister Msimang's attempts to promote beetroot, lemon, garlic, and olive oil as an alternative to antiretrovirals (ARV) medication. Subsequently, when South Africa slowly began a universal ARV roll-out program, but remained hesitant in terms of budget constraints, the TAC campaigned against the moral assumption that some lives were more expendable than others (Nattrass 2004, 175).[32]

Yet, what remains one of the most puzzling questions is why the TAC—run by a committed elite and a few thousand activists on the local level—despite vocal leaders, like Zackie Achmat, successful court cases, media criticism of the government, and alignment with organizations like Médecins Sans Frontières, was never able to spark a "voters revolution" or a "civic political revolution" similar to the 2000 blacklist campaign in South Korea. In a nation where more than 5 million people were infected with HIV and where most victims had limited access to treatment and health care, there was something at stake. Yet, during the last two elections HIV/AIDS was not a major issue. In my opinion this can only be explained by the general weakness of civil society and the lack of access, for average South Africans, to information, information technology, and education. To end on a positive note, the situation has changed dramatically under President Jacob Zuma,[33] since the treatment of HIV/AIDS now has the highest priority with the widespread distribution of antiretrovirals in public facilities, thanks to the sustained pressure that TAC put on an unwilling government.

DEMOCRATIC DEEPENING IN THE AGE OF INTERNET

Over the last two decades South Korea has become one of the success stories of information technology. Furthermore, as was shown by the significant HDI

Table 10.3 Information and Communication Technology in South Korea and South Africa

Indicator	*Country*	*1980*	*1990*	*2000*	*2007*
Information and communication technology expenditure per capita (current U.S.$)	South Korea	—	—	—	1,991
	South Africa	—	—	—	560
Internet users (thousand)	South Korea	—	10	19,040	36,211
	South Africa	—	0	2,400	3,966
Internet users (per 100 people)	South Korea	—	0	41	75
	South Africa	—	0	5	8

Note: From World Development Report Data Base, accessed from http://databank.worldbank.org/ddp/home.do?Step=3&id=4.

increases, from 0.722 in 1980 to 0.927 in 2007 (Table 10.1), South Korea has made great strides forward in education levels. By 2007 75 % of its population were internet users, but even more significant, already in 2001, more than half of the population was connected E.-J. Lee (2005, 55).

Therefore, one cannot understand processes of democratic deepening in South Korea without taking into account that the country is among the most highly wired in the world, as was shown by the 10 million (!) signatures that were collected in the anti-impeachment campaign. According to Ryoo (2009, 32) even the election of Roh Moo-Hyun was partly due to "his internet-based fan club, 'Nosamo'." The second blacklist campaign in 2004 even "refrained from holding outdoor rallies and promoted its efforts solely through the Internet by creating its own website to inform the public" (A.E. Kim 2006, 531).

It is unsurprising, therefore, that a relatively new term—"Netizen," the wired citizen in the information age—keeps on surfacing, when describing the role of civil society in the public sphere in South Korea (Armstrong 2007, 4; E.-J. Lee 2005, 53; Ryoo 2009, 33). These netizens form various alliances, which can be formed—and disbanded—extremely fast, are relatively fluid, and are part of numerous e-communities. These communities can be about sharing the love of sports, environmental concerns or politics, and so on. Particularly important in the field of public opinion and politics has been the emergence of very influential alternative media, like Ohmynews launched in 2002—"motto: every citizen is a reporter"[34]—that have become crucial alternative public spheres, breaking the monopolies of the mainstream conservative news media and conservative political forces (E.-J. Lee 2005, 60). By 2002 South Korea's conservative newspapers had lost their monopoly position regarding the news. In that year many netizens turned to internet for political information and analysis (Ryoo 2009, 32), and Ohmynews was receiving around 20 million hits per day. According to Ryoo (2009, 33), "citizen eParticipation is characterised by convenient access to detailed information, free expression and the exchange of political opinions, online activism led by politicised agenda, and the active formation of cyber groups and culture . . . . Korean . . . 'netizens' . . . no longer passively accept the agenda put forward by the traditional media, and they are now producers of messages."

Also the civil society organizations, discussed previously, like the People's Solidarity for Participatory Democracy (PSPD), have launched their own websites, blogs, and so forth.[35] Moreover, NGOs and civil society initiatives have turned their attention to the world at large. Civil society is no longer concerned with only issues that are relevant for the Korean nation state and its immediate neighbors. An organization, like Good Neighbors, is active in development assistance in many different countries.

Taking Heller's (2009, 124) definition of democratic deepening, all these processes point in the right direction since they contribute to the increasing capability of subordinate groups to shape South Korean politics and give voice to those who were rather voiceless before the age of the internet.

When going back to Table 10.3, it becomes clear that there are huge differences between South Korea and South Africa concerning the advances in information technology. In 2007 only 8 out of 100 South Africans had access to the internet. Wt is clear that South Africa is far behind in the digital revolution. In fact, with only 8 out of 100 people connected to the internet, it is clear that the situation is extremely worrying, with most South Africans clearly on the wrong side of the "digital divide," as Hobsbawm coined it. When we combine this with the fact that South Africa is one of the most unequal societies in the world with a Gini Coefficient of 57.8 (UNDP 2009), it is reasonable to assume that the masses have little capacity to be full citizens in the age of internet. On top of this, the HDI, in which education levels are represented, is slipping from rank 107th in 2000 to rank 129th in 2007. This is also illustrated by the dismal secondary school Matric results, with the exception of some good (private) schools in the large cities. On a tertiary level a handful of formerly "white" universities are renowned, while former Bantustan institutions are still poor performers.

When grappling with the relationship of poverty and development the work of Amartya Sen (1999) has been instrumental in broadening our understanding. In *Development as Freedom* he argues that development can only be achieved through the expansion of freedom, while not ignoring "deprivations . . . such as unemployment, ill health, lack of education, and social exclusion" (Sen 1999, 108). Sen, therefore, defines poverty as "the deprivation of basic capabilities rather than merely as lowness of incomes" (ibid., 87). Such deprivations lead to unfreedoms and, as a consequence, to bottlenecks in processes of development and processes of democratic deepening as Heller (2009) has argued. This is why post-2001 South Korea's democracy is deepening and processes of democratic deepening are stalling in South Africa.

CONCLUDING REMARKS

In early 2011 the world witnessed the so-called Facebook revolution in the Middle East and North Africa (MENA) region, when Tahrir Square became etched into our collective memory. Consequently, many commentators ask whether this revolutionary wave could wash over Sub-Saharan Africa and countries like South Africa? When examining the evidence in this chapter, particularly concerning the still rather fragmented state of civil society and the low levels of education and access to the internet, I would say not yet.

There are some striking similarities when we compare the role of civil society organizations in South Korea and South Africa in processes of democratic deepening. In the 1980s both countries showed a heightened intensity of the democratic struggles, the early to mid-1990s marked the democratic transition, while the late 1990s confronted both countries with the harsh realities of the global markets. Moreover, both countries experienced similar popular uprisings around 1980, while the late 1980s saw the rise of powerful, mass-based civil society movements. In South Korea the National Coalition for Democracy Movement was established in 1986 and the Mass Democratic Movement was established in 1988. In both countries a marked shift took place in terms of the involvement of the masses, particularly through the mass labor unions. Subsequently, in the early to mid-1990s civil society organizations in both countries significantly weakened when the progressive forces entered the political arena. NGO staff cooperated with their new progressive governments and ultimately left their organizations to join the government. While at the same time losing their cause, the capacity of civil society was severely compromised. This leaves us to consider the huge difference that emerged in the new millennium, with an emphasis on the role of organized labor and the role of information technology.

As was shown previously, in South Africa COSATU became part of the tripartite alliance and joined NEDLAC, the socio-economic consultative body. Although, at times, it did organize protests and strikes and won minor victories, it became part and parcel of the ruling government, thwarting its much-needed independence. As other NGOs never really recovered, only TAC became a real critical voice opposite the government. In South Korea, the independent labor movement stayed independent by leaving the tri-partite commission.

Furthermore, the impeachment of progressive President Roh Moo-hyun by the conservative forces offered South Korean civil society the opportunity to deepen the democratization process that began in the 1980s, making use of the internet and high education levels. In South Africa, on the other hand, quality education and information technology is not at the disposal of the masses (although many people have cell phones, air time is frequently the problem).

In conclusion I would argue that South Africa should take its cues from South Korea. More concerted efforts to fight poverty and the legacies of Apartheid, massive investments in human resources through education and health, and lastly, substantial investments in information technology are needed. Finally, regarding the lessons of organized labor in South Korea, one can only hope that COSATU quits the tripartite alliance sooner rather than later. In terms of the East-South turn, discussed by Nederveen Pieterse (2011), a Korean wave on the African continent, in an inspirational sense and possibly in a material sense, whereby South Korean organizations like Good Neighbors seek East-South ties with civil society organizations in Africa, could assist processes of democratic deepening by strengthening the role of civil society in the public sphere.

NOTES

1. The "international spread of Korean popular culture" (Jung 2009, 66).
2. Although we must remember that in those days the average black South African was also extremely poor in terms of Human Development.
3. It was ranked 107th in 2000 while South Korea then ranked 27th in terms of Human Development Index.
4. Online News Hour, Interview by Jim Leher with President Kim Dae-jung on June 9, 1998. Accessed February 9, 2012 from http://www.pbs.org/newshour/bb/asia/jan-june98/kim_6–9a.html.
5. According to Y. Lee (2005, 55), in 2001 24.4 million South Koreans had access to the internet, 51.5% of the population.
6. Critical scholars may disagree and point to the (neo-colonial) role of the U.S. in the last six decades.
7. The term 'black' is of course contentious, but since the term is still widely used in South Africa to describe South Africans of "African"—in itself contentious—origin, I use it in this chapter.
8. In 1951 the Bantu Authorities Act was passed which laid the foundation for the road to "independent" bantustans. In 1959, after the Promotion of Bantu Self-Government Act was passed, the government proclaimed that eight African "national units" would be recognized.
9. For this chapter I focus on the last three decades. However, both countries also witnessed earlier struggles against the dictatorial regimes.
10. "Scientific" here refers to theoretical and intellectual orientation by the students who were, for example, inspired by Latin American liberation theory (Cumings 2007, 23).
11. Bantu education.
12. UDF's Secretarial Report, February 1986, quoted by Van Kessel (2000, 37).
13. For example Hanbo.
14. Cho, Dae-Yop (2006, 95) describes the role of large citizens organizations in terms of the need to "counter giant state power."

15. "NGOs receive project-based funding and other financial support including some forms of tax-exempt status and postal discounts" (E. Kim 2009, 891).
16. Before the democratic transition three major government-related organizations were The New Village Movement (Saemaeul Undong), the Right Life Movement Council, and the Korean Federation of Freedom (Isozaki 2002, 306).
17. Of course, truly autonomous civil society organizations simply do not exist since "all organizations, governing bodies and institutions are to some degree influenced by their surrounding institutional arena" (Nauta 2004, 53).
18. The Korea Tripartite Commission: http://www.lmg.go.kr/english/e_index.asp.
19. The last KCTU affiliate was legalized in 1999 (see http://kctu.org/kctu).
20. Mandela referred to the security forces, responsible for destabilization through instigation of violence on the Rand around the mining hostels and in KwaZulu Natal, as "the third force."
21. The Convention for a Democratic South Africa deadlocked several times until it was replaced by the Multi-Party Negotiating Forum.
22. The Inkatha Freedom Party became strongly associated with a Zulu identity.
23. Some also term it "the tripartite and a half alliance" as SANCO is considered part of the alliance as well: "Sanco: We do not accept junior-partner status" (see http://www.mg.co.za/article/2009–09–23-sanco-we-do-not-accept-juniorpartner-status).
24. Often white.
25. People were arrested, tortured, and sometimes killed.
26. It, in fact, contains many valuable ideas and plans that found their way—albeit altered and adapted—to several Green Papers and White Papers published by the government in later years, after it had become more acquainted with budgetary, legal, and institutional constraints. For example, the Green Paper on Land Policy (1996) and the White Paper on South African Land Policy in 1997.
27. As a foreign researcher I was also allowed to attend such meetings and express my opinion (e.g., the Eastern Cape Province Land Reform Steering Committee; Nauta 2004).
28. In 2004 the "traditionally white" National Party, until then an opposition party, even merged with the ANC, to secure Cabinet posts.
29. For an excellent analysis, see Buhlungu (2008).
30. "The People's Solidarity for Participatory Democracy raised eight questions about the Joint Investigation Group's final report, putting together doubts and suspicions which have been circulated in cyberspace by leftist circles since the naval incident on March 26. . . . When a local NGO sends a letter to the U.N. Security Council refuting the truthfulness of the result of a multinational investigation into the sinking of the Navy patrol craft Cheonan, it may demonstrate social diversity in this country. But it could also damage national credibility (*Korea Herald* 2010, June 15. Accessed February 9, 2012 from http://www.koreaherald.com/opinion/Detail.jsp?newsMLId=20100615000481).
31. "On 10 December 1998, International Human Rights Day, a group of about15 people protested on the steps of St George's Cathedral in Cape Town to demand medical treatment for people living with the virus that causes AIDS" (TAC, n.d., "An Overview," 2). Accessed February 9, 2012 from http://www.tac.org.za/Documents/MTCTPrevention/mtcthist.rtf
32. Trevor Manuel is alleged to have stated at an internal cabinet meeting, "It does not make financial sense to spend money on people dying anyway, who are not even productive in the first place" (cited in Gumede 2005, 163). Whether or not this quote is authentic, the government's policies spoke for themselves.

33. Zuma himself has also been a controversial figure in the past, in terms of HIV/AIDS—for example, during his alleged rape trial when he suggested that a shower had a positive effect in preventing HIV infection.
34. See http://english.ohmynews.com/.
35. See http://www.peoplepower21.org/.

REFERENCES

Alemán, J. 2004. "Social Movements and Democratic Consolidation in South Korea, 1987–1999." Presented at the 2004 Annual Meeting of the American Political Science Association, Hilton, Chicago, September 2–5.

ANC. 1994. *The Reconstruction and Development Programme: a Policy Framework*. Johannesburg: Umanyano Publications.

Armstrong, C.K. 2007. "Introduction." In *Korean Society: Civil Society, Democracy and the State*, edited by C.K. Armstrong, 1–8. London: Routledge.

Bassett, C., and M. Clarke. 2008. "The Zuma Affair, Labour and the Future of Democracy in South Africa." *Third World Quarterly* 29(4): 787–803.

Beinart, W. and Colin Bundy. 1987. *Hidden Struggles in Rural South Africa*. London: James Currey.

Bernstein, Henry. 1996. *The Agrarian Question in South Africa*. London: Frank Cass.

Buhlungu, S. 2008. "Gaining Influence but Losing Power? COSATU Members and the Democratic Transformation of South Africa." *Social Movement Studies*, 7(1): 31–42.

Bundy, C. 1988. *The Rise and Fall of the South African Peasantry*. Cape Town: David Philip.

Chandhoke, N. 2006. "The Limits of Global Civil Society." In *Global Civil Society 2002*, edited by M. Glasius, M. Kaldor & H. Anheier. Oxford: Oxford University Press.

Charney, C. 1991. "Vigilantes, Clientelism, and the South African State". *Transformation* 16: 1–28

Cho, Dae-Yop. 2006. "Korean Citizens' Movement Organizations: Their Ideologies, Resources, and Action Repertoires." *Korea Journal* 46(2): 68–98. Accessed April 20, 2010 from http://www.ekoreajournal.net.

Cho, W. 2005. "The General Election in South Korea, April 2004." *Electoral Studies* 24(3): 511–551.

Choi, J. 2000. "Democratization, Civil Society, and the Civil Social Movement in Korea: The Significance of the Citizens' Alliance for the 2000 General Elections." *Korea Journal* 40(3): 26–57.

COSATU. 2005. Joint COSATU, SACC TAC Statement. Accessed May 10, 2010 from http://www.cosatu.org.za/docs/pr/2005/pr1123.html

COSATU. 1996. A Draft Programme for the Alliance. Accessed November 9, 2002 from www.cosatu.org.za/docs.

Cumings, B. 2007. "Civil Society in West and East." In *Korean Society: Civil Society, Democracy and the State*, edited by C.K. Armstrong, 9–32. London: Routledge.

Department of Finance. 1998. Growth, Employment and Redistribution: a Macroeconomic Strategy. Accessed February 9, 2012 from http://www.info.gov.za/view/DownloadFileAction?id=70507

Department of Land Affairs. 1997. *White Paper on South African Land Policy*. Pretoria: Department of Land Affairs.

Friedman, S., and M. Reitzes. 1996. "Democratization or Bureaucratization?: Civil Society, the Public Sphere and the State in Post-Apartheid South Africa." *Transformation* 29: 55–73.

Grebe, E. 2008. "Transnational networks of influence in South African AIDS treatment activism", *CSSR Working Paper 222*, Centre for Social Science Research. Accessed March 15, 2011 from http://www.cssr.uct.ac.za/

Gumede, W.M. 2005. *Thabo Mbeki and the Battle for the Soul of the ANC*. Cape Town: Zebra Press.

Heller, P. 2009. "Democratic Deepening in India and South Africa." In *Journal of Asian and African Studies* 2009 44(1): 123–149.

Hundt, D. 2005. "A Legitimate Paradox: Neo-liberal Reform and the Return of the State in Korea." *The Journal of Development Studies* 41(2): 242–258.

Isozaki, N. 2002. "South Korea: Advocacy for Democratisation." In *The State and NGOs: Perspectives from Asia*, edited by S. Shigetomi, 288–310. Singapore: Institute of Southeast Asian Studies.

Jung, Eun-Young. 2009. "Transnational Korea: A Critical Assessment of the Korean Wave in Asia and the United States." *South-East Review of Asian Studies* 31, 2009: 69–80.

Kaarsholm, P. 2009. "Public Spheres, Hidden Politics and Struggles over Space: Boundaries of Public Engagement in Post-Apartheid South Africa." In *Social Dynamics* 35(2): 411–422.

Kaldor, M. 2003. "The Idea of Global Civil Society." In *International Affairs*, 79(3): 583–593.

Kim, Andrew Eungi. 2006. "Civic Activism and Korean Democracy: the Impact of Blacklisting Campaigns in the 2000 and 2004 General Elections." *The Pacific Review* 19(4): 519–542.

Kim, Dong-Choon. 2006. "Growth and Crisis of the Korean Citizens' Movement." *Korea Journal* 46(2): 99–128. Accessed from http://www.ekoreajournal.net.

Kim, Euiyoung. 2009. "The Limits of Ngo-Government Relations in South Korea." *Asian Survey* 49(5): 873–894.

Kim, S. 2007. "Civil Society and Democratization in South Korea." In *Korean Society: Civil Society, Democracy and the State*, edited by C.K. Armstrong, 53–71. London: Routledge.

Kim, Yeong-soon. 2010. "Institutions of Interest Representation and the Welfare State in Post-Democratization Korea." *Asian Perspective* 34(1): 159–189.

Koo, H. 2007. "Engendering Civil Society: the Role of the Labour Movement." In *Korean Society: Civil Society, Democracy and the State*, edited by C.K. Armstrong, 73–94. London: Routledge.

Lee, Eun-Jung. 2005. "Internetmacht und soziale Bewegung in Südkorea." *Welt Trends* 48(13): 53–65. Accessed from http://www.welttrends.de/downloads/WT48_Lee.pdf

Lee, N. 2007. "The South Korean Student Movement: Undongkwŏn as Counterpublic Sphere." In *Korean Society: Civil Society, Democracy and the State*, edited by C.K. Armstrong, 95–120. London: Routledge.

Lee, Youngjae. 2005. "Law, Politics, and Impeachment: The Impeachment of Roh Moo-hyun from a Comparative Constitutional Perspective." *New York University Public Law and Legal Theory Working Papers*. NELLCO Legal Scholarship Repository. Accessed February 9, 2012 from http://lsr.nellco.org/nyu plltwp/4.

Lee, Y. S. Chung, and H. Jang. 2008. "Labor and Politics in East Asia: The Case of Failure of the Encompassing Labor Organization in Korea." *Asian Perspective* 32(3): 111–138.

Lewis, L.S. 2007. "Commemorating Kwangju: The 5.18 Movement and Civil Society at the Millennium." In *Korean Society: Civil Society, Democracy and the State*, edited by C.K. Armstrong, 145–166. London: Routledge.

Mafeje, A. 1978. "Soweto and Its Aftermath." *Review of African Political Economy*. 5(11): 17–30.

Mamdani, Mahmood. 1996. *Citizen and Subject: Contemporary Africa and the Legacy of Late Colonialism.* Princeton: Princeton University Press.
Nattrass, N. 2004. *The Moral economy of AIDS in South Africa.* Cambridge: Cambridge University Press.
Nauta, W. 2004. *The Implications of Freedom: the changing role of land sector NGOs in a transforming South Africa.* Münster: Lit Verlag.
Nederveen Pieterse, J. 2011. "Global rebalancing: crisis and the East-South turn." In *Development & Change*, 42(1): 22–48.
The Nobel Foundation. 2000. "Kim Dae-Jung Biography." Accessed April 14, 2010 from http://nobelprize.org/nobel_prizes/peace/laureates/2000/dae-jung-bio.html.
Ryoo, Woongjae. 2009. "The Public Sphere and the Rise of South Korean Civil Society." *Journal of Contemporary Asia* 39(1): 23–35.
Sen, A. 1999. *Development as Freedom.* New York: Anchor Books.
Surplus People Project. 1983. *Forced Removals in South Africa: the SPP reports, Vol.1 General Overview.* Cape Town: The Surplus People Project.
UNDP. 2009. *Human Development Report 2009.* New York: UNDP.
UNDP. 2010. International Human Development Indicators. Accessed May 21, 2010 from: http://hdrstats.undp.org/en/buildtables
Van Kessel, I. 2000. *Beyond Our Wildest Dreams: the United Democratic Front and the transformation of South Africa.* Charlottesville: University Press of Virginia.
Walraven, B. 2003. "Dit Lant bij ons Coree Genaemt: Korea in de Tijd van Hamel." In *De Wereld van Hendrik Hamel* by V. Roeper and B. Walraven. Amsterdam: SUN.
Washington Post. 2003. "Mbeki Says Diplomacy Needed for Zimbabwe." *Washington Post*, Accessed September 25, 2003 from http://www.washingtonpost.com/
World Bank. 2010. World Development Report Data base. Accessed May 21, 2010 from: http://databank.worldbank.org/ddp/home.do?Step=3&id=4
Yanagimachi, I. 2004. "Chaebol Reform and Corporate Governance in Korea." *Policy and Governance Working Paper Series No.18.* The Graduate School of Media and Governance, Keio University, Japan.

Contributors

Lynne Ciochetto is an Associate Professor at the Institute of Communication Design, University of Massey, New Zealand. Her research interests reflect her interdisciplinary background: sociology, anthropology, development studies and graphic design. Her recent focus has been the exploration of advertising and globalization in terms of social and cultural change. 2 key areas have emerged: case studies of the globalization of advertising in specific countries: Russia, India, China, Vietnam and Thailand. Complementing this approach are thematic studies of the market sectors: men, children and women. Her latest research direction is an exploration of the environmental impact of the growth in consumption in emerging economies that is stimulated by advertising and the media. Another area of interest is the documentation of signage. Her book *Advertising and globalization in the emerging economies of Brazil, Russia, India and China* was published by Routledge London in December 2011.

Min Gong is a professor of Economics and the Vice Director of the Center for Macroeconomic Research at Xiamen University, Fujian. She holds a Ph.D. in economics from Fudan University, Shangai; served as a visiting scholar at the Institution for Economic Research at Hitotsubashi University, Tokyo; and as a Freeman Fellow at the Center for East Asian and Pacific Studies at the University of Illinois at Urbana-Champaign. Her research field includes economic growth, macroeconomic policy, and international economics.

John M. Hobson is Professor of Politics and International Relations at the University of Sheffield and co-director of the Political Economy Research. His main research interest lies in the critique of Eurocentrism and the reconstruction of a non-Eurocentric account of inter-civilizational relations, past and present. His two most recent books are *The Eastern Origins of Western Civilisation* (Cambridge University Press 2004) and *Everyday Politics of the World Economy* (Cambridge University Press 2007, co-edited with Leonard Seabrooke). He also has edited a volume of J.A. Hobson's unpublished 1930s lectures entitled *The Struggle for the International Mind* (Routledge, 2011), and is currently finishing off a book manuscript entitled, "Defending the Western Interest: Historical Sociology of Eurocentrism in International Theory, 1760–2010."

Jin-Ho Jang is Assistant Professor in the School of General Studies at Gwangju Institute of Science and Technology in South Korea and teaches sociology and globalization studies. His research areas include sociology of finance, corporate governance, neoliberalism, social welfare, and global political economy. He has published "Analyzing Neoliberalism as Financial Hegemony: History, Dynamics, and Actors," "Should Financialized Capitalism Be a Model for the Future of South Korea?" both in Korean, and "Neoliberalism in South Korea: The Dynamics of Financialization" in English.

Jongtae Kim is Humanities Korea (HK) Research Professor in the Asiatic Research Institute (ARI) at Korea University, Seoul. He earned his Ph.D. in sociology from the University of Illinois at Urbana Champaign, U.S. His research interests include global sociology, cultural studies, development studies, historical sociology, and international relations, with a regional focus on Korea and East Asia. Before beginning his academic career, he worked as a journalist for about 10 years for *The Hankyoreh*, a leading progressive Korean daily newspaper based in Seoul.

Seung Kuk Kim is Professor of Sociology at Pusan National University and director of the Brain Korea 21 Project team of the Department of Sociology. He received his Ph.D. from Indiana University at Bloomington and his M.A. and B.A. from Seoul National University. His main research interest lies in the postmodern reformulation of libertarianism and the critical examination of the approaches to the building of East Asian Community. He served as the president of the Korean Sociological Association, Korean Society for Social Theory, and Korean Sociological Association for East Asia. He was a founding member of the East Asian Sociologists Network in 2002 and since then has organized annually the East Asian Sociologists Conference in China, Japan, and Korea. He is now a member of the Presidential Committee on Social Cohesion.

Peilin Li received his Ph.D. from Sorbonne in Paris and is Director of the Institute of Sociology at the Chinese Academy of Social Sciences, Beijing. Dr. Peilin Li is also President of the Chinese Sociological Association.

Hyun-Chin Lim is Professor of Sociology and Director of Asia Center, Seoul National University. He received his B.A. and M.A. in Sociology from Seoul National University and his Ph.D. in Sociology from Harvard University. He was President of Korean Sociological Association and Dean of College of Social Sciences, Seoul National University. Currently, he is the President of Korean Association of Political Sociology.

Wiebe Nauta is a sociologist of development at the Faculty of Arts and Social Sciences, Maastricht University. He has conducted extensive research in the Eastern Cape Province of South Africa since 1996, with a particular focus on the role of civil society in the field of the land sector and more recently in the field of HIV/AIDS. For the past three years he has also undertaken comparative work on the role of civil society in South Africa, South Korea, and Brazil in a transnational perspective. Publications include "Saving Depraved Africans in a Neoliberal Age: Critically Examining Mainstream Approaches to HIV/AIDS" in the *Journal of Developing Societies* (2010, vol. 26, no. 3) and "Mobilising Brazil as 'Significant Other' in the Fight for HIV/AIDS Treatment in South Africa: The Treatment Action Campaign (TAC) and Its Global Allies," in *African Engagements: Africa Negotiating an Emerging Multipolar World* (2011, Brill), edited by T. Dietz et al.

Jan Nederveen Pieterse is Mellichamp professor of Global Studies and Sociology at University of California Santa Barbara. Recent books are *Globalization and Culture: Global Mélange* (2nd ed., Rowman & Littlefield 2010), *Development Theory: Deconstructions/ Reconstructions* (2nd ed., Sage 2010), *Is There Hope for Uncle Sam? Beyond the American Bubble* (Zed 2008), *Ethnicities and Global Multiculture: Pants for an Octopus* (Rowman & Littlefield 2007), *Globalization or Empire?* (Routledge 2004). For more information see http://www.jannederveenpieterse.com.

Hidetaka Yoshimatsu is Professor of Politics and International Relations at Ritsumeikan Asia Pacific University, Japan. His current research interests include Japan's foreign policy and regionalism in East Asia. His publications include *The Political Economy of Regionalism in East Asia: Integrative Explanation for Dynamics and Challenges* (Palgrave 2008) and *Japan and East Asia in Transition: Trade Policy, Crisis and Evolution, and Regionalism* (Palgrave 2003).

Index

For Product Safety Concerns and Information please contact our EU representative GPSR@taylorandfrancis.com
Taylor & Francis Verlag GmbH, Kaufingerstraße 24, 80331 München, Germany

www.ingramcontent.com/pod-product-compliance
Ingram Content Group UK Ltd.
Pitfield, Milton Keynes, MK11 3LW, UK
UKHW022000180926
475701UK00003B/114
* 9 7 8 0 4 1 5 5 3 7 3 9 1 *